The FURTHER ADVENTURES of NICK WILSON

CREATED BY

EDDIE GORODETSKY & **MARC ANDREYKO**

IMAGE COMICS, INC.

Robert Kirkman: Chief Operating Officer

Erik Larsen: Chief Financial Officer

Todd McFarlane: President

Marc Silvestri: Chief Executive Officer

Jim Valentino: Vice President

Eric Stephenson: Publisher / Chief Creative Officer

Corey Hart: Director of Sales

Jeff Boison: Director of Publishing Planning & Book Trade Sales

Chris Ross: Director of Digital Sales

Jeff Stang: Director of Specialty Sales

Kat Salazar: Director of PR & Marketing

Drew Gill: Art Director

Heather Doornink: Production Director

Nicole Lapalme: Controller

IMAGECOMICS.COM

thefurtheradventuresofnickwilson.com

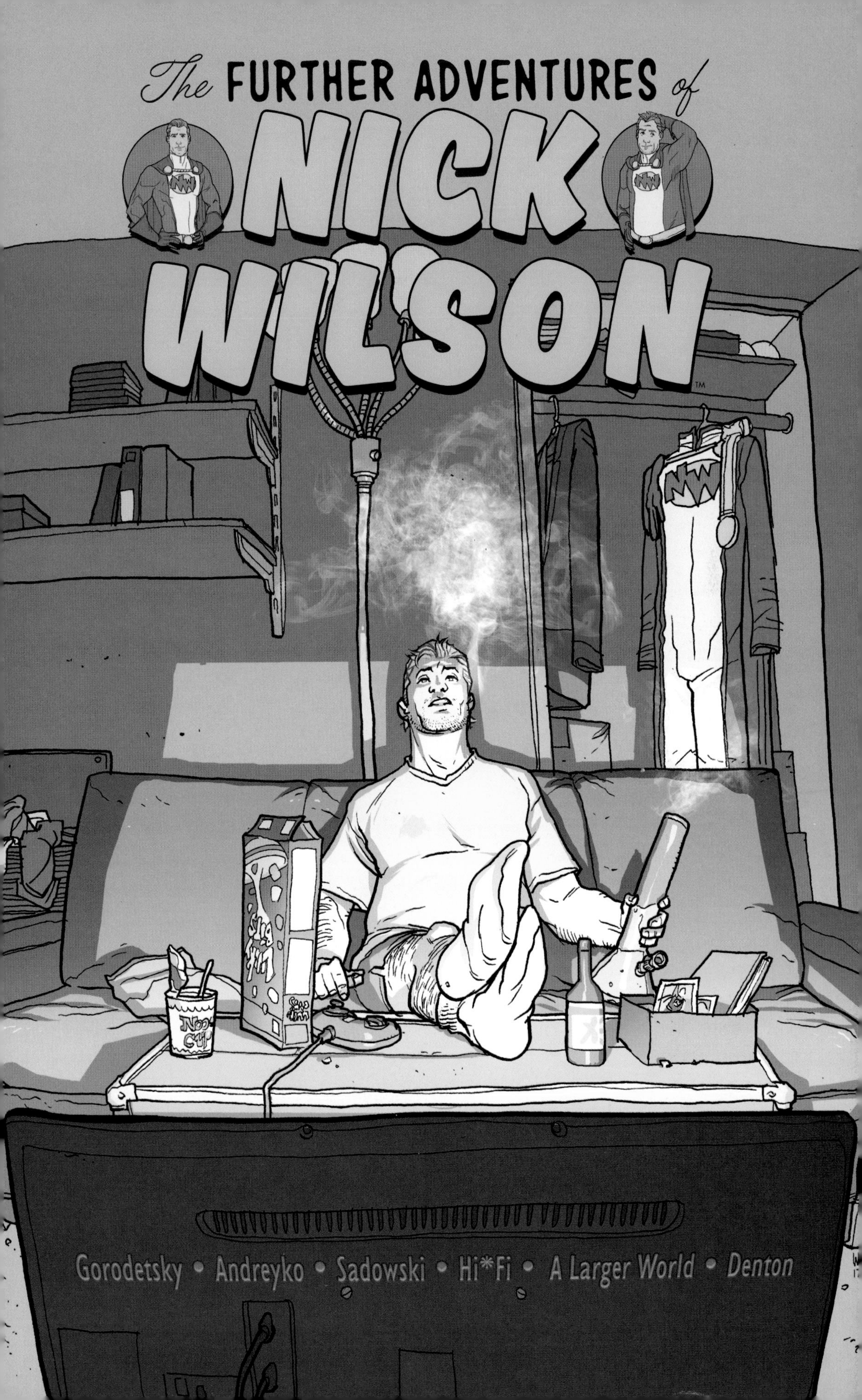
The FURTHER ADVENTURES of
NICK WILSON™
Gorodetsky • Andreyko • Sadowski • Hi*Fi • A Larger World • Denton

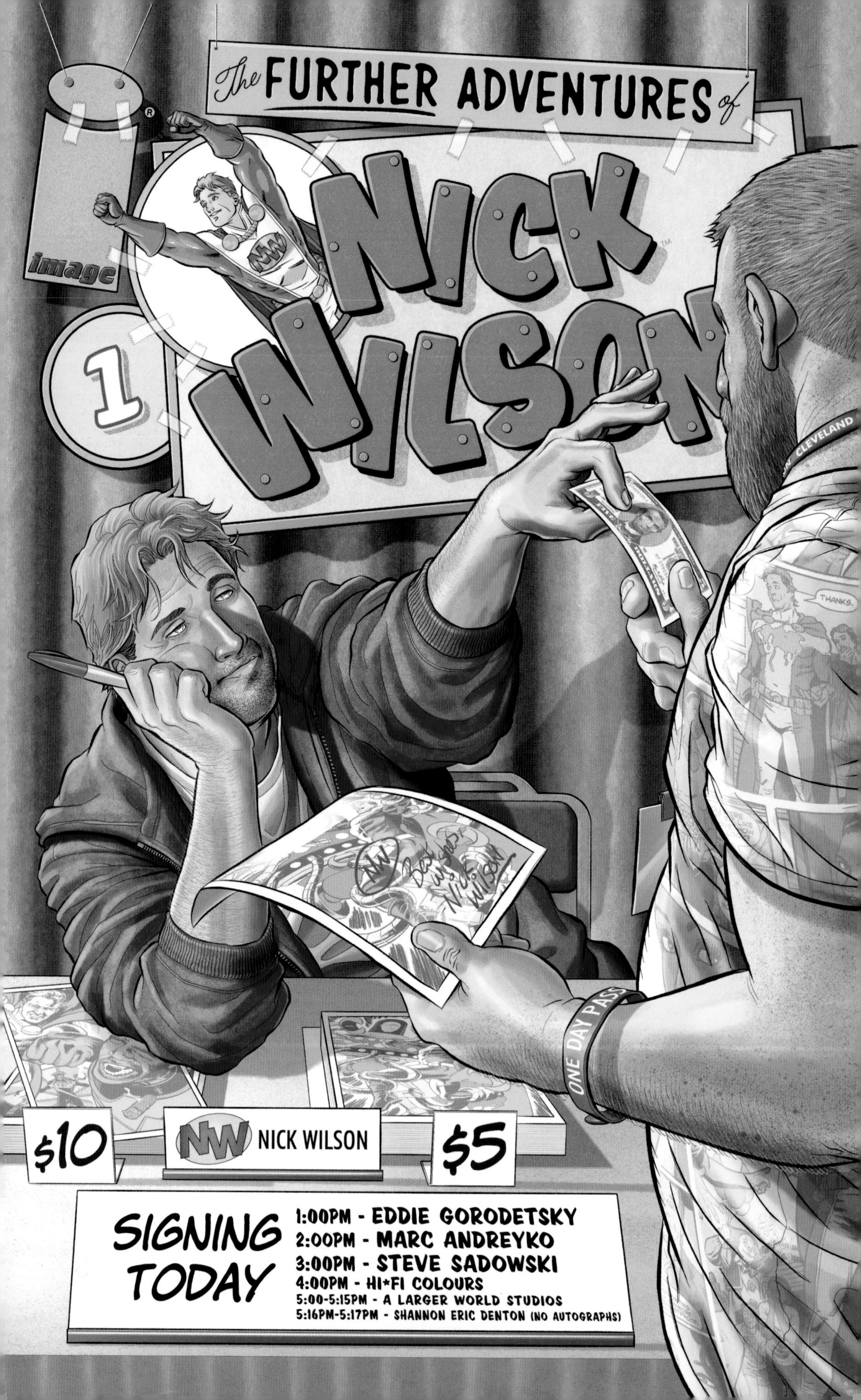

image
The FURTHER ADVENTURES of
NICK WILSON™
1
CLEVELAND
THANKS.
ONE DAY PASS
$10
NW NICK WILSON
$5
SIGNING TODAY
1:00PM - EDDIE GORODETSKY
2:00PM - MARC ANDREYKO
3:00PM - STEVE SADOWSKI
4:00PM - HI*FI COLOURS
5:00-5:15PM - A LARGER WORLD STUDIOS
5:16PM-5:17PM - SHANNON ERIC DENTON (NO AUTOGRAPHS)

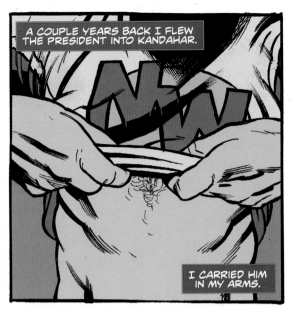

A COUPLE YEARS BACK I FLEW THE PRESIDENT INTO KANDAHAR.

I CARRIED HIM IN MY ARMS.

HE COULDN'T TAKE AIR FORCE ONE BECAUSE IT WAS A COVERT MISSION.

HE WORE A BLINDFOLD AND EARBUDS. WHO WOULD'VE GUESSED THE LEADER OF THE FREE WORLD WAS A NERVOUS FLYER?

HE DIDN'T WANT ME TO KNOW HE THREW UP IN HIS MOUTH A LITTLE.

KLIK

BUT I COULD SMELL IT.

OF COURSE BACK THEN, I COULD SMELL A DOG PASSING WIND TWO STATES OVER.

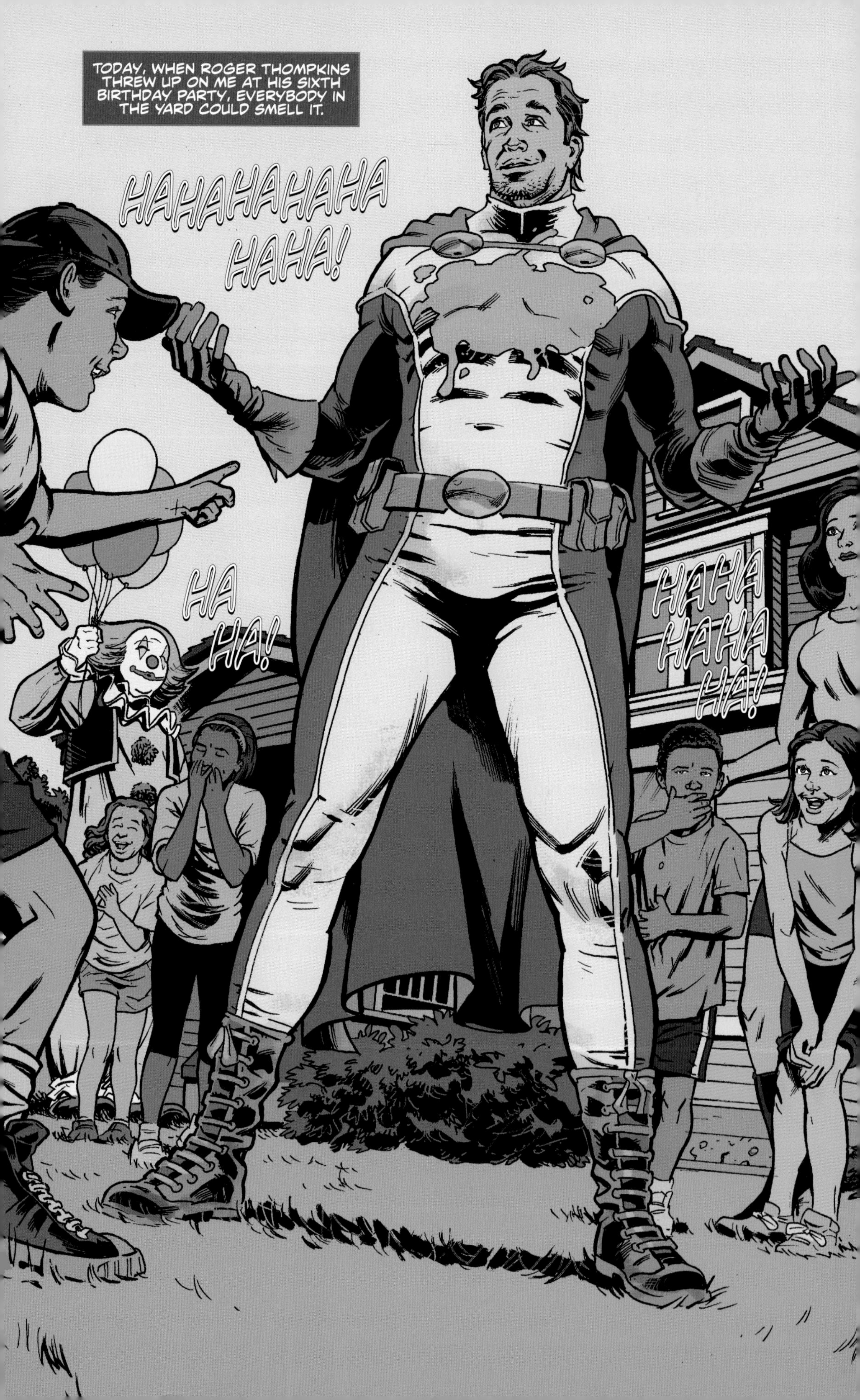
TODAY, WHEN ROGER THOMPKINS THREW UP ON ME AT HIS SIXTH BIRTHDAY PARTY, EVERYBODY IN THE YARD COULD SMELL IT.
HAHAHAHAHAHA HAHA!
HA HA!
HAHA HAHA HA!

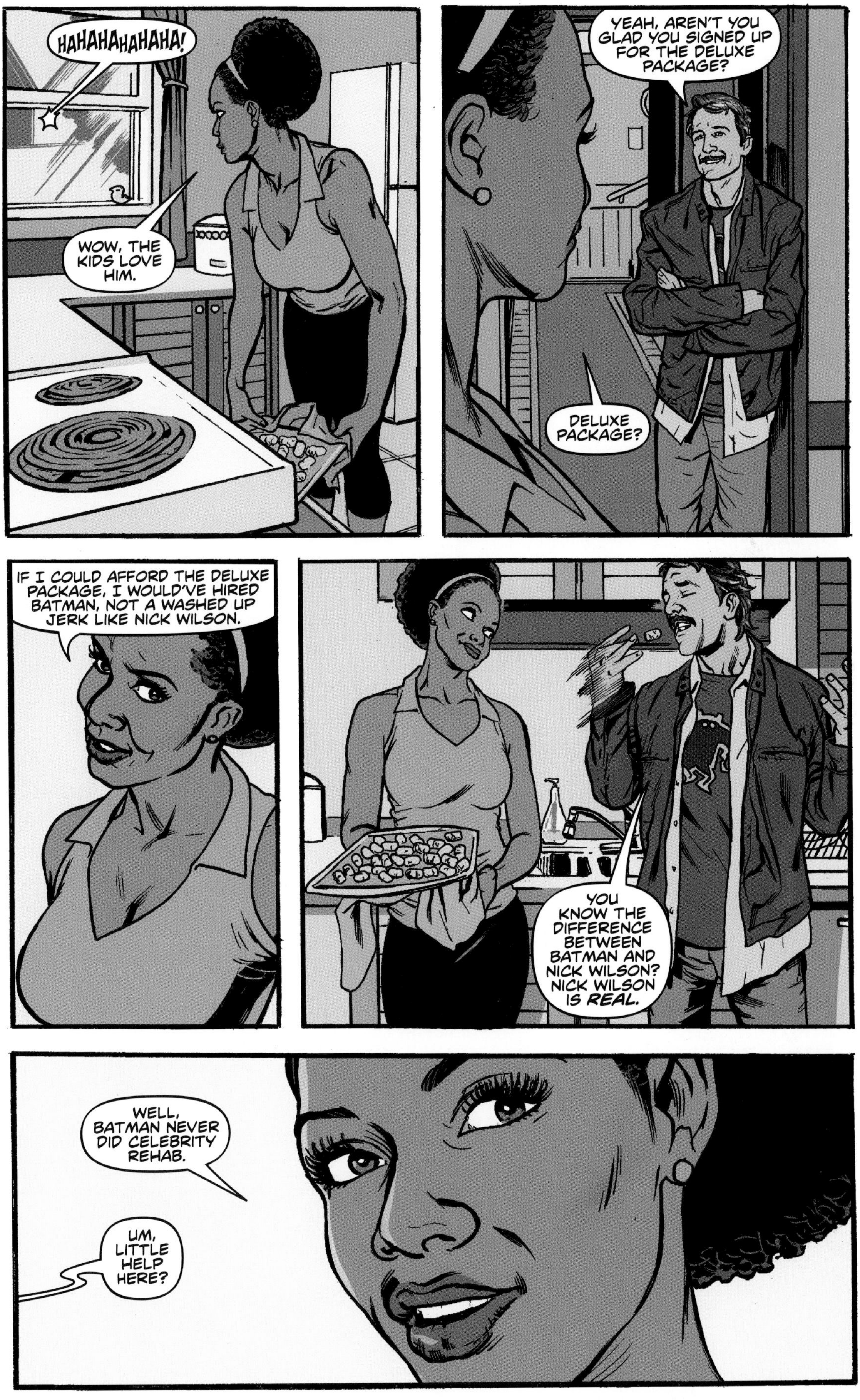
HAHAHAHAHAHA!
WOW, THE KIDS LOVE HIM.
YEAH, AREN'T YOU GLAD YOU SIGNED UP FOR THE DELUXE PACKAGE?
DELUXE PACKAGE?
IF I COULD AFFORD THE DELUXE PACKAGE, I WOULD'VE HIRED BATMAN, NOT A WASHED UP JERK LIKE NICK WILSON.
YOU KNOW THE DIFFERENCE BETWEEN BATMAN AND NICK WILSON? NICK WILSON IS *REAL*.
WELL, BATMAN NEVER DID CELEBRITY REHAB.
UM, LITTLE HELP HERE?

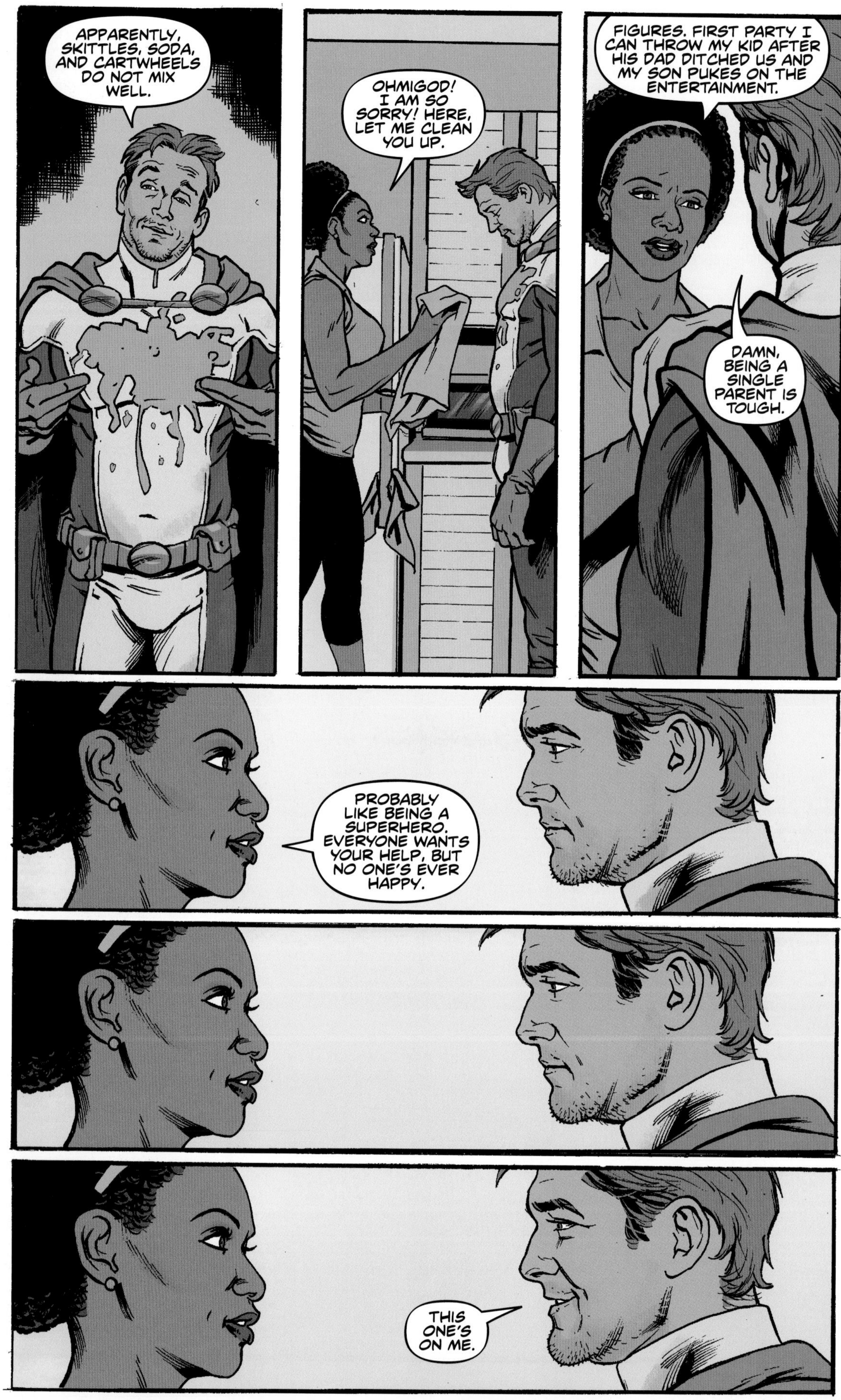
APPARENTLY, SKITTLES, SODA, AND CARTWHEELS DO NOT MIX WELL.
OHMIGOD! I AM SO SORRY! HERE, LET ME CLEAN YOU UP.
FIGURES. FIRST PARTY I CAN THROW MY KID AFTER HIS DAD DITCHED US AND MY SON PUKES ON THE ENTERTAINMENT.
DAMN, BEING A SINGLE PARENT IS TOUGH.
PROBABLY LIKE BEING A SUPERHERO. EVERYONE WANTS YOUR HELP, BUT NO ONE'S EVER HAPPY.
THIS ONE'S ON ME.

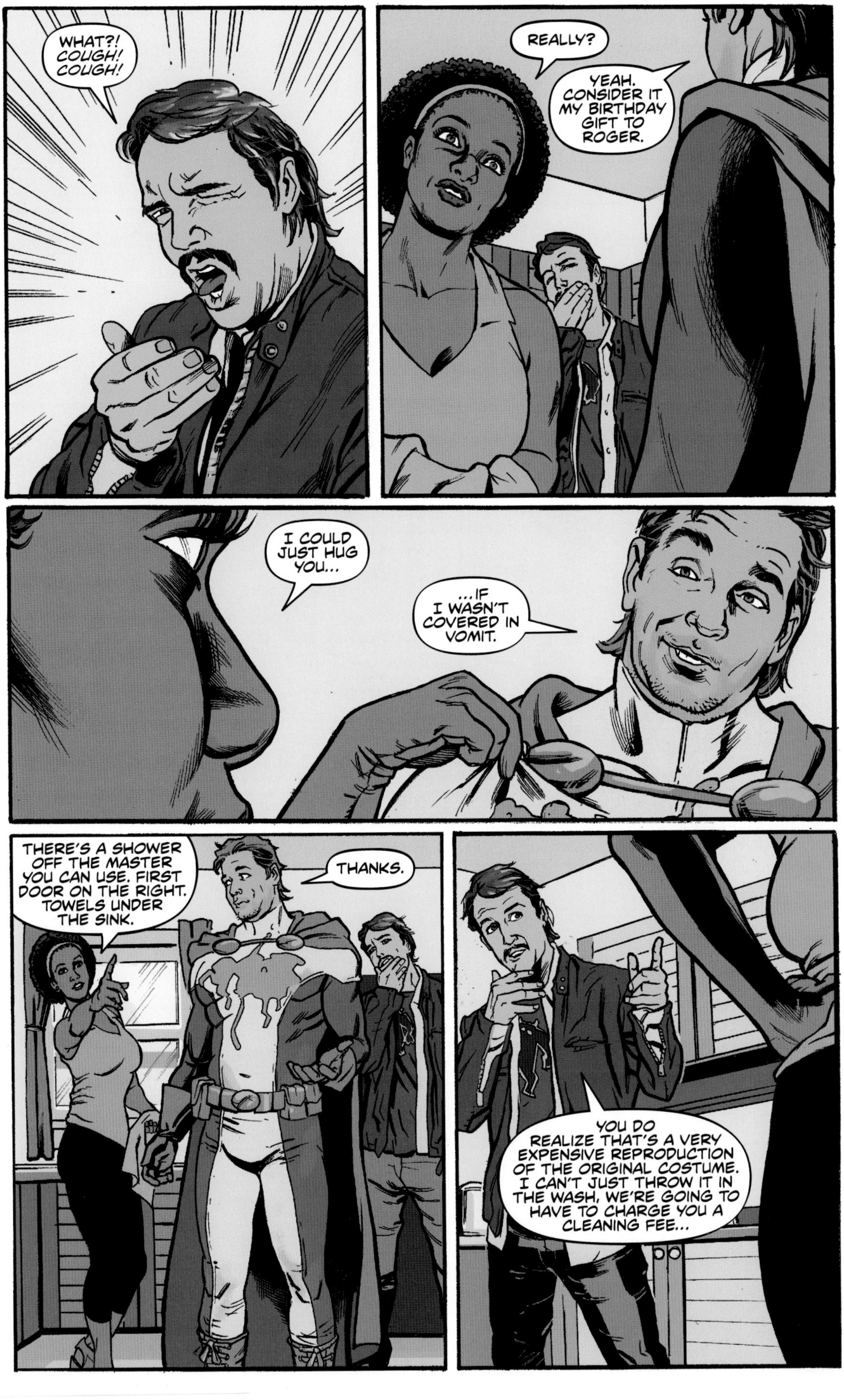
WHAT?! COUGH! COUGH!
REALLY?
YEAH. CONSIDER IT MY BIRTHDAY GIFT TO ROGER.
I COULD JUST HUG YOU...
...IF I WASN'T COVERED IN VOMIT.
THERE'S A SHOWER OFF THE MASTER YOU CAN USE. FIRST DOOR ON THE RIGHT. TOWELS UNDER THE SINK.
THANKS.
YOU DO REALIZE THAT'S A VERY EXPENSIVE REPRODUCTION OF THE ORIGINAL COSTUME. I CAN'T JUST THROW IT IN THE WASH, WE'RE GOING TO HAVE TO CHARGE YOU A CLEANING FEE...

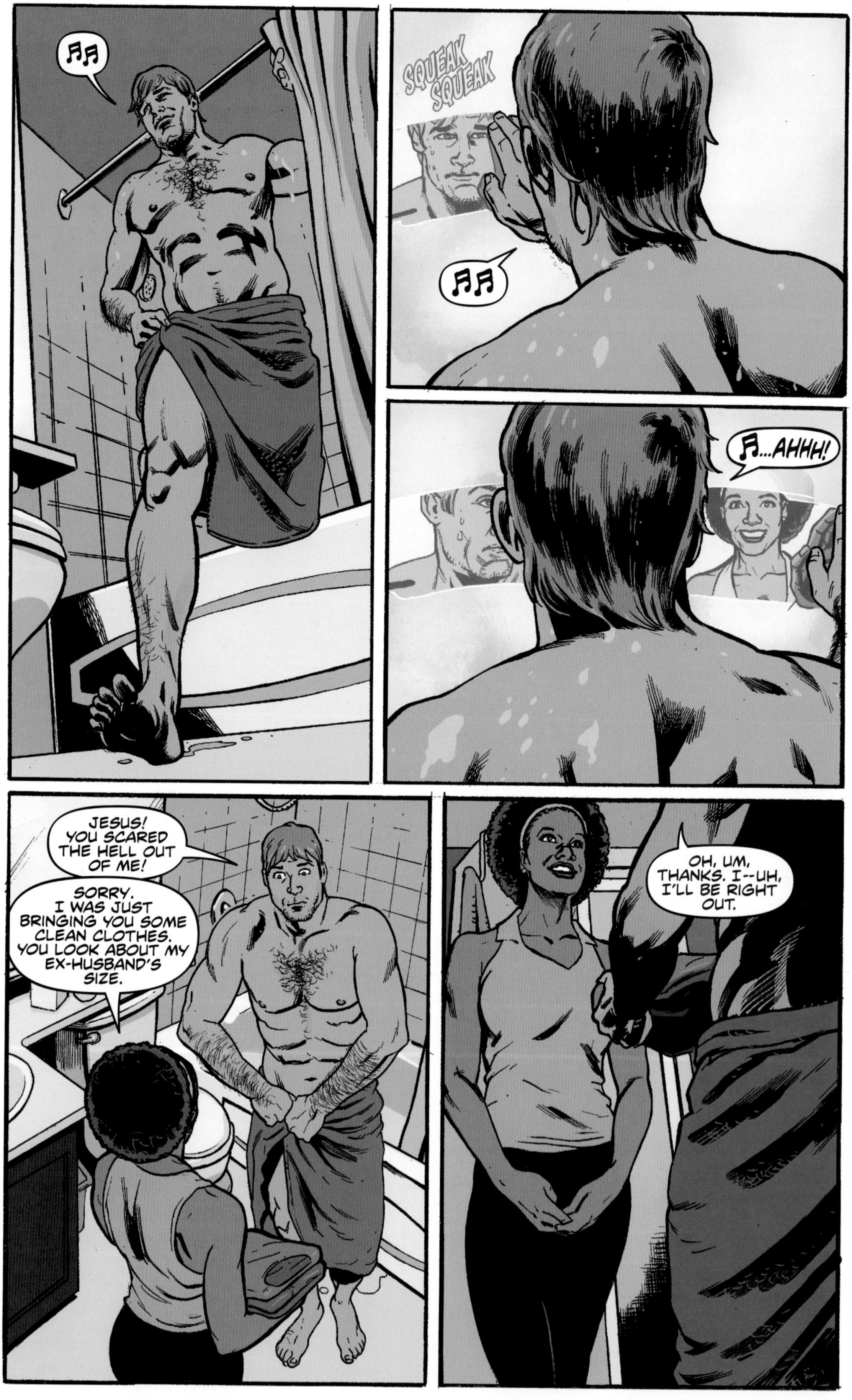
♬♬
SQUEAK SQUEAK
♬♬
♬...AHHH!
JESUS! YOU SCARED THE HELL OUT OF ME!
SORRY. I WAS JUST BRINGING YOU SOME CLEAN CLOTHES. YOU LOOK ABOUT MY EX-HUSBAND'S SIZE.
OH, UM, THANKS. I--UH, I'LL BE RIGHT OUT.

YOU WERE RIGHT. FIT LIKE A GLOVE. HOW DO I LOOK?

HONESTLY? ONLY SLIGHTLY LESS RIDICULOUS THAN YOU DID IN YOUR "SUPER SUIT."

BUT THE LACK OF VOMIT SEALS THE DEAL FOR ME.

YOU ARE MUCH HANDSOMER THAN THE REAL NICK WILSON.

I DON'T KNOW ABOUT THAT.

I JUST WISH THERE WAS SOME WAY I COULD THANK YOU.

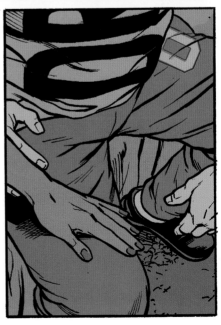

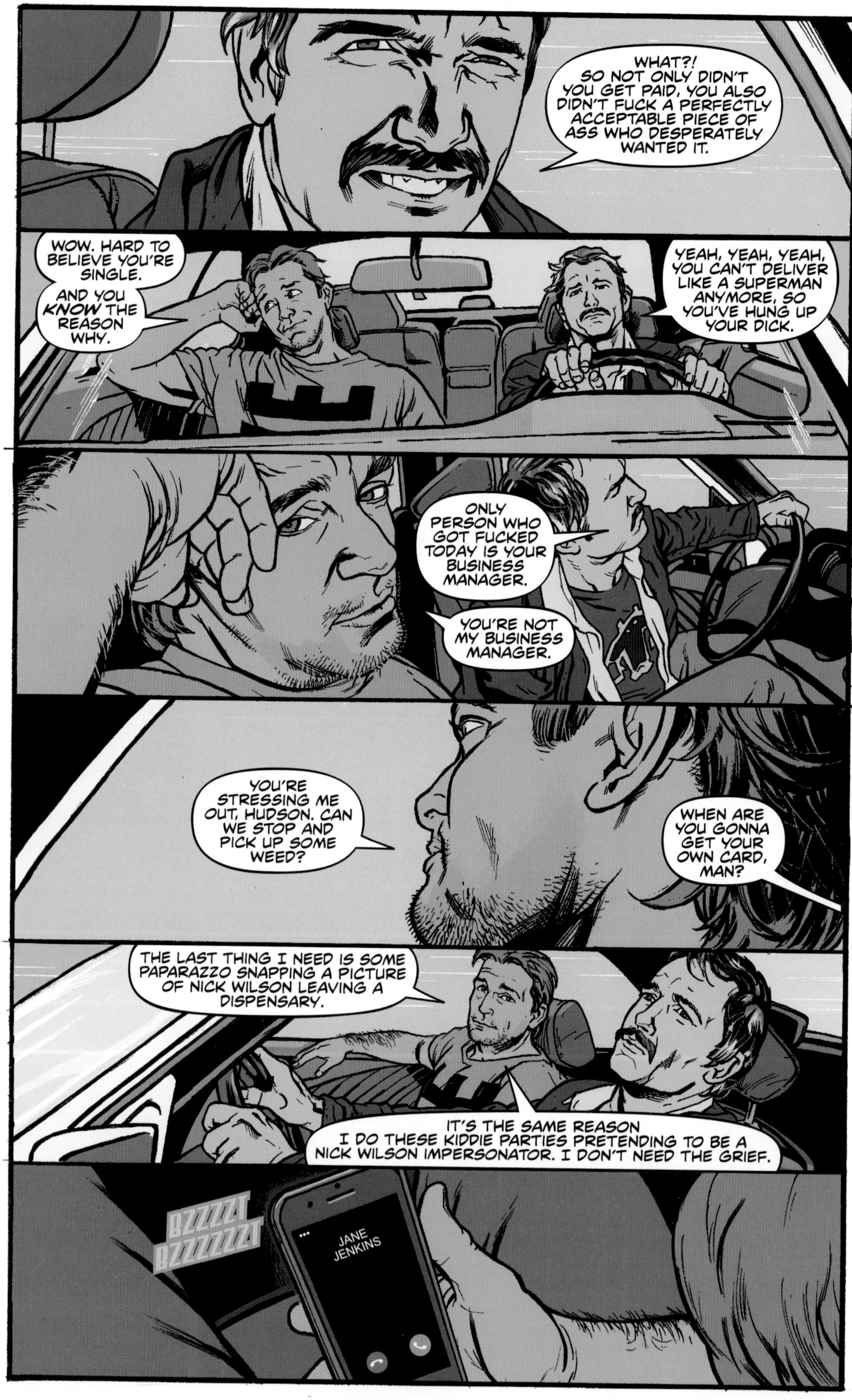
WHAT?! SO NOT ONLY DIDN'T YOU GET PAID, YOU ALSO DIDN'T FUCK A PERFECTLY ACCEPTABLE PIECE OF ASS WHO DESPERATELY WANTED IT.
WOW. HARD TO BELIEVE YOU'RE SINGLE.
AND YOU KNOW THE REASON WHY.
YEAH, YEAH, YEAH, YOU CAN'T DELIVER LIKE A SUPERMAN ANYMORE, SO YOU'VE HUNG UP YOUR DICK.
ONLY PERSON WHO GOT FUCKED TODAY IS YOUR BUSINESS MANAGER.
YOU'RE NOT MY BUSINESS MANAGER.
YOU'RE STRESSING ME OUT, HUDSON. CAN WE STOP AND PICK UP SOME WEED?
WHEN ARE YOU GONNA GET YOUR OWN CARD, MAN?
THE LAST THING I NEED IS SOME PAPARAZZO SNAPPING A PICTURE OF NICK WILSON LEAVING A DISPENSARY.
IT'S THE SAME REASON I DO THESE KIDDIE PARTIES PRETENDING TO BE A NICK WILSON IMPERSONATOR. I DON'T NEED THE GRIEF.
BZZZZT BZZZZZZT
JANE JENKINS

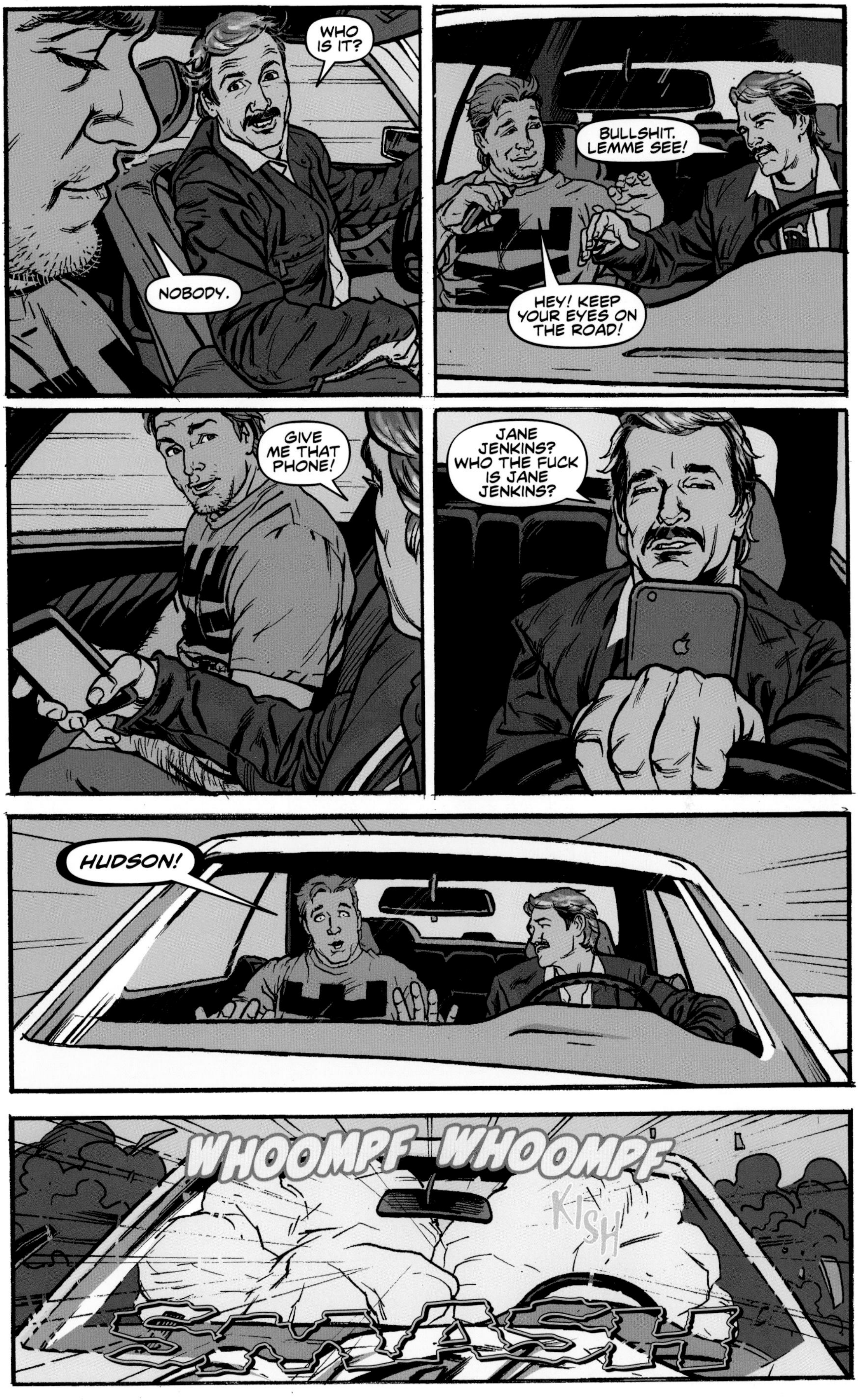
WHO IS IT?
NOBODY.
BULLSHIT. LEMME SEE!
HEY! KEEP YOUR EYES ON THE ROAD!
GIVE ME THAT PHONE!
JANE JENKINS? WHO THE FUCK IS JANE JENKINS?
HUDSON!
WHOOMPF WHOOMPF
KISH

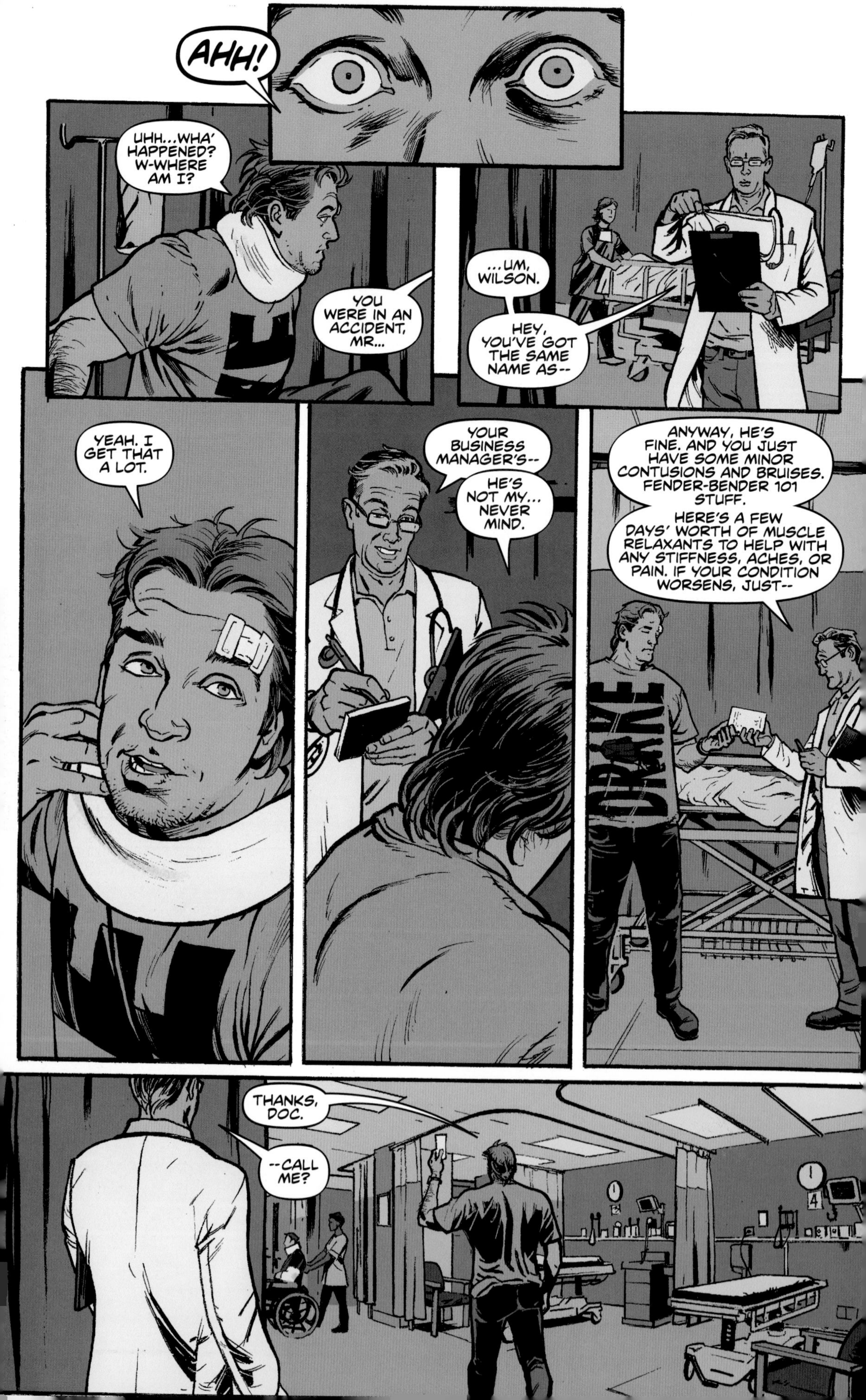
AHH!
UHH...WHA' HAPPENED? W-WHERE AM I?
YOU WERE IN AN ACCIDENT, MR...
...UM, WILSON.
HEY, YOU'VE GOT THE SAME NAME AS--
YEAH. I GET THAT A LOT.
YOUR BUSINESS MANAGER'S--
HE'S NOT MY... NEVER MIND.
ANYWAY, HE'S FINE. AND YOU JUST HAVE SOME MINOR CONTUSIONS AND BRUISES. FENDER-BENDER 101 STUFF.
HERE'S A FEW DAYS' WORTH OF MUSCLE RELAXANTS TO HELP WITH ANY STIFFNESS, ACHES, OR PAIN. IF YOUR CONDITION WORSENS, JUST--
THANKS, DOC.
--CALL ME?

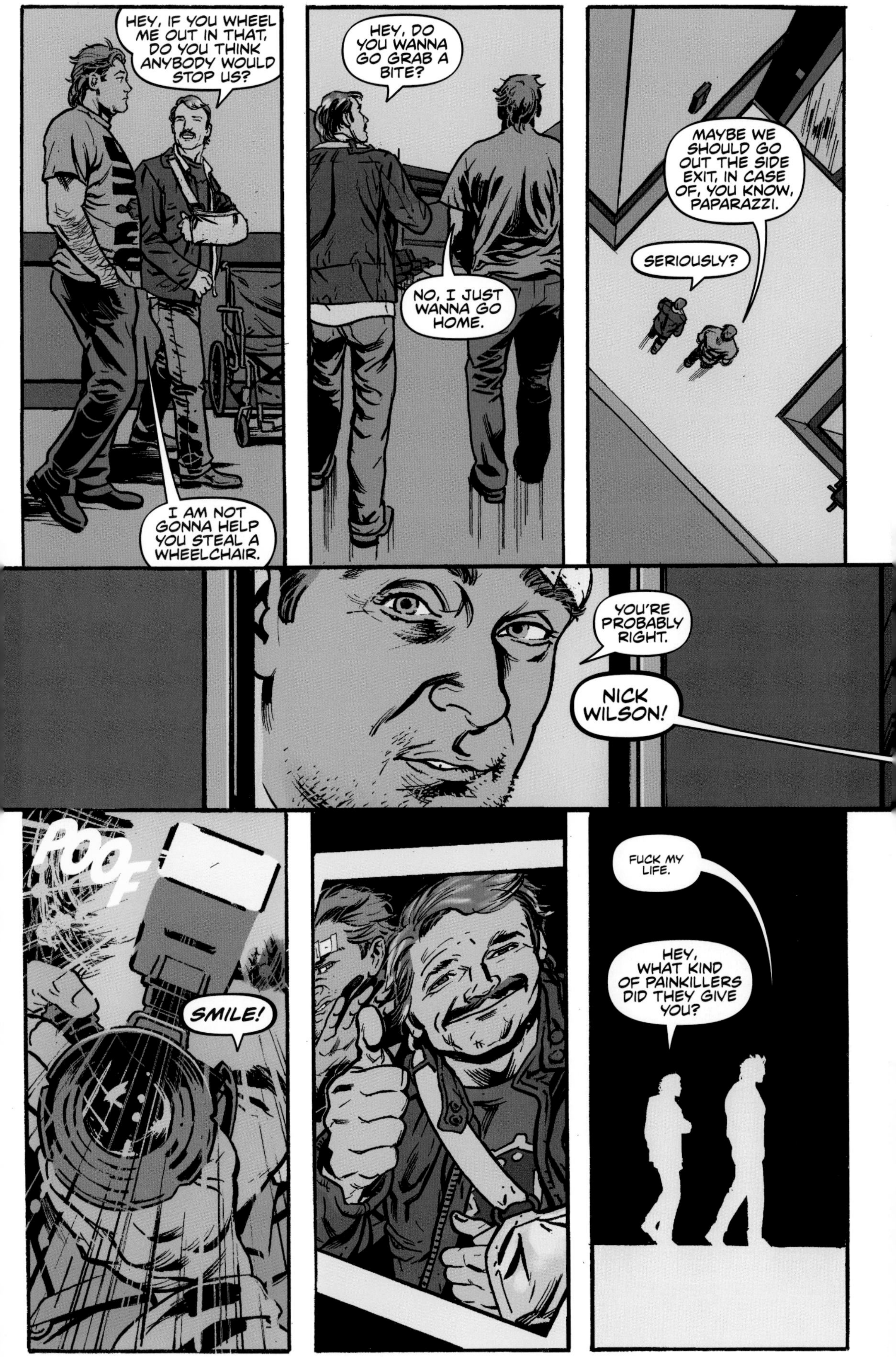
HEY, IF YOU WHEEL ME OUT IN THAT, DO YOU THINK ANYBODY WOULD STOP US?
I AM NOT GONNA HELP YOU STEAL A WHEELCHAIR.
HEY, DO YOU WANNA GO GRAB A BITE?
NO, I JUST WANNA GO HOME.
MAYBE WE SHOULD GO OUT THE SIDE EXIT, IN CASE OF, YOU KNOW, PAPARAZZI.
SERIOUSLY?
YOU'RE PROBABLY RIGHT.
NICK WILSON!
POOF
SMILE!
FUCK MY LIFE.
HEY, WHAT KIND OF PAINKILLERS DID THEY GIVE YOU?

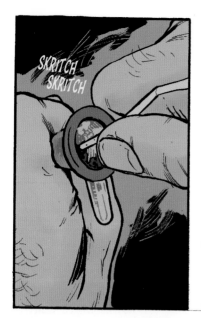

SKRITCH
SKRITCH

...AND THAT PUTS ANOTHER MARK IN THE LOSS COLUMN FOR OUR BELEAGUERED BROWNS.

PIZZA TIME

TCHIK

HE USED TO BE FLYING HIGH, BUT NOW HE'S REAR-ENDING MINIVANS, LOCAL BOY NICK WILSON IS BACK IN THE NEWS.

COUGH! COUGH! COUGH!

OH CRAP, HERE WE GO.

NEWS

3 wkyc
EXCLUSIVE

FOR THREE YEARS HE WAS THE HOTTEST STORY ON THE PLANET...

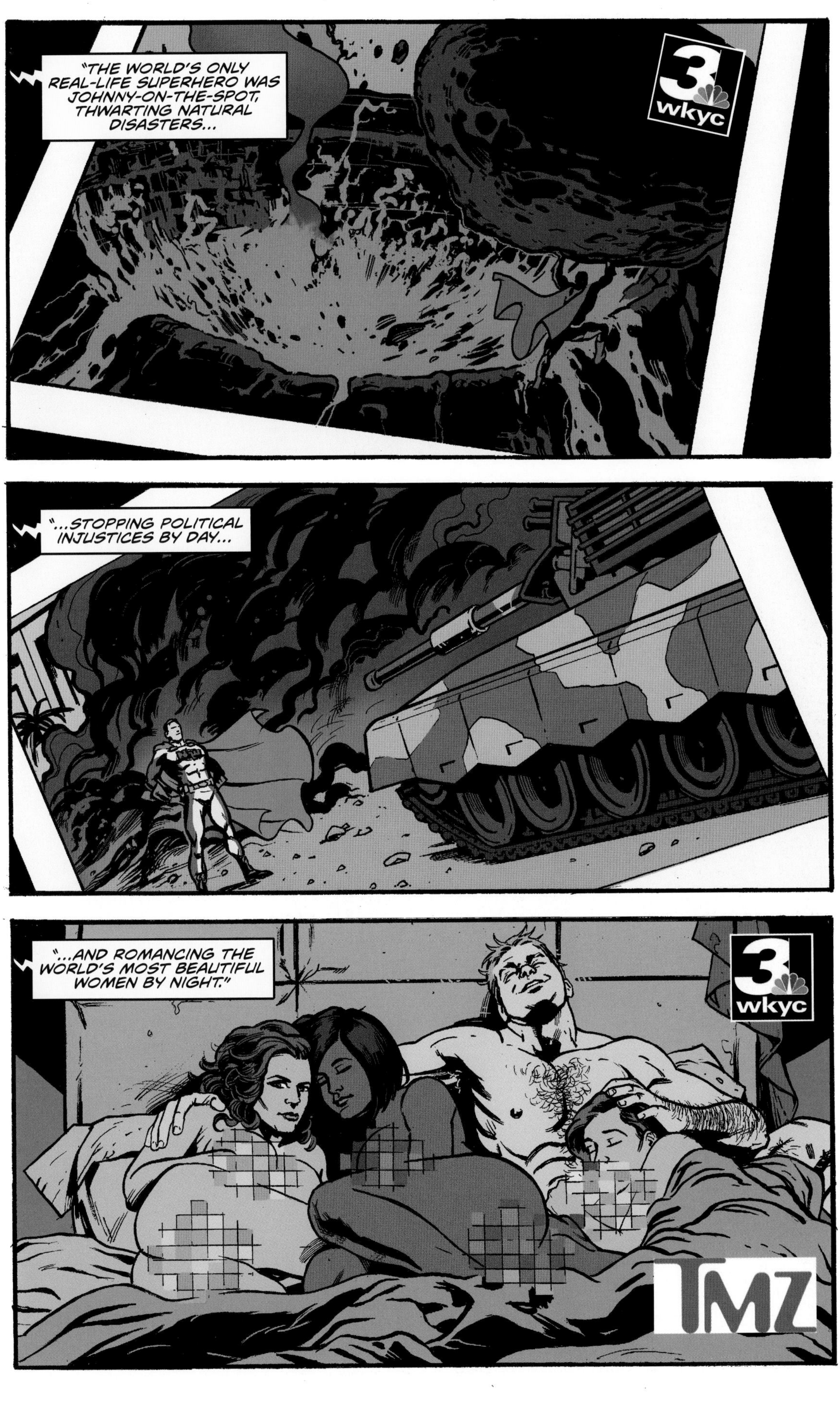
"THE WORLD'S ONLY REAL-LIFE SUPERHERO WAS JOHNNY-ON-THE-SPOT, THWARTING NATURAL DISASTERS...
3 wkyc
"...STOPPING POLITICAL INJUSTICES BY DAY...
"...AND ROMANCING THE WORLD'S MOST BEAUTIFUL WOMEN BY NIGHT."
3 wkyc
TMZ

EXCLUSIVE

3 wkyc

"THE NOW POWERLESS FORMER HERO WAS IN A FENDER BENDER THIS AFTERNOON THAT LANDED HIM IN A LOCAL ER AND WKYC HAS THIS EXCLUSIVE PHOTO OF WILSON LEAVING THE HOSPITAL."

AND WE THOUGHT JOHNNY MANZIEL WAS A LOSER.

OH, GIL, THAT'S SO *MEAN!* HAHAHAHAHA!

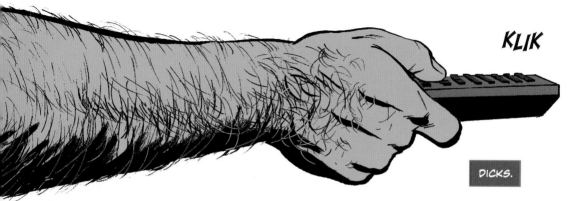

KLIK

DICKS.

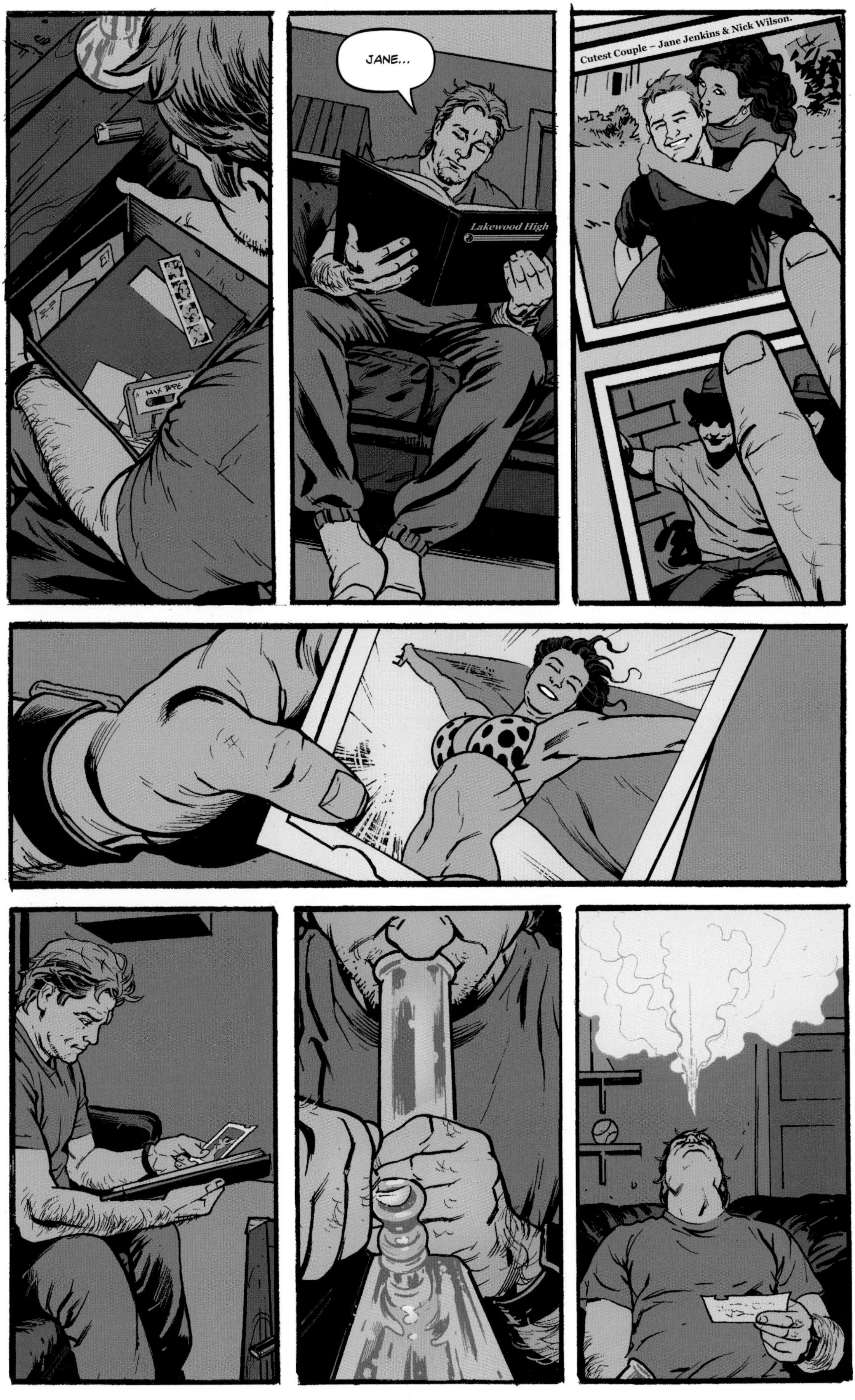
MIX TAPE
JANE...
Lakewood High
Cutest Couple – Jane Jenkins & Nick Wilson.

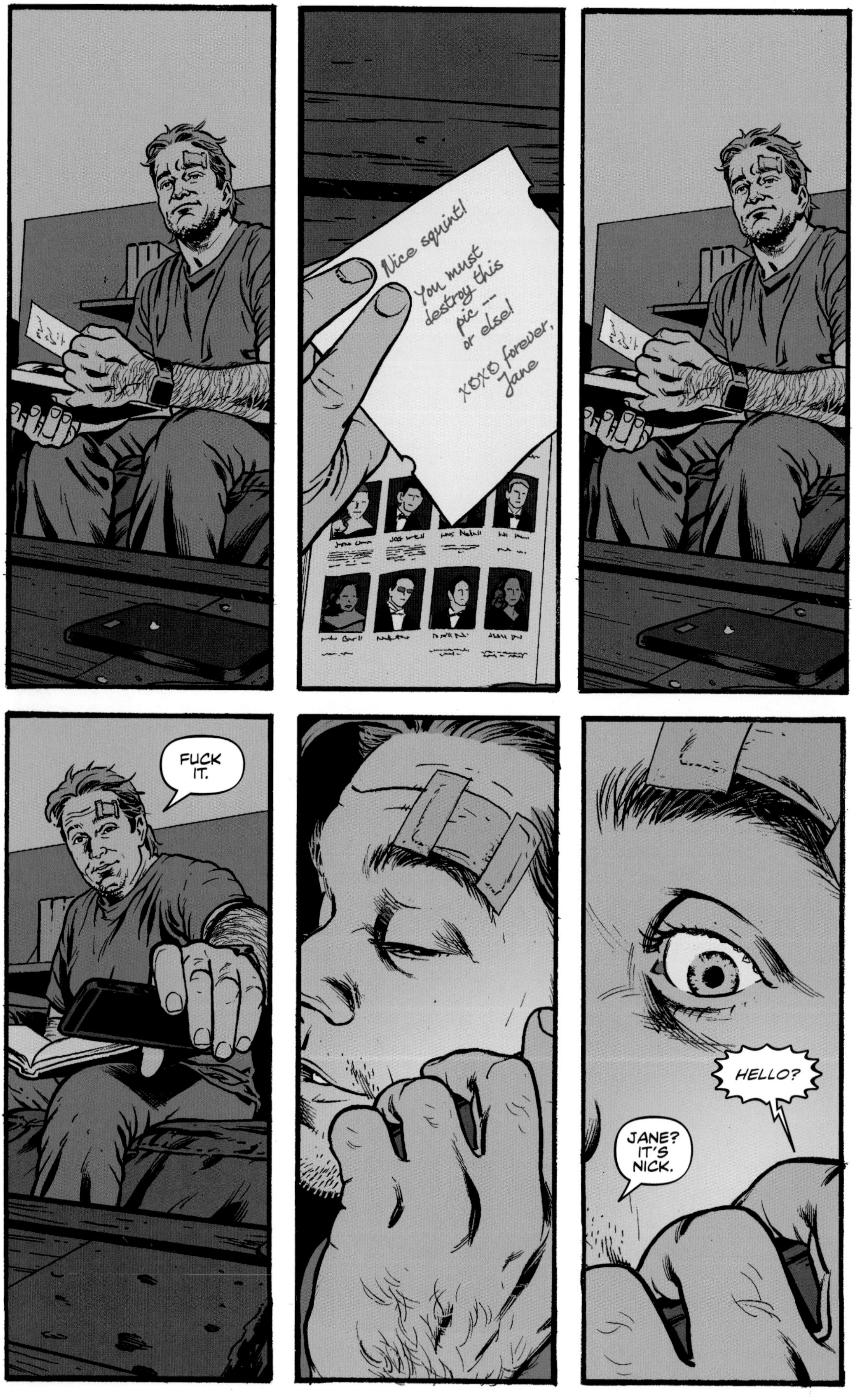
Nice squint!
You must destroy this pic -- or else!
XOXO forever, Jane
FUCK IT.
HELLO?
JANE? IT'S NICK.

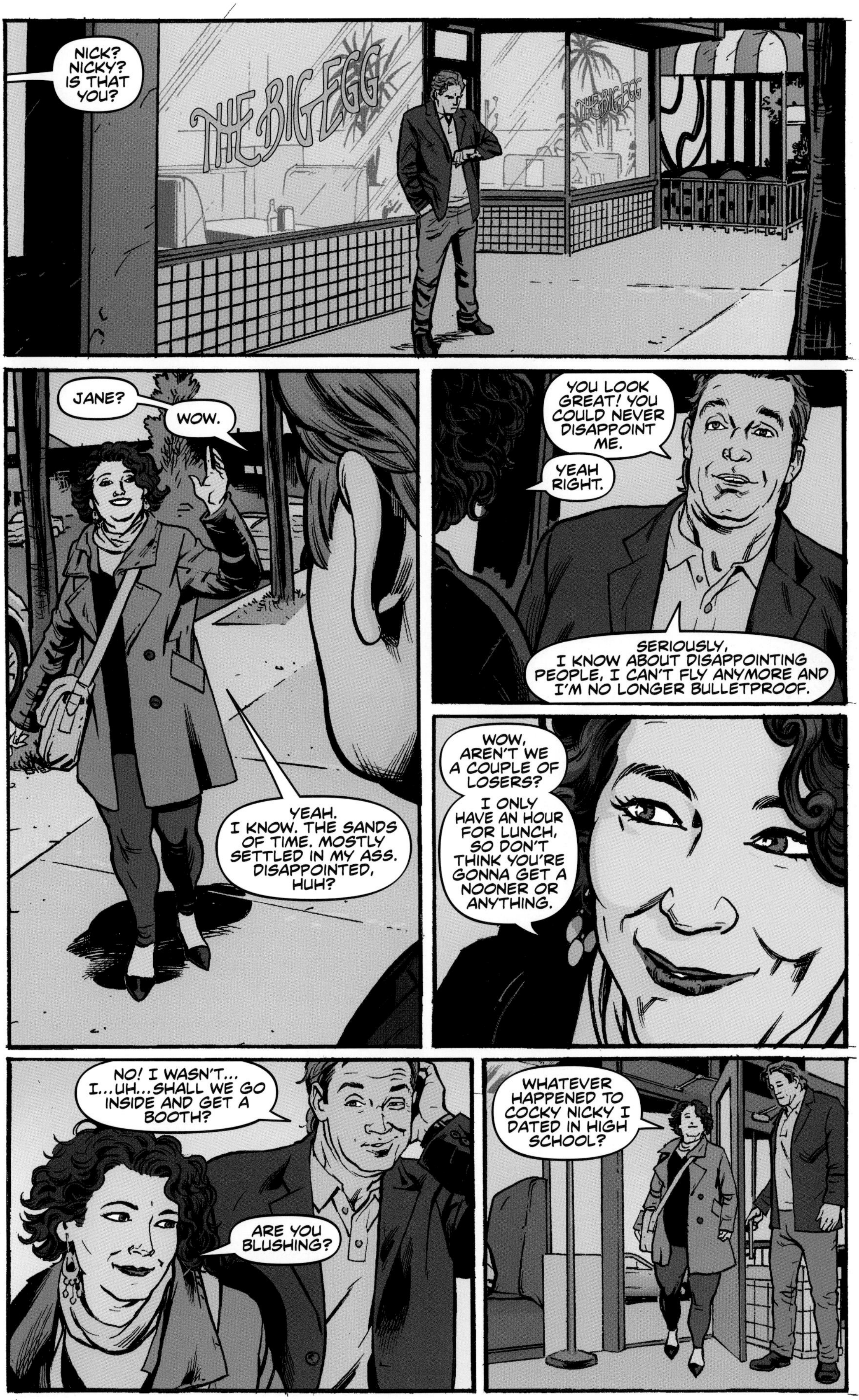
NICK? NICKY? IS THAT YOU?
JANE?
WOW.
YEAH. I KNOW. THE SANDS OF TIME. MOSTLY SETTLED IN MY ASS. DISAPPOINTED, HUH?
YOU LOOK GREAT! YOU COULD NEVER DISAPPOINT ME.
YEAH RIGHT.
SERIOUSLY, I KNOW ABOUT DISAPPOINTING PEOPLE, I CAN'T FLY ANYMORE AND I'M NO LONGER BULLETPROOF.
WOW, AREN'T WE A COUPLE OF LOSERS?
I ONLY HAVE AN HOUR FOR LUNCH, SO DON'T THINK YOU'RE GONNA GET A NOONER OR ANYTHING.
NO! I WASN'T... I...UH...SHALL WE GO INSIDE AND GET A BOOTH?
ARE YOU BLUSHING?
WHATEVER HAPPENED TO COCKY NICKY I DATED IN HIGH SCHOOL?

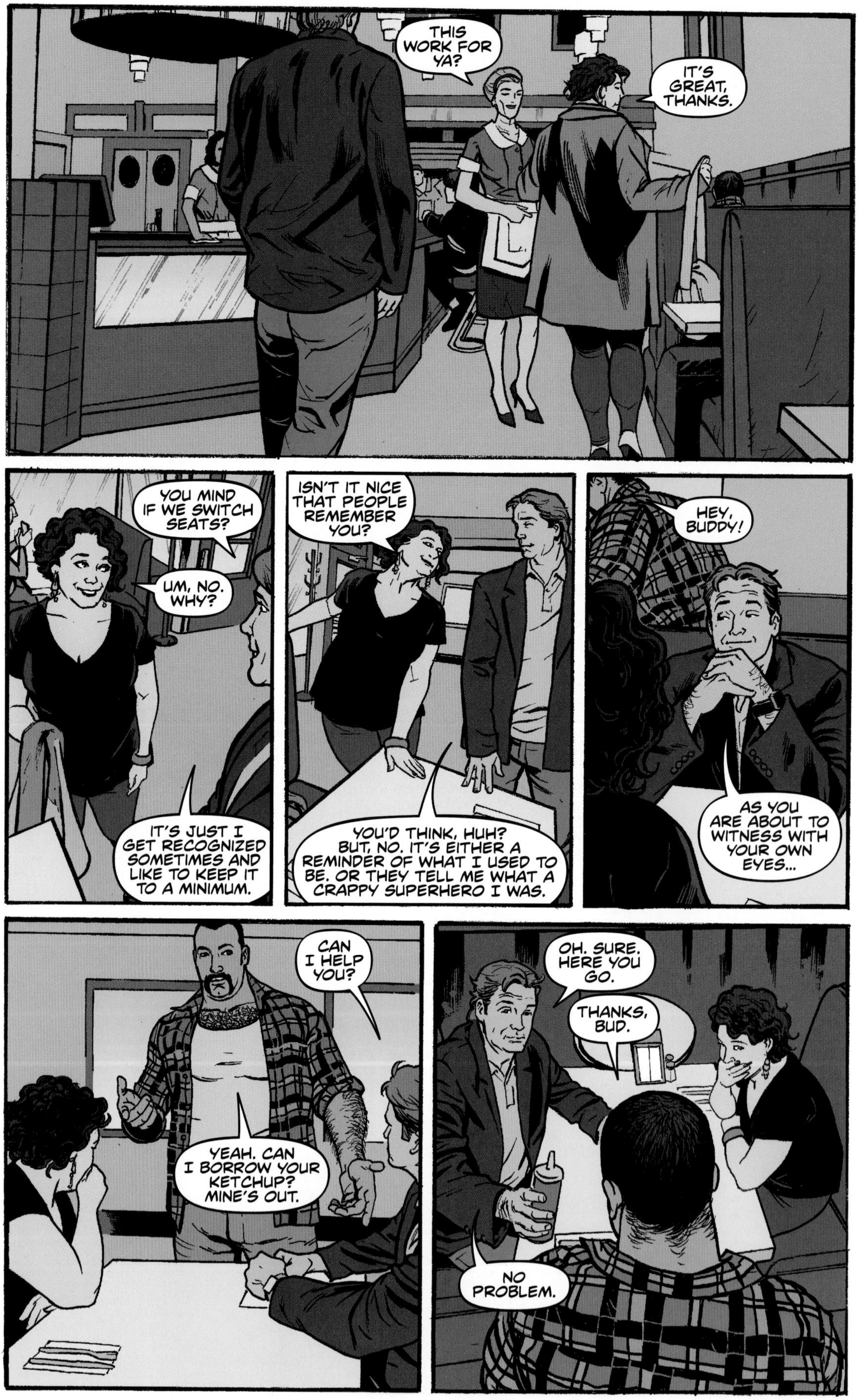
THIS WORK FOR YA?
IT'S GREAT, THANKS.
YOU MIND IF WE SWITCH SEATS?
UM, NO. WHY?
IT'S JUST I GET RECOGNIZED SOMETIMES AND LIKE TO KEEP IT TO A MINIMUM.
ISN'T IT NICE THAT PEOPLE REMEMBER YOU?
YOU'D THINK, HUH? BUT, NO. IT'S EITHER A REMINDER OF WHAT I USED TO BE. OR THEY TELL ME WHAT A CRAPPY SUPERHERO I WAS.
HEY, BUDDY!
AS YOU ARE ABOUT TO WITNESS WITH YOUR OWN EYES...
CAN I HELP YOU?
YEAH. CAN I BORROW YOUR KETCHUP? MINE'S OUT.
OH. SURE. HERE YOU GO.
THANKS, BUD.
NO PROBLEM.

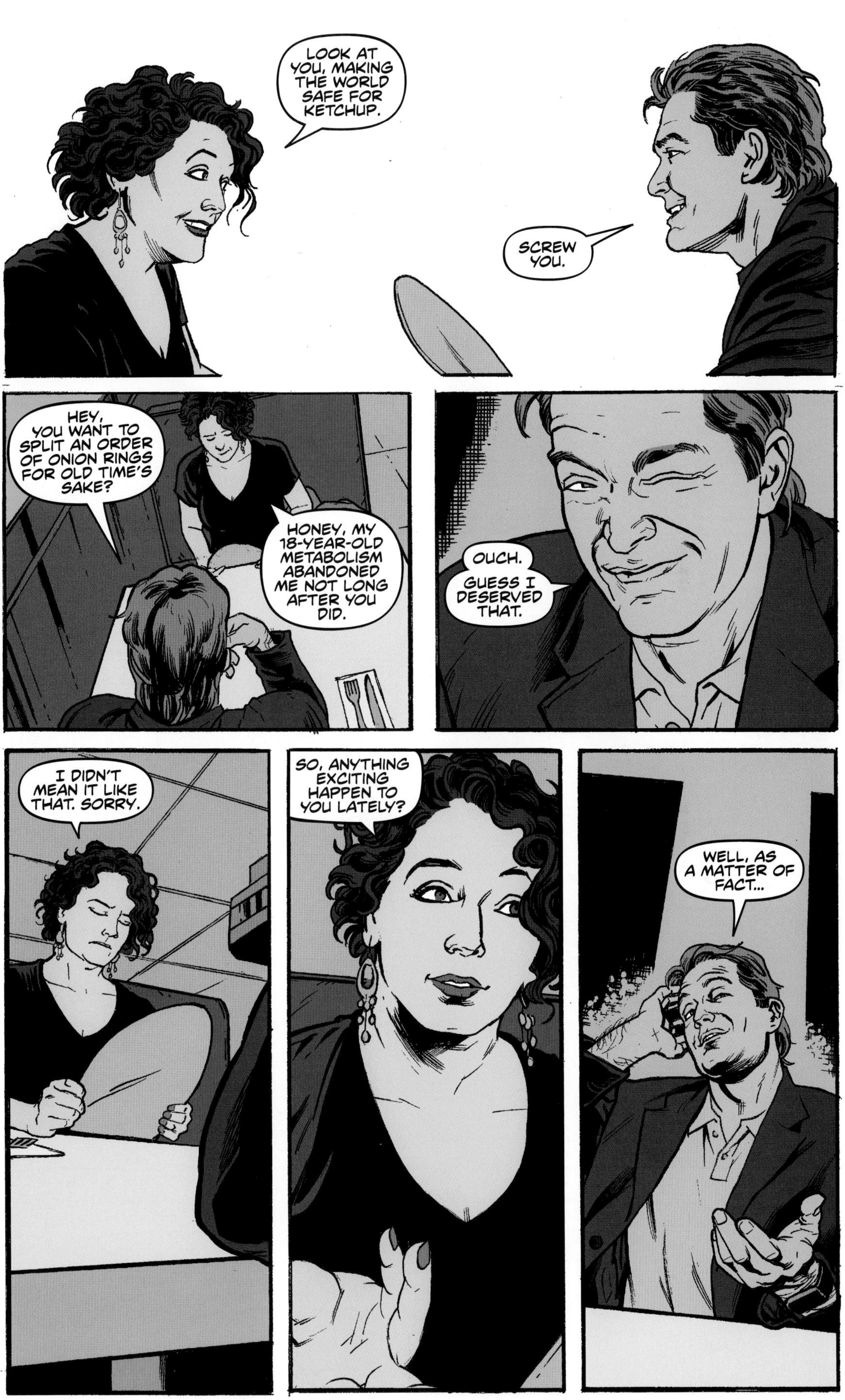
LOOK AT YOU, MAKING THE WORLD SAFE FOR KETCHUP.
SCREW YOU.
HEY, YOU WANT TO SPLIT AN ORDER OF ONION RINGS FOR OLD TIME'S SAKE?
HONEY, MY 18-YEAR-OLD METABOLISM ABANDONED ME NOT LONG AFTER YOU DID.
OUCH. GUESS I DESERVED THAT.
I DIDN'T MEAN IT LIKE THAT. SORRY.
SO, ANYTHING EXCITING HAPPEN TO YOU LATELY?
WELL, AS A MATTER OF FACT...

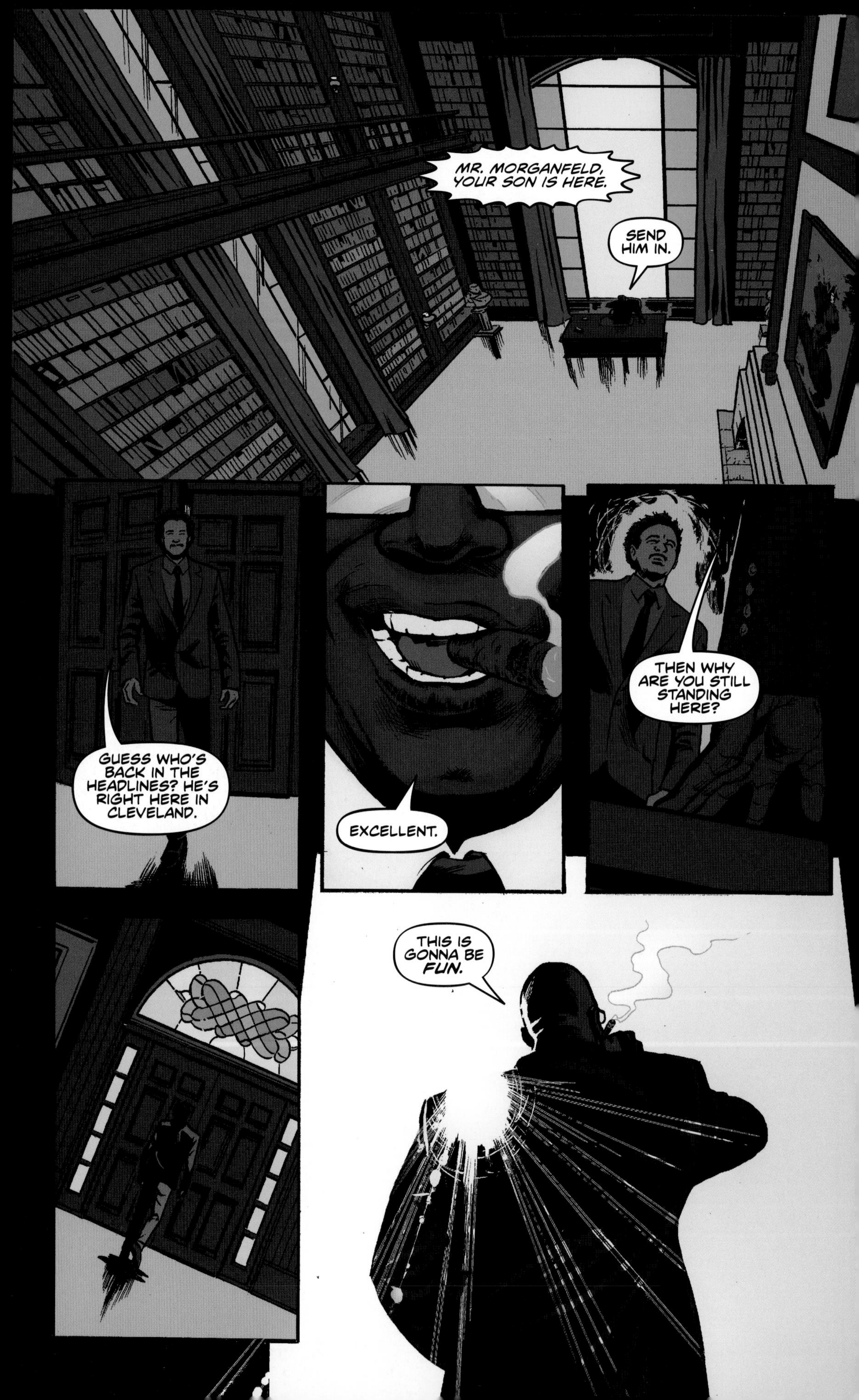
MR. MORGANFELD, YOUR SON IS HERE.
SEND HIM IN.
GUESS WHO'S BACK IN THE HEADLINES? HE'S RIGHT HERE IN CLEVELAND.
EXCELLENT.
THEN WHY ARE YOU STILL STANDING HERE?
THIS IS GONNA BE *FUN*.

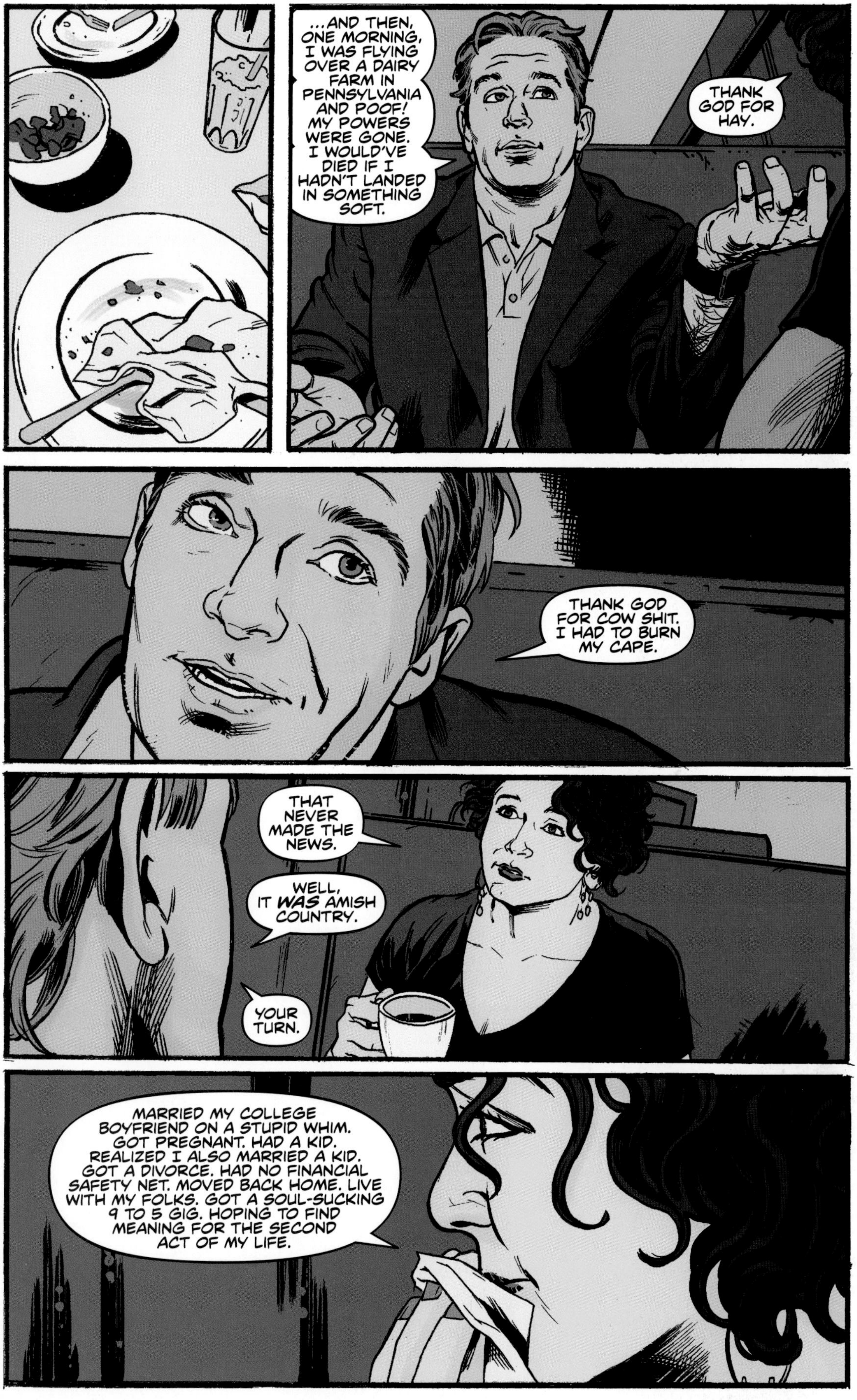
...AND THEN, ONE MORNING, I WAS FLYING OVER A DAIRY FARM IN PENNSYLVANIA AND POOF! MY POWERS WERE GONE. I WOULD'VE DIED IF I HADN'T LANDED IN SOMETHING SOFT.
THANK GOD FOR HAY.
THANK GOD FOR COW SHIT. I HAD TO BURN MY CAPE.
THAT NEVER MADE THE NEWS.
WELL, IT *WAS* AMISH COUNTRY.
YOUR TURN.
MARRIED MY COLLEGE BOYFRIEND ON A STUPID WHIM. GOT PREGNANT. HAD A KID. REALIZED I ALSO MARRIED A KID. GOT A DIVORCE. HAD NO FINANCIAL SAFETY NET. MOVED BACK HOME. LIVE WITH MY FOLKS. GOT A SOUL-SUCKING 9 TO 5 GIG. HOPING TO FIND MEANING FOR THE SECOND ACT OF MY LIFE.

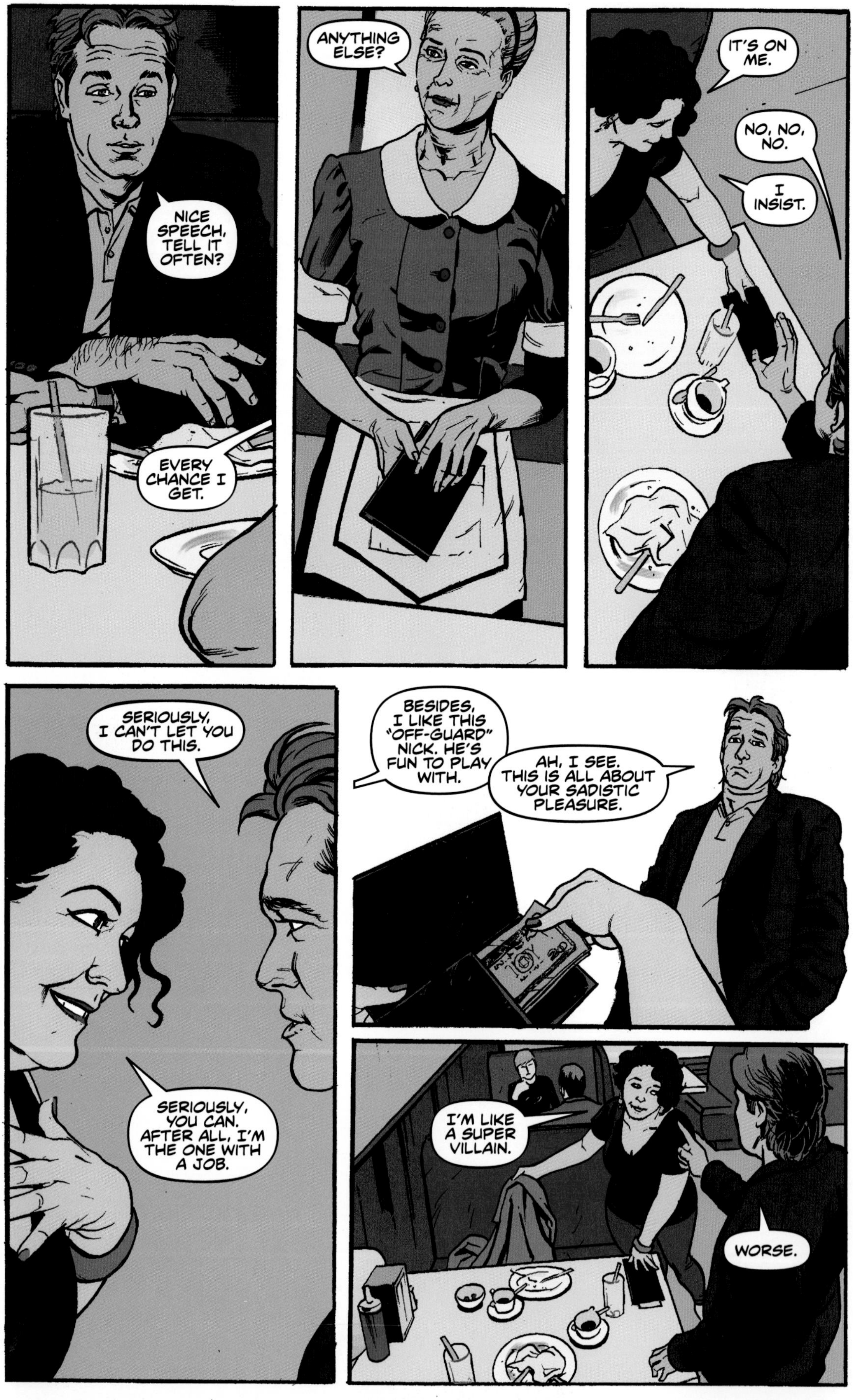
NICE SPEECH, TELL IT OFTEN?
EVERY CHANCE I GET.
ANYTHING ELSE?
IT'S ON ME.
NO, NO, NO.
I INSIST.
SERIOUSLY, I CAN'T LET YOU DO THIS.
SERIOUSLY, YOU CAN. AFTER ALL, I'M THE ONE WITH A JOB.
BESIDES, I LIKE THIS "OFF-GUARD" NICK. HE'S FUN TO PLAY WITH.
AH, I SEE. THIS IS ALL ABOUT YOUR SADISTIC PLEASURE.
I'M LIKE A SUPER VILLAIN.
WORSE.

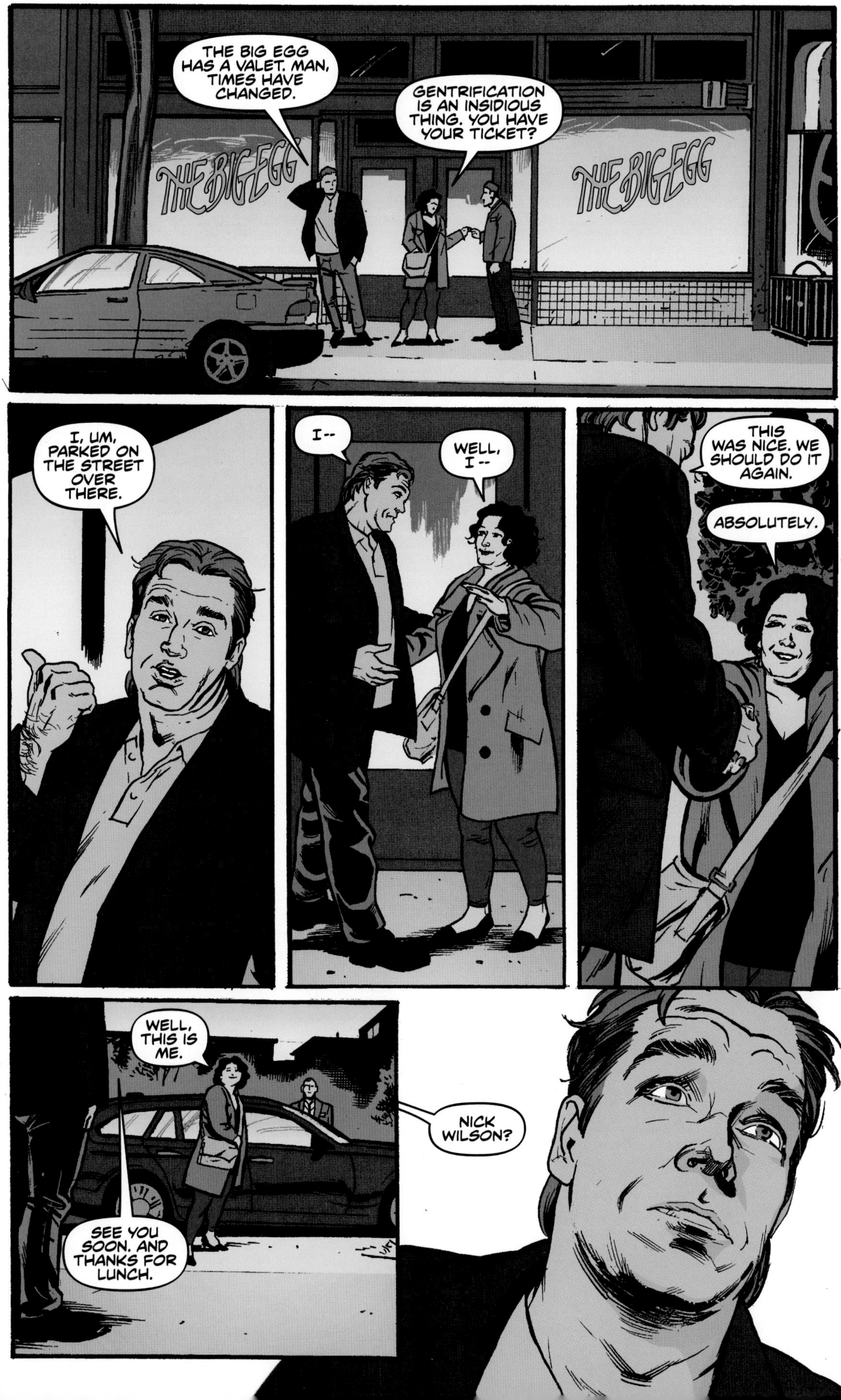
THE BIG EGG HAS A VALET. MAN, TIMES HAVE CHANGED.
GENTRIFICATION IS AN INSIDIOUS THING. YOU HAVE YOUR TICKET?
THE BIG EGG
THE BIG EGG
I, UM, PARKED ON THE STREET OVER THERE.
I--
WELL, I --
THIS WAS NICE. WE SHOULD DO IT AGAIN.
ABSOLUTELY.
WELL, THIS IS ME.
SEE YOU SOON. AND THANKS FOR LUNCH.
NICK WILSON?

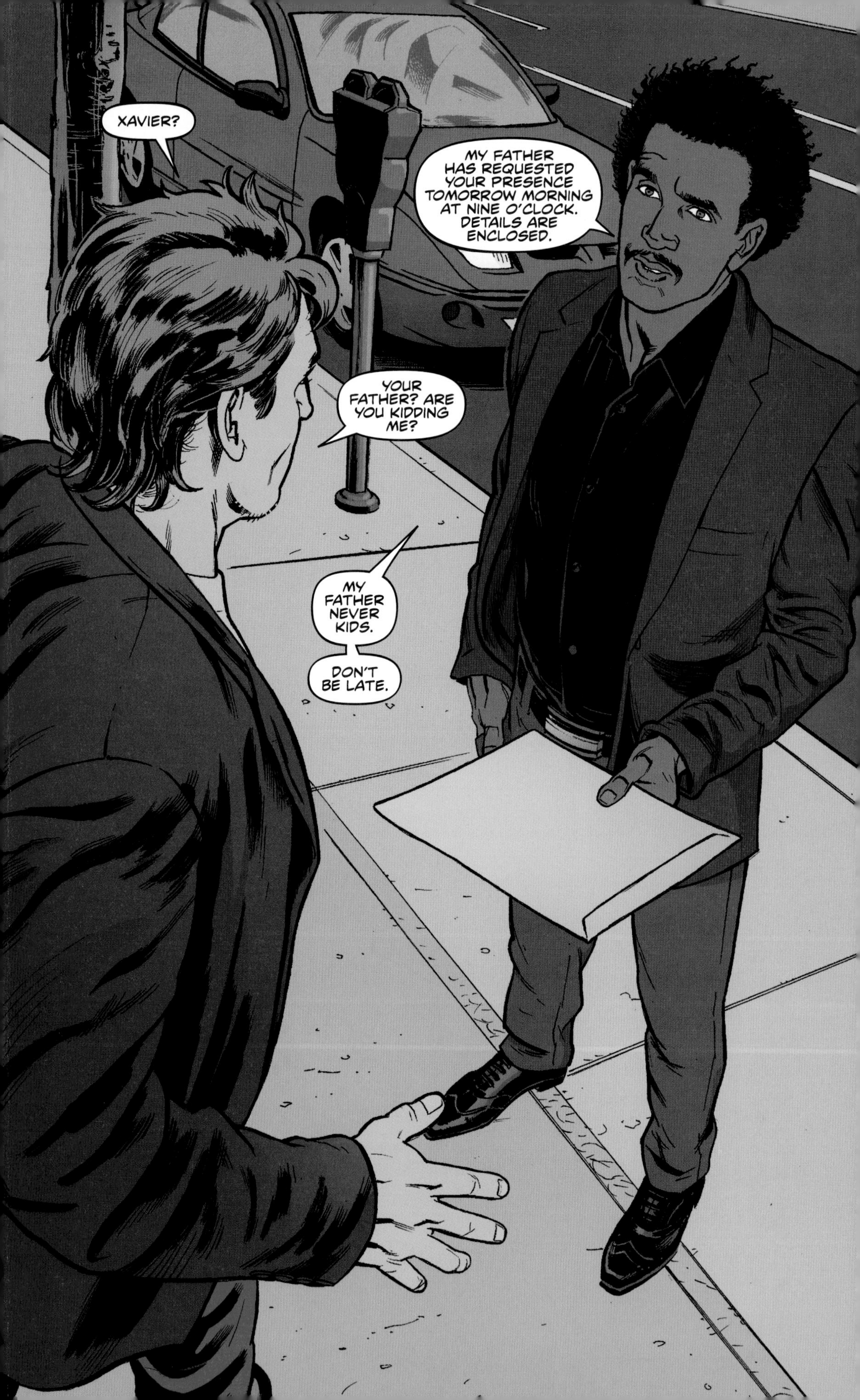
XAVIER?
MY FATHER HAS REQUESTED YOUR PRESENCE TOMORROW MORNING AT NINE O'CLOCK. DETAILS ARE ENCLOSED.
YOUR FATHER? ARE YOU KIDDING ME?
MY FATHER NEVER KIDS.
DON'T BE LATE.

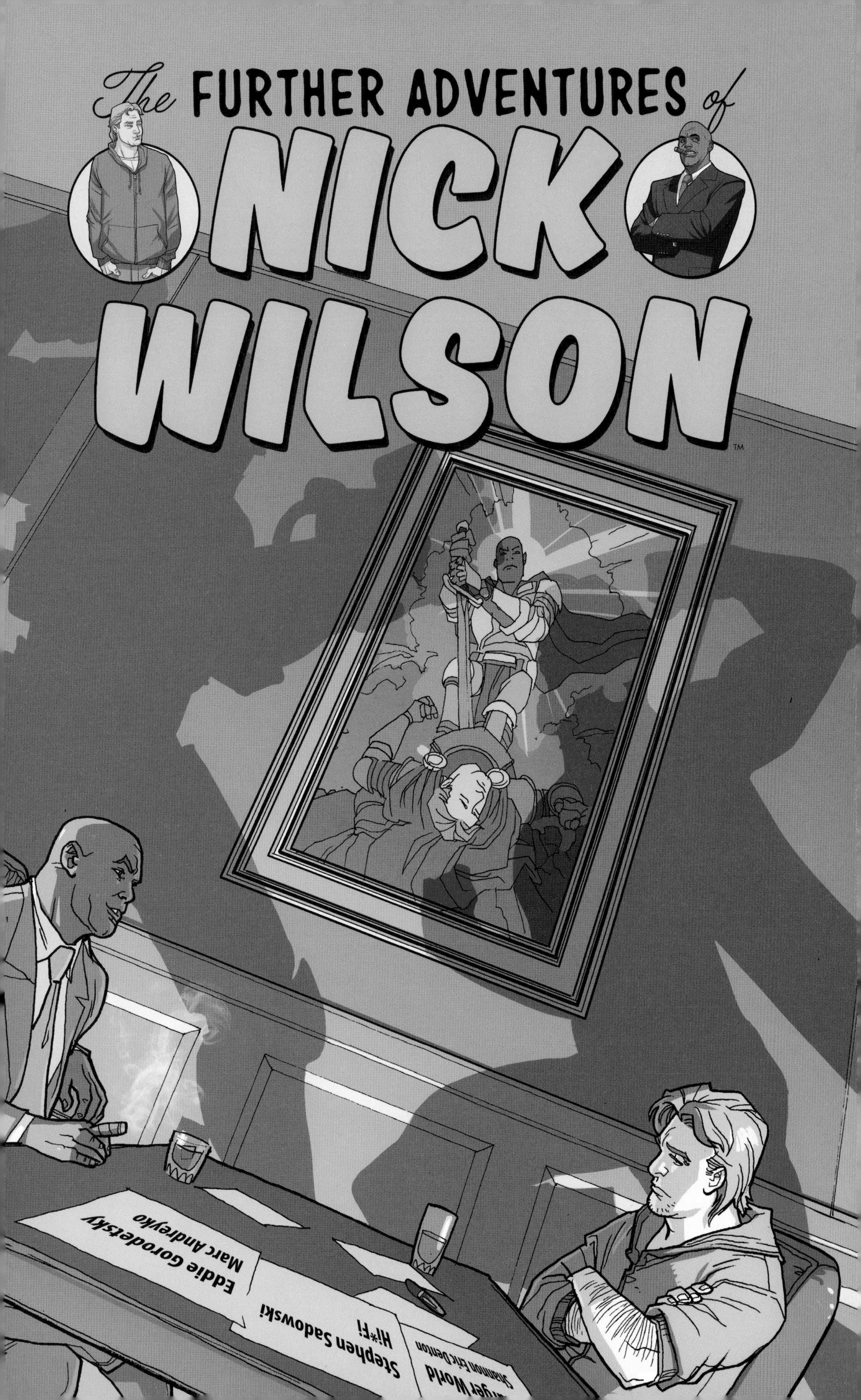

The FURTHER ADVENTURES of
NICK WILSON™
Eddie Gorodetsky
Marc Andreyko
Stephen Sadowski
Hi*Fi
Shannon Eric Denton

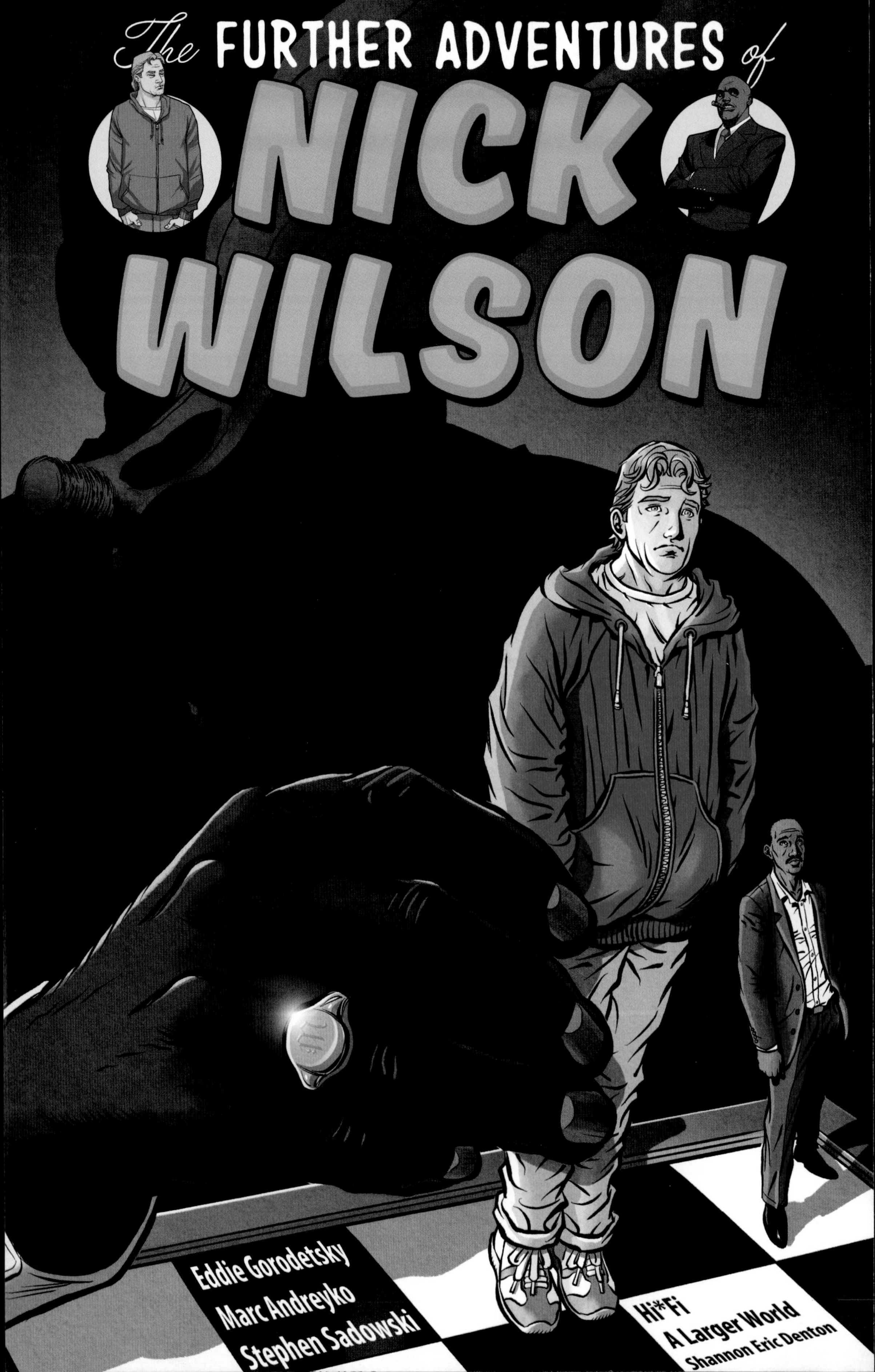
The FURTHER ADVENTURES of
NICK WILSON
Eddie Gorodetsky
Marc Andreyko
Stephen Sadowski
Hi*Fi
A Larger World
Shannon Eric Denton

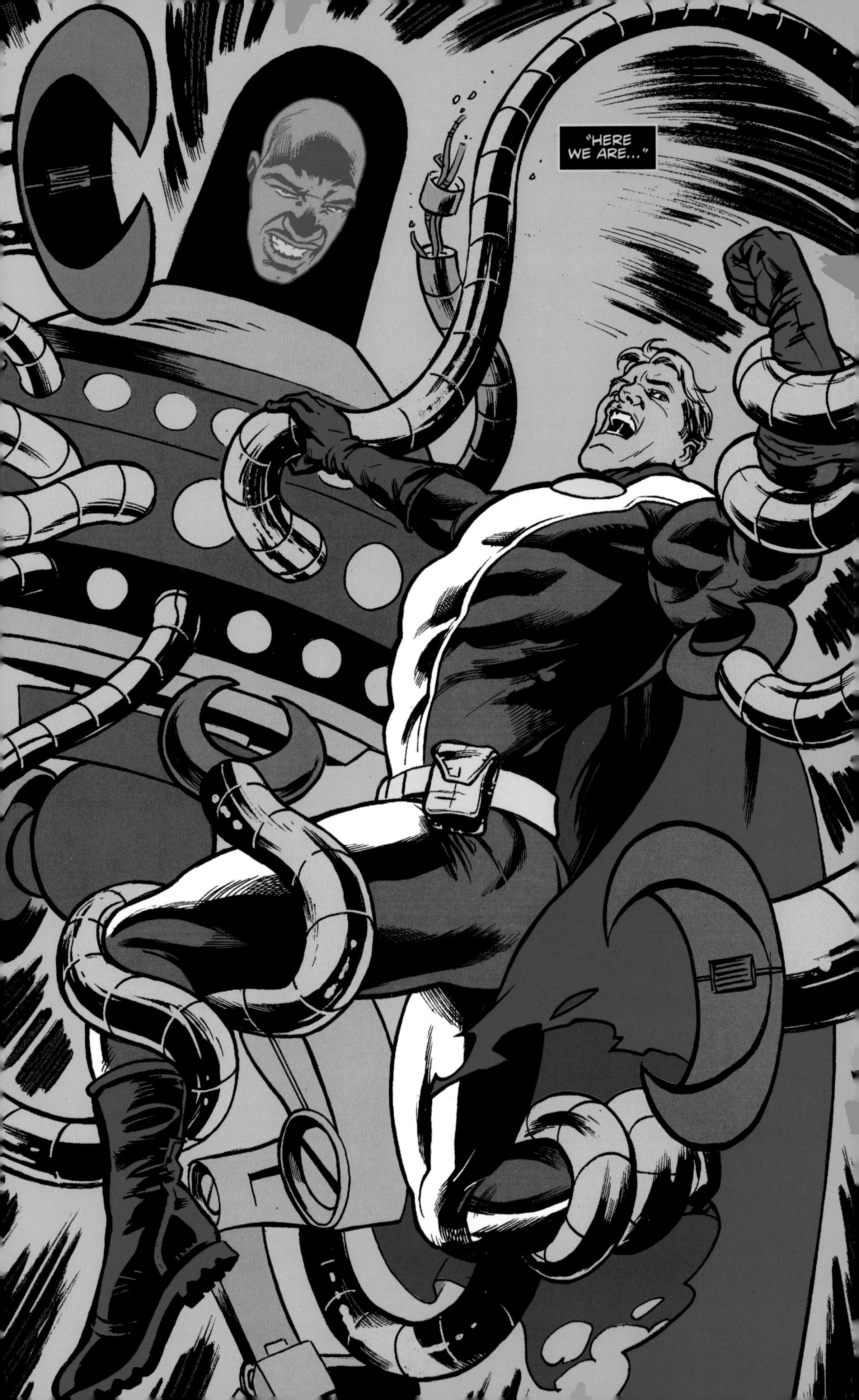
"HERE WE ARE..."

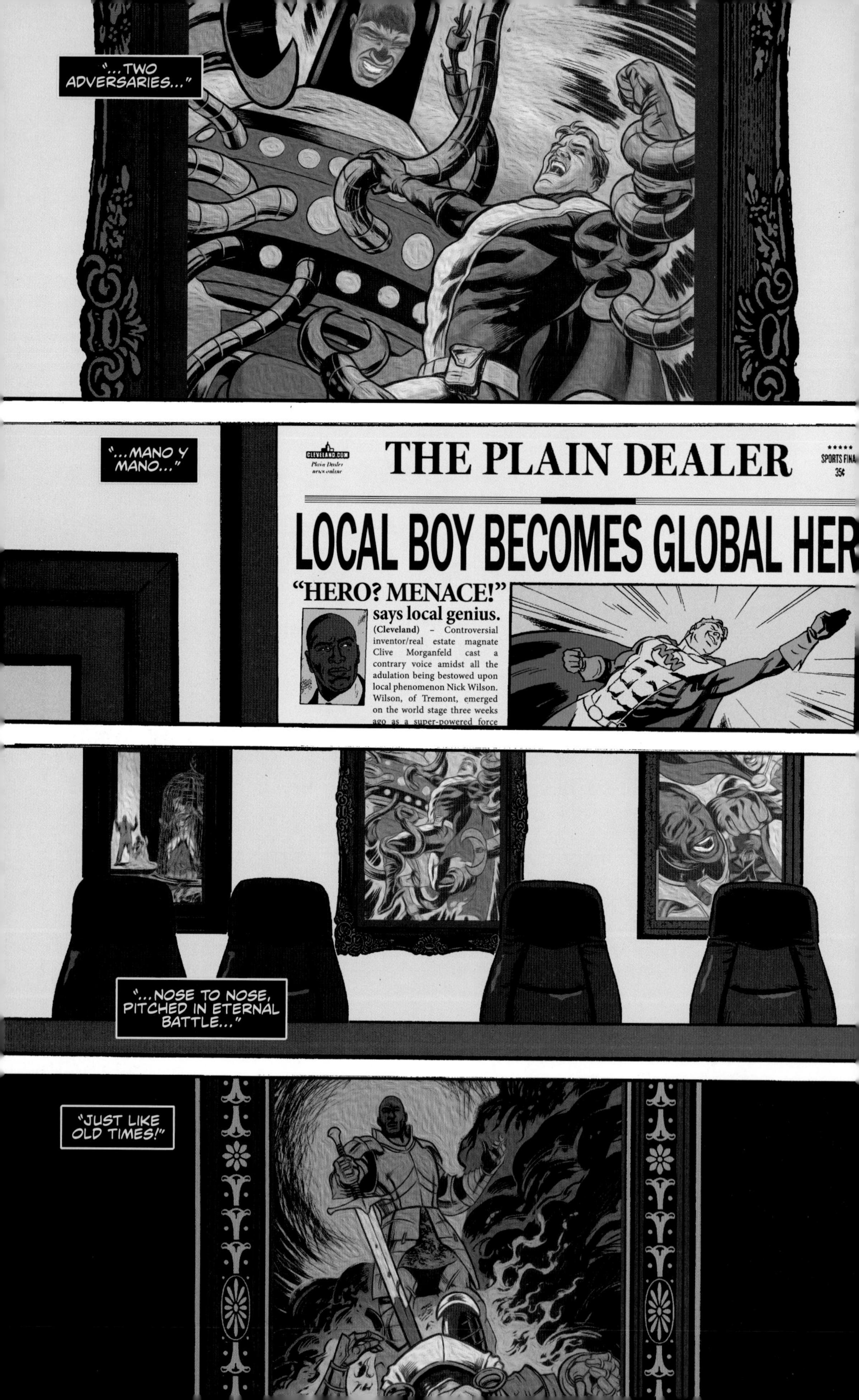
"...TWO ADVERSARIES..."
"...MANO Y MANO..."
CLEVELAND.COM
Plain Dealer news online
THE PLAIN DEALER
SPORTS FINA
35¢
LOCAL BOY BECOMES GLOBAL HER
"HERO? MENACE!"
says local genius.
(Cleveland) – Controversial inventor/real estate magnate Clive Morganfeld cast a contrary voice amidst all the adulation being bestowed upon local phenomenon Nick Wilson. Wilson, of Tremont, emerged on the world stage three weeks ago as a super-powered force
MW
"...NOSE TO NOSE, PITCHED IN ETERNAL BATTLE..."
"JUST LIKE OLD TIMES!"

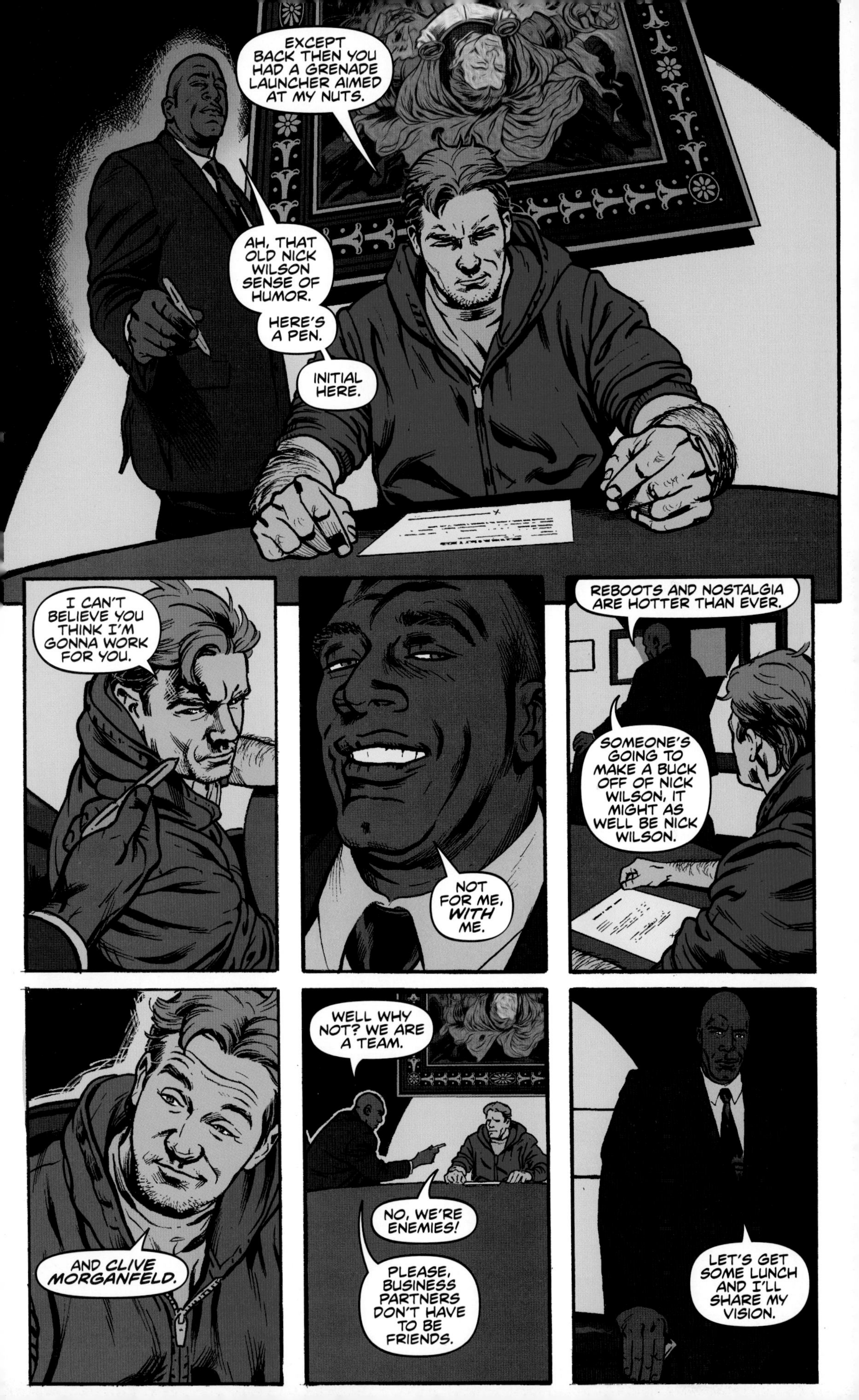
EXCEPT BACK THEN YOU HAD A GRENADE LAUNCHER AIMED AT MY NUTS.
AH, THAT OLD NICK WILSON SENSE OF HUMOR.
HERE'S A PEN.
INITIAL HERE.
I CAN'T BELIEVE YOU THINK I'M GONNA WORK FOR YOU.
NOT FOR ME, *WITH* ME.
REBOOTS AND NOSTALGIA ARE HOTTER THAN EVER.
SOMEONE'S GOING TO MAKE A BUCK OFF OF NICK WILSON, IT MIGHT AS WELL BE NICK WILSON.
AND *CLIVE MORGANFELD.*
WELL WHY NOT? WE ARE A TEAM.
NO, WE'RE ENEMIES!
PLEASE, BUSINESS PARTNERS DON'T HAVE TO BE FRIENDS.
LET'S GET SOME LUNCH AND I'LL SHARE MY VISION.

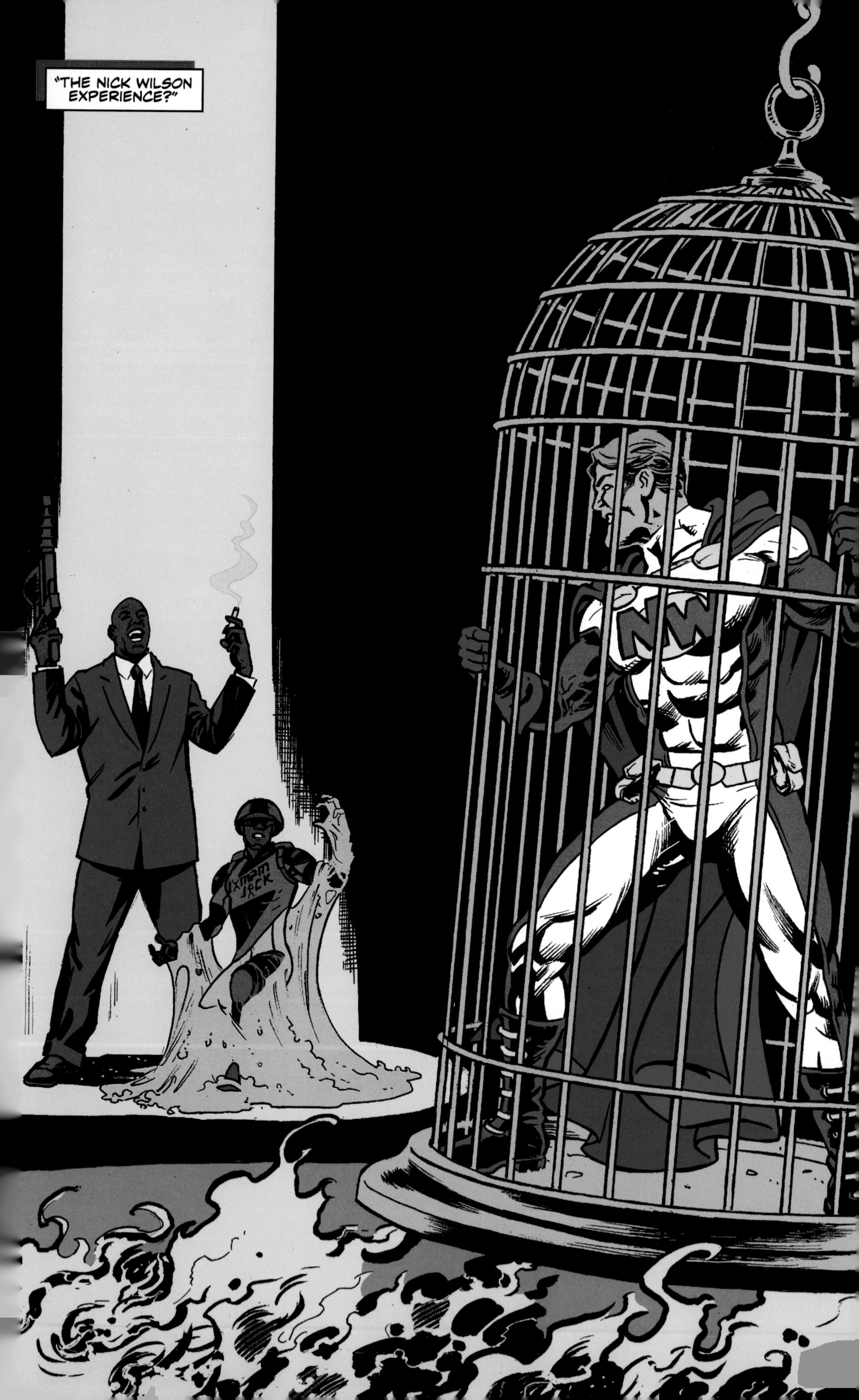
"THE NICK WILSON EXPERIENCE?"

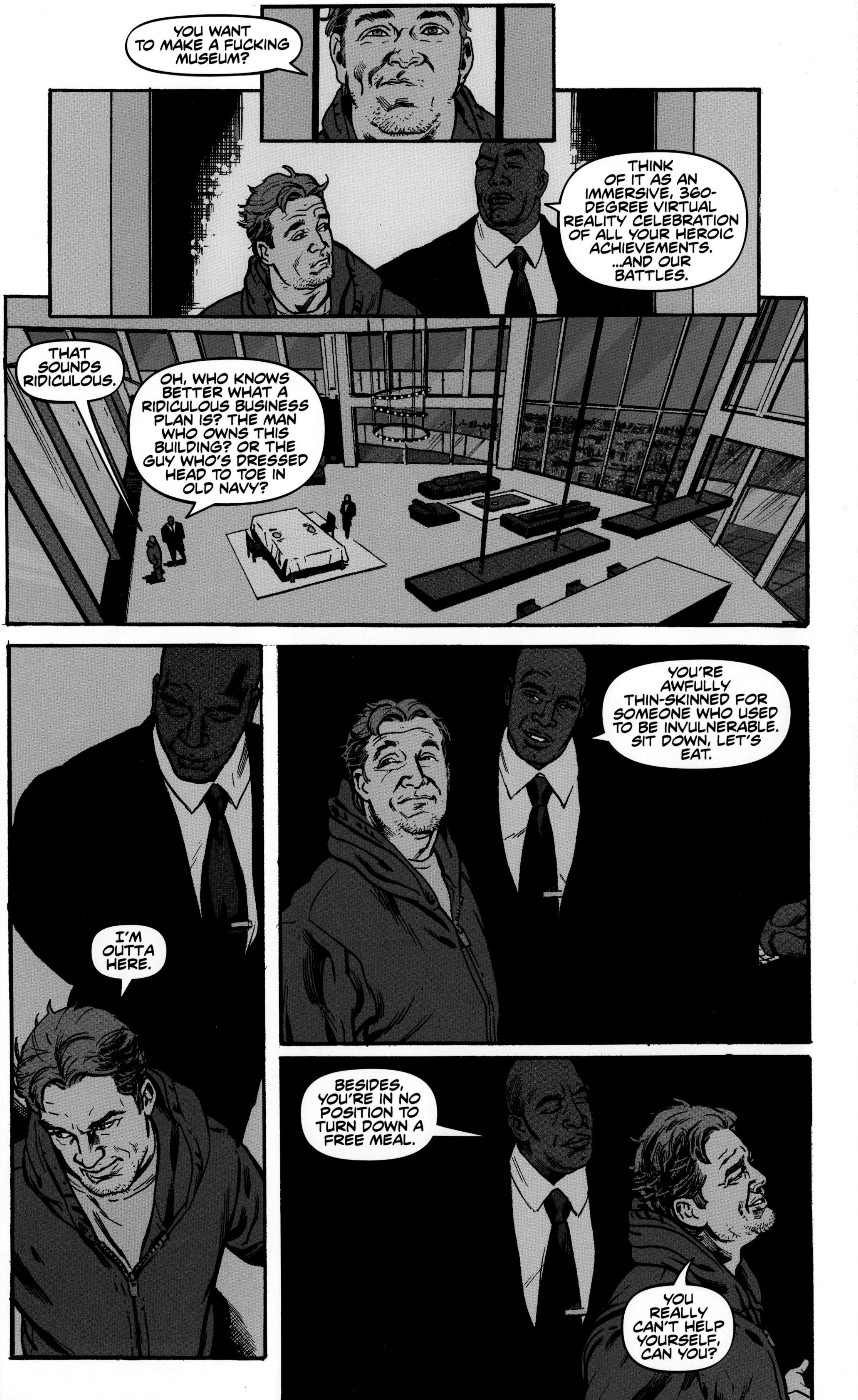
YOU WANT TO MAKE A FUCKING MUSEUM?
THINK OF IT AS AN IMMERSIVE, 360-DEGREE VIRTUAL REALITY CELEBRATION OF ALL YOUR HEROIC ACHIEVEMENTS. ...AND OUR BATTLES.
THAT SOUNDS RIDICULOUS.
OH, WHO KNOWS BETTER WHAT A RIDICULOUS BUSINESS PLAN IS? THE MAN WHO OWNS THIS BUILDING? OR THE GUY WHO'S DRESSED HEAD TO TOE IN OLD NAVY?
I'M OUTTA HERE.
YOU'RE AWFULLY THIN-SKINNED FOR SOMEONE WHO USED TO BE INVULNERABLE. SIT DOWN, LET'S EAT.
BESIDES, YOU'RE IN NO POSITION TO TURN DOWN A FREE MEAL.
YOU REALLY CAN'T HELP YOURSELF, CAN YOU?

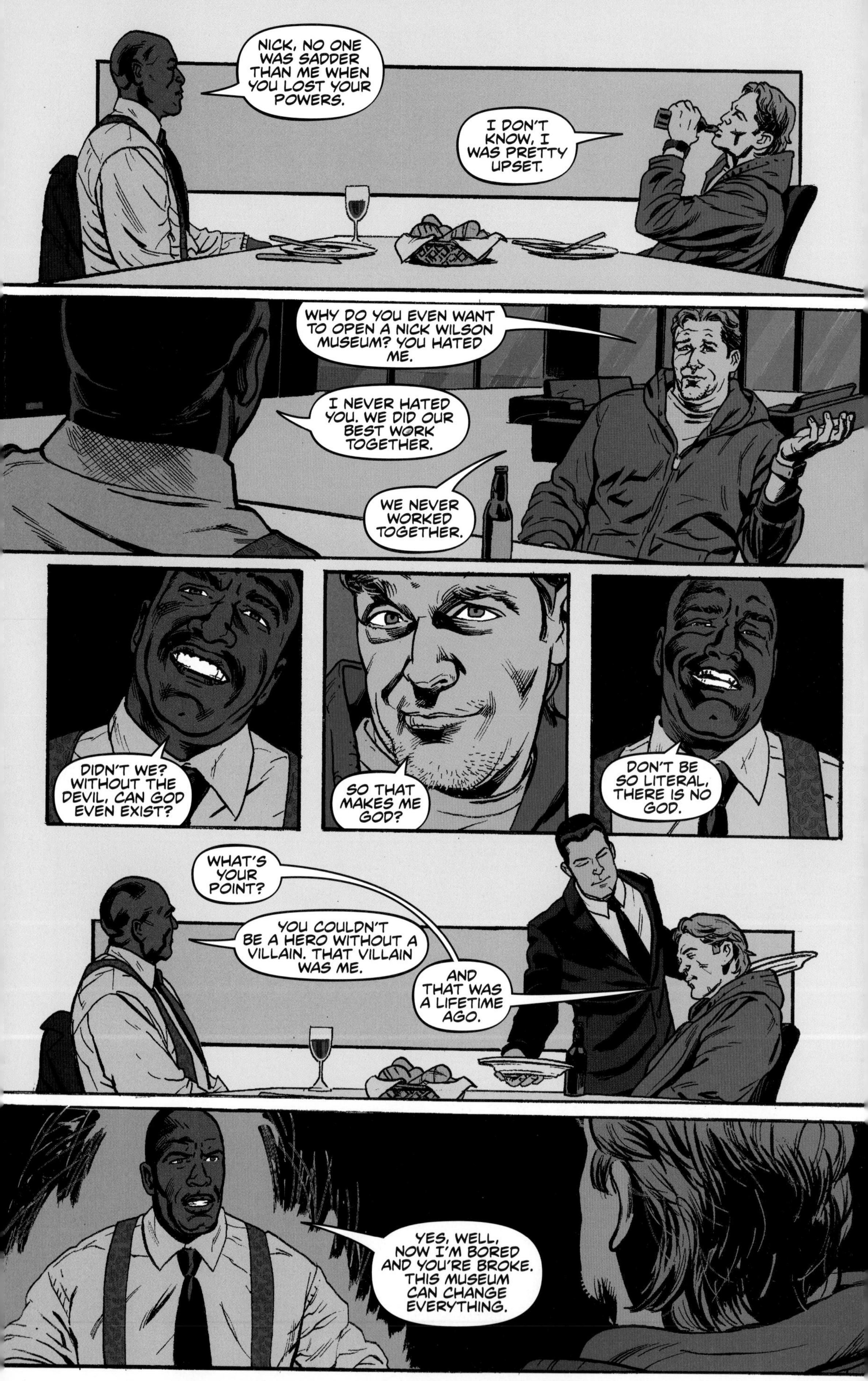
NICK, NO ONE WAS SADDER THAN ME WHEN YOU LOST YOUR POWERS.
I DON'T KNOW, I WAS PRETTY UPSET.
WHY DO YOU EVEN WANT TO OPEN A NICK WILSON MUSEUM? YOU HATED ME.
I NEVER HATED YOU. WE DID OUR BEST WORK TOGETHER.
WE NEVER WORKED TOGETHER.
DIDN'T WE? WITHOUT THE DEVIL, CAN GOD EVEN EXIST?
SO THAT MAKES ME GOD?
DON'T BE SO LITERAL, THERE IS NO GOD.
WHAT'S YOUR POINT?
YOU COULDN'T BE A HERO WITHOUT A VILLAIN. THAT VILLAIN WAS ME.
AND THAT WAS A LIFETIME AGO.
YES, WELL, NOW I'M BORED AND YOU'RE BROKE. THIS MUSEUM CAN CHANGE EVERYTHING.

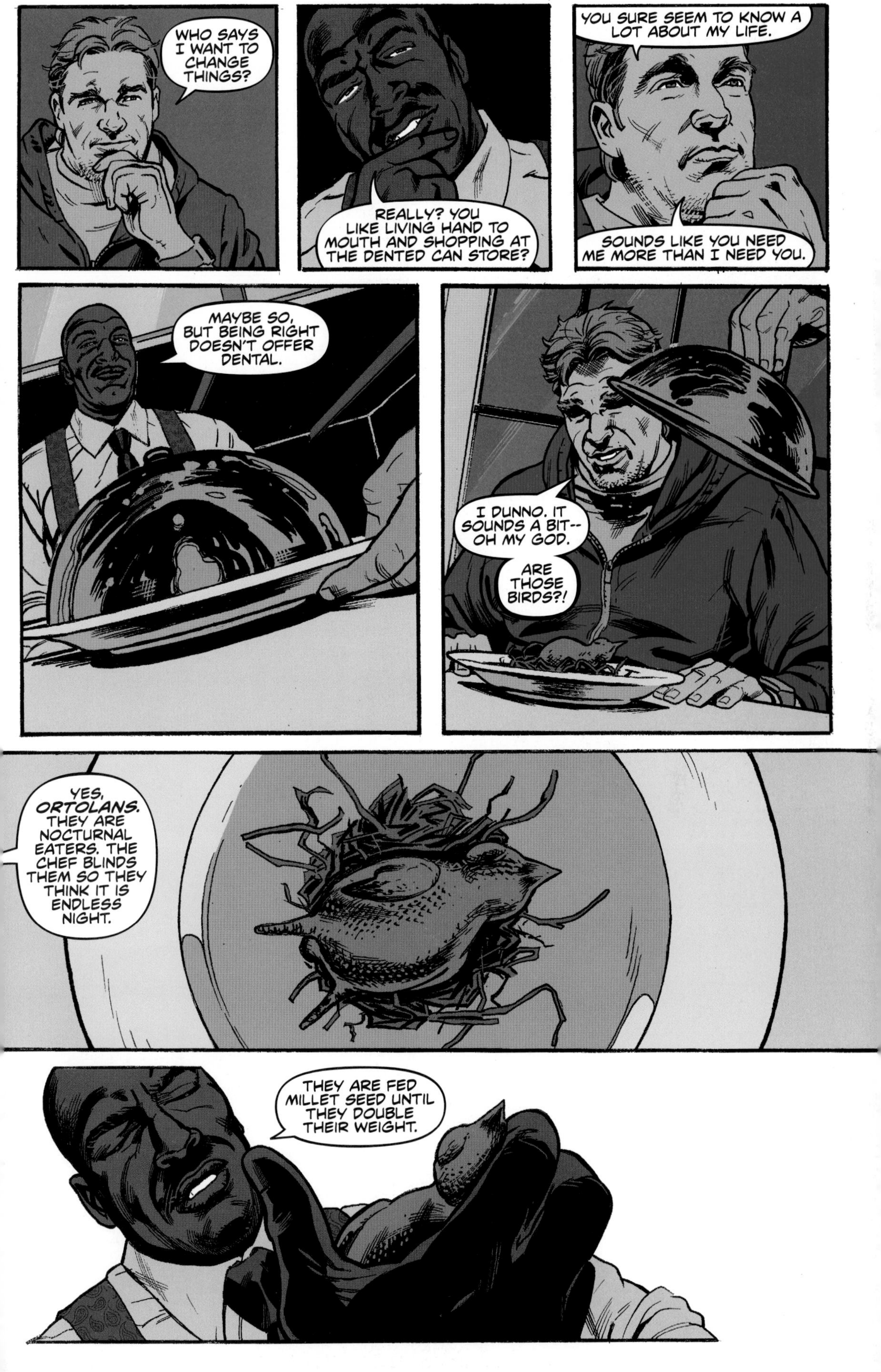
WHO SAYS I WANT TO CHANGE THINGS?
REALLY? YOU LIKE LIVING HAND TO MOUTH AND SHOPPING AT THE DENTED CAN STORE?
YOU SURE SEEM TO KNOW A LOT ABOUT MY LIFE.
SOUNDS LIKE YOU NEED ME MORE THAN I NEED YOU.
MAYBE SO, BUT BEING RIGHT DOESN'T OFFER DENTAL.
I DUNNO. IT SOUNDS A BIT-- OH MY GOD.
ARE THOSE BIRDS?!
YES, ORTOLANS. THEY ARE NOCTURNAL EATERS. THE CHEF BLINDS THEM SO THEY THINK IT IS ENDLESS NIGHT.
THEY ARE FED MILLET SEED UNTIL THEY DOUBLE THEIR WEIGHT.

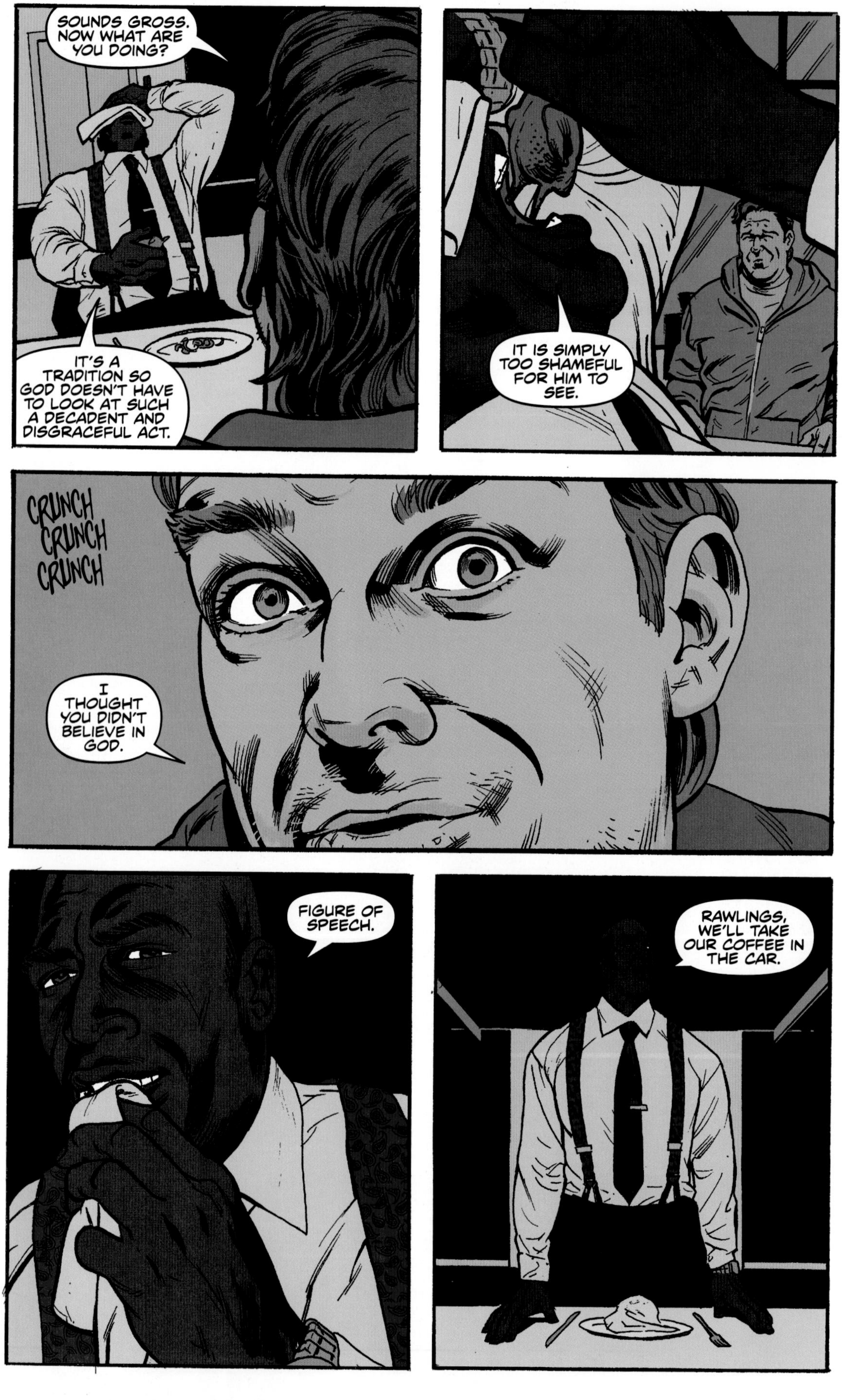
SOUNDS GROSS. NOW WHAT ARE YOU DOING?
IT'S A TRADITION SO GOD DOESN'T HAVE TO LOOK AT SUCH A DECADENT AND DISGRACEFUL ACT.
IT IS SIMPLY TOO SHAMEFUL FOR HIM TO SEE.
CRUNCH CRUNCH CRUNCH
I THOUGHT YOU DIDN'T BELIEVE IN GOD.
FIGURE OF SPEECH.
RAWLINGS, WE'LL TAKE OUR COFFEE IN THE CAR.

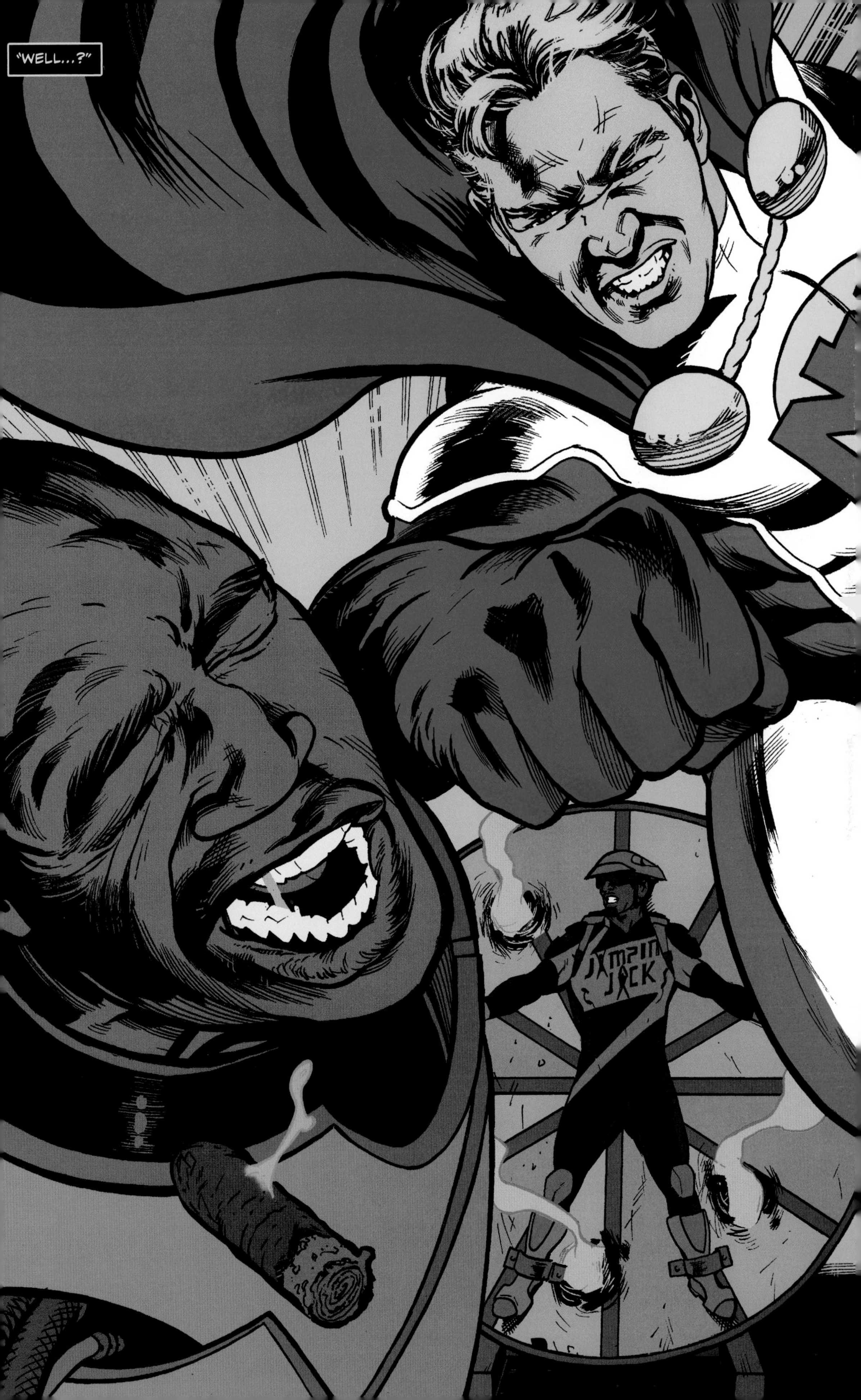
"WELL...?"
JUMPIN JACK

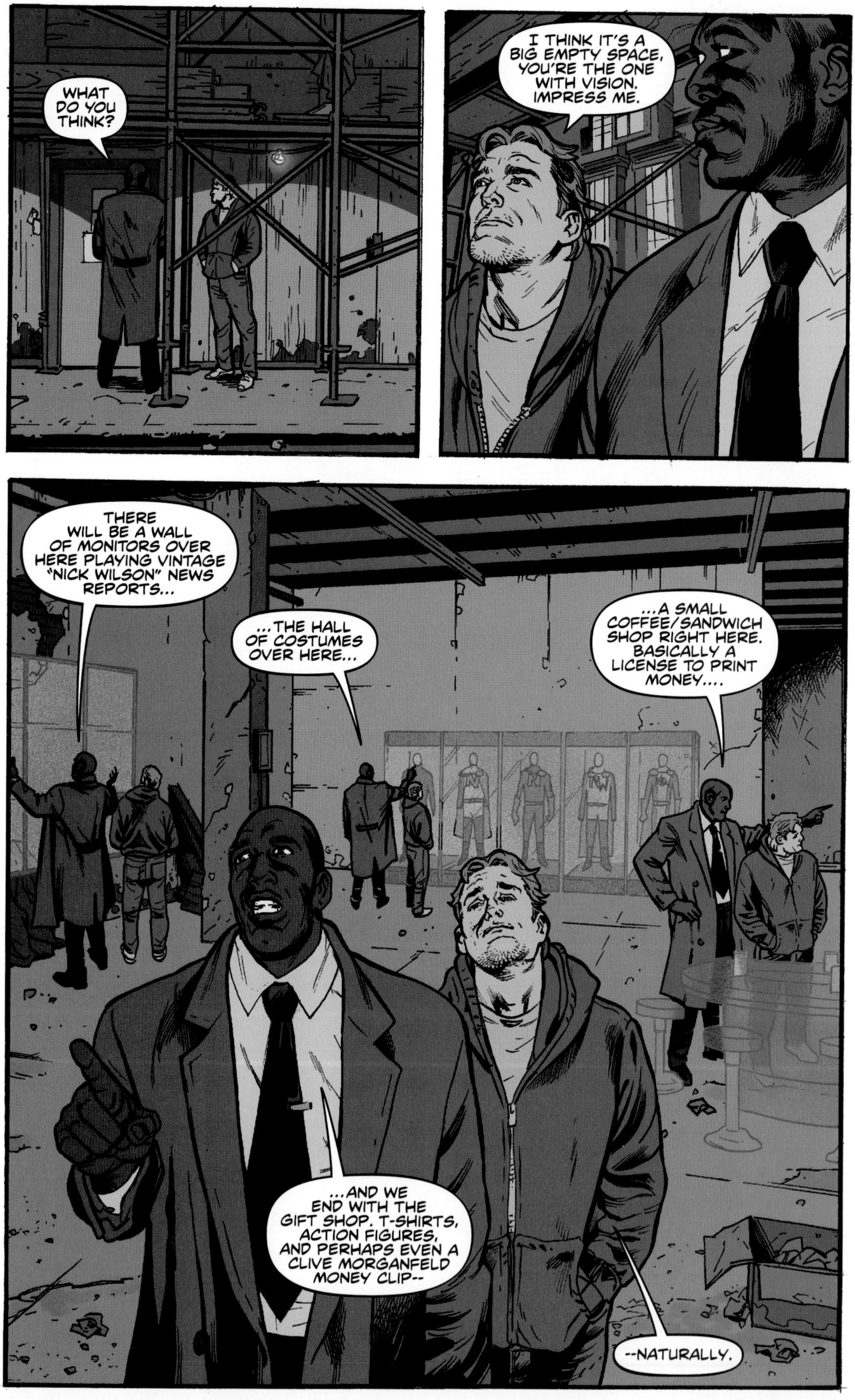
WHAT DO YOU THINK?
I THINK IT'S A BIG EMPTY SPACE, YOU'RE THE ONE WITH VISION. IMPRESS ME.
THERE WILL BE A WALL OF MONITORS OVER HERE PLAYING VINTAGE "NICK WILSON" NEWS REPORTS...
...THE HALL OF COSTUMES OVER HERE...
...A SMALL COFFEE/SANDWICH SHOP RIGHT HERE. BASICALLY A LICENSE TO PRINT MONEY....
...AND WE END WITH THE GIFT SHOP. T-SHIRTS, ACTION FIGURES, AND PERHAPS EVEN A CLIVE MORGANFELD MONEY CLIP--
--NATURALLY.

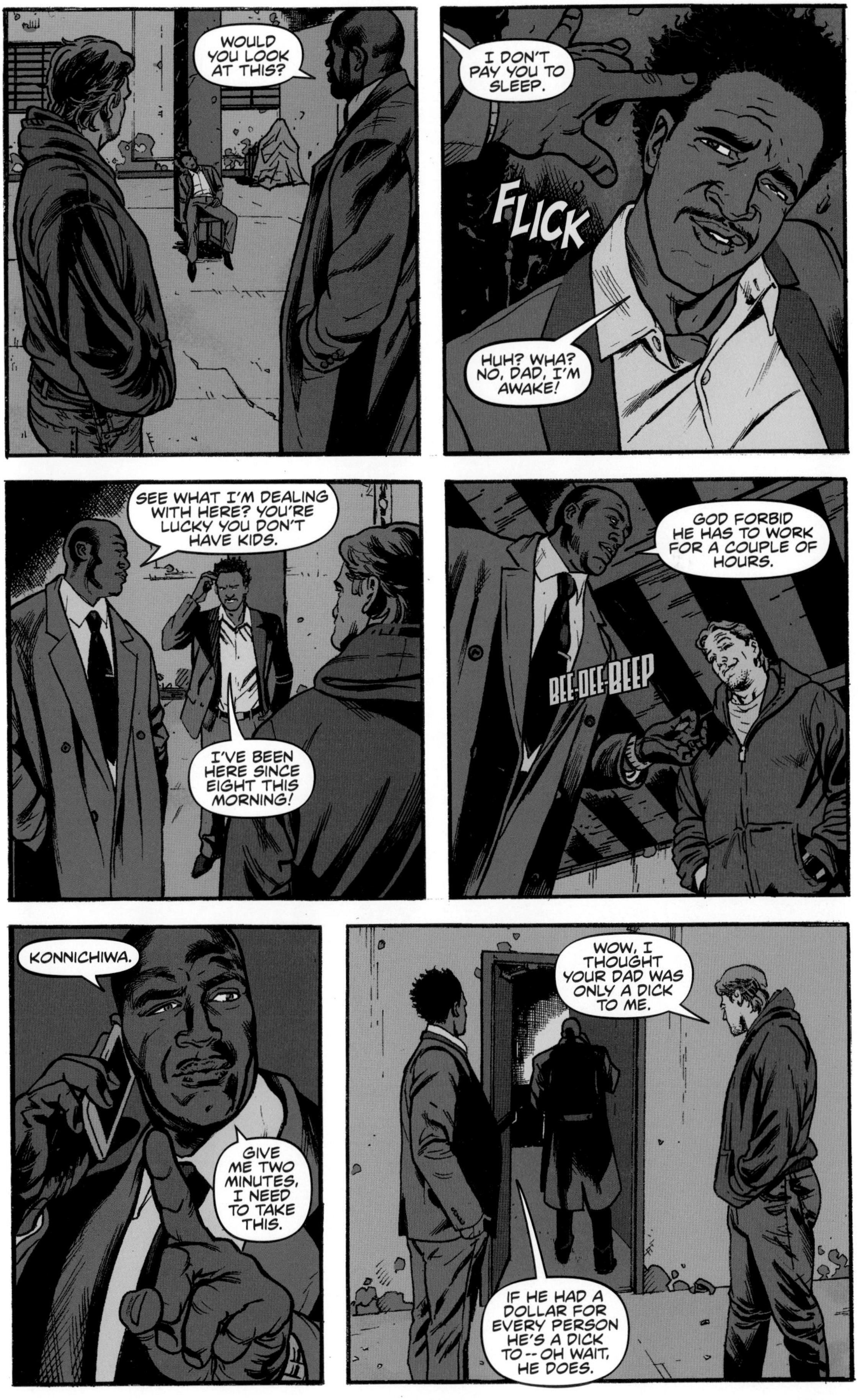
WOULD YOU LOOK AT THIS?
I DON'T PAY YOU TO SLEEP.
FLICK
HUH? WHA? NO, DAD, I'M AWAKE!
SEE WHAT I'M DEALING WITH HERE? YOU'RE LUCKY YOU DON'T HAVE KIDS.
I'VE BEEN HERE SINCE EIGHT THIS MORNING!
GOD FORBID HE HAS TO WORK FOR A COUPLE OF HOURS.
BEE-DEE-BEEP
KONNICHIWA.
GIVE ME TWO MINUTES, I NEED TO TAKE THIS.
WOW, I THOUGHT YOUR DAD WAS ONLY A DICK TO ME.
IF HE HAD A DOLLAR FOR EVERY PERSON HE'S A DICK TO -- OH WAIT, HE DOES.

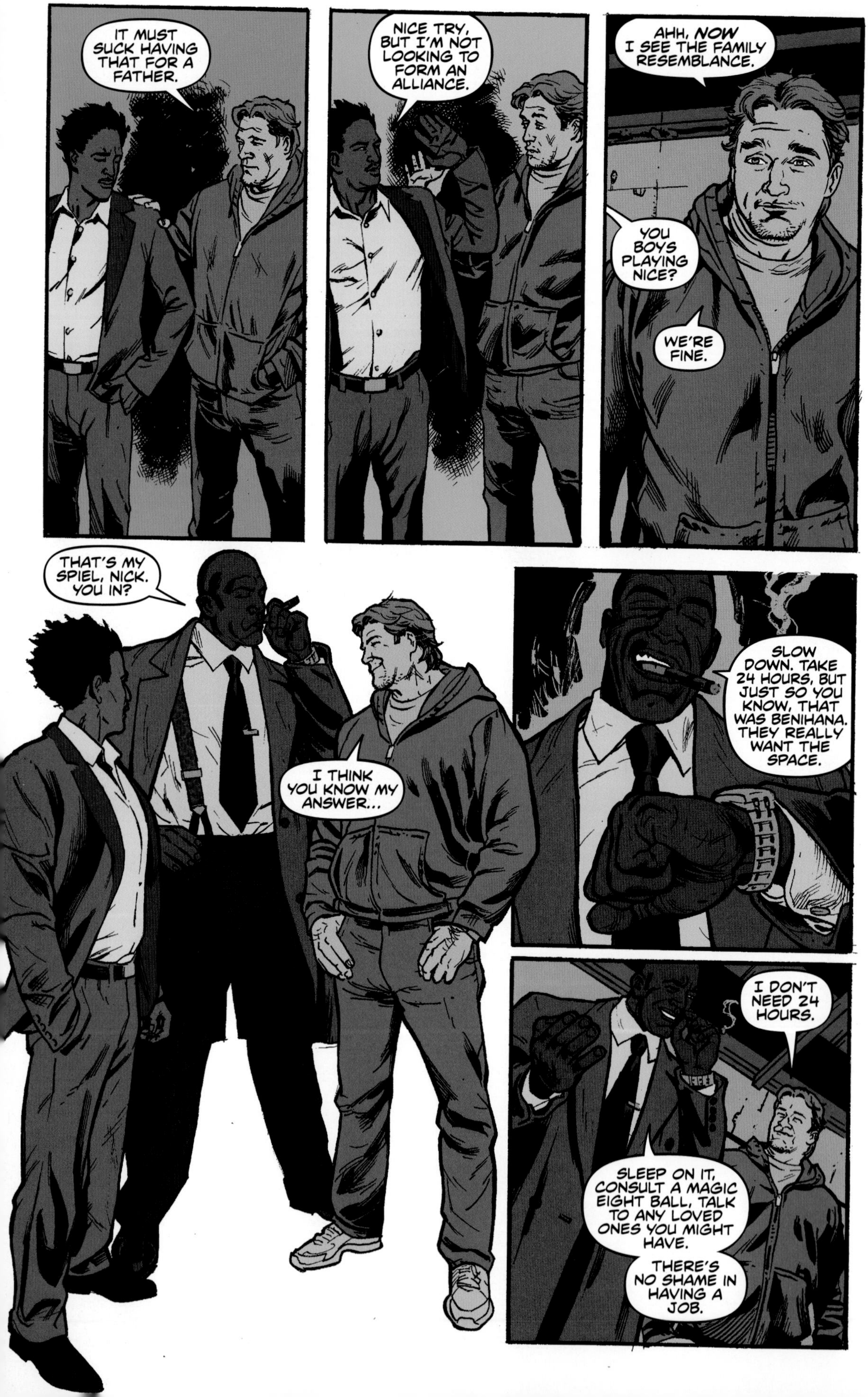
IT MUST SUCK HAVING THAT FOR A FATHER.
NICE TRY, BUT I'M NOT LOOKING TO FORM AN ALLIANCE.
AHH, *NOW* I SEE THE FAMILY RESEMBLANCE.
YOU BOYS PLAYING NICE?
WE'RE FINE.
THAT'S MY SPIEL, NICK. YOU IN?
I THINK YOU KNOW MY ANSWER...
SLOW DOWN. TAKE 24 HOURS, BUT JUST SO YOU KNOW, THAT WAS BENIHANA. THEY REALLY WANT THE SPACE.
I DON'T NEED 24 HOURS.
SLEEP ON IT, CONSULT A MAGIC EIGHT BALL, TALK TO ANY LOVED ONES YOU MIGHT HAVE.
THERE'S NO SHAME IN HAVING A JOB.

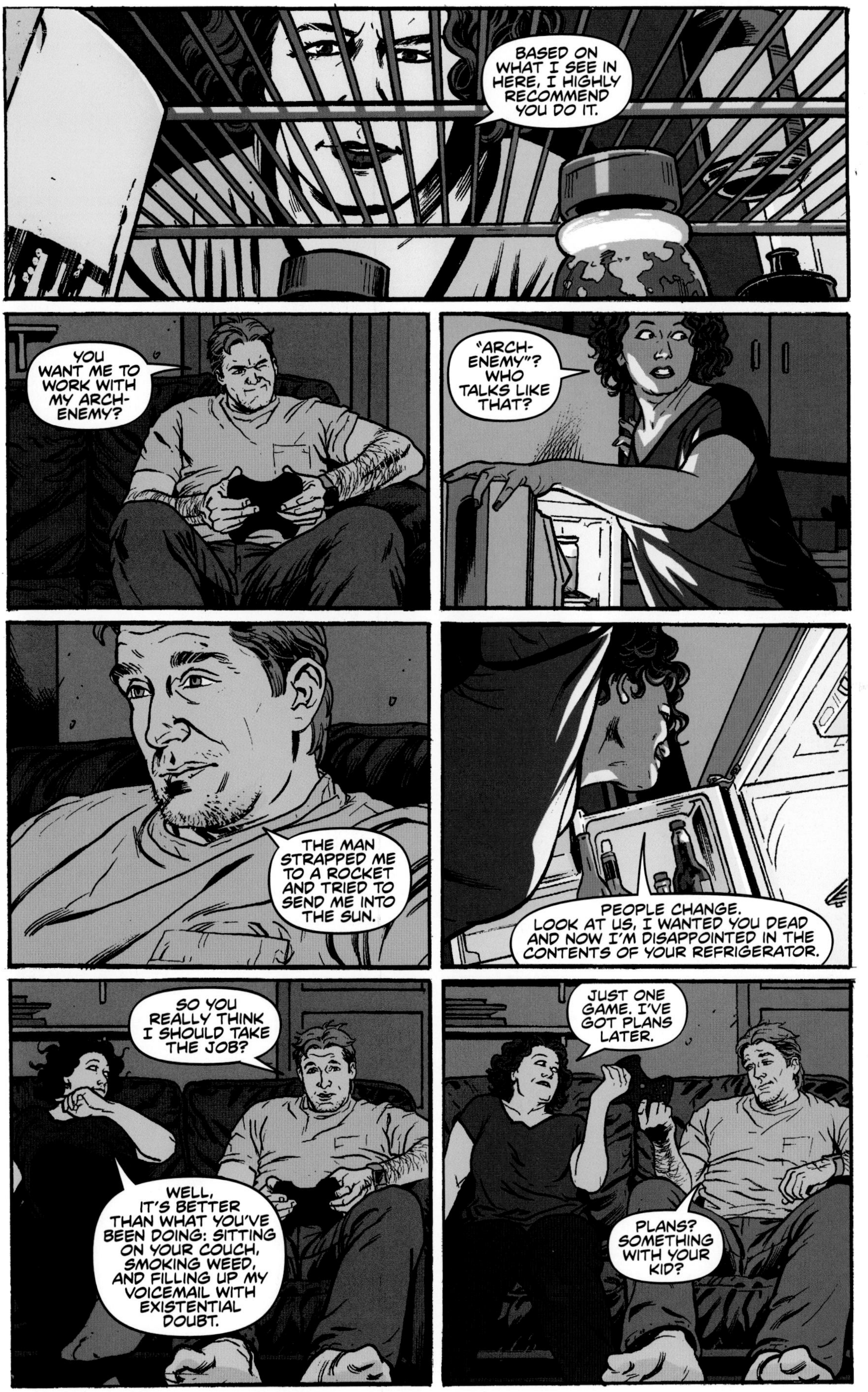
BASED ON WHAT I SEE IN HERE, I HIGHLY RECOMMEND YOU DO IT.
YOU WANT ME TO WORK WITH MY ARCH-ENEMY?
"ARCH-ENEMY"? WHO TALKS LIKE THAT?
THE MAN STRAPPED ME TO A ROCKET AND TRIED TO SEND ME INTO THE SUN.
PEOPLE CHANGE. LOOK AT US, I WANTED YOU DEAD AND NOW I'M DISAPPOINTED IN THE CONTENTS OF YOUR REFRIGERATOR.
SO YOU REALLY THINK I SHOULD TAKE THE JOB?
WELL, IT'S BETTER THAN WHAT YOU'VE BEEN DOING: SITTING ON YOUR COUCH, SMOKING WEED, AND FILLING UP MY VOICEMAIL WITH EXISTENTIAL DOUBT.
JUST ONE GAME. I'VE GOT PLANS LATER.
PLANS? SOMETHING WITH YOUR KID?

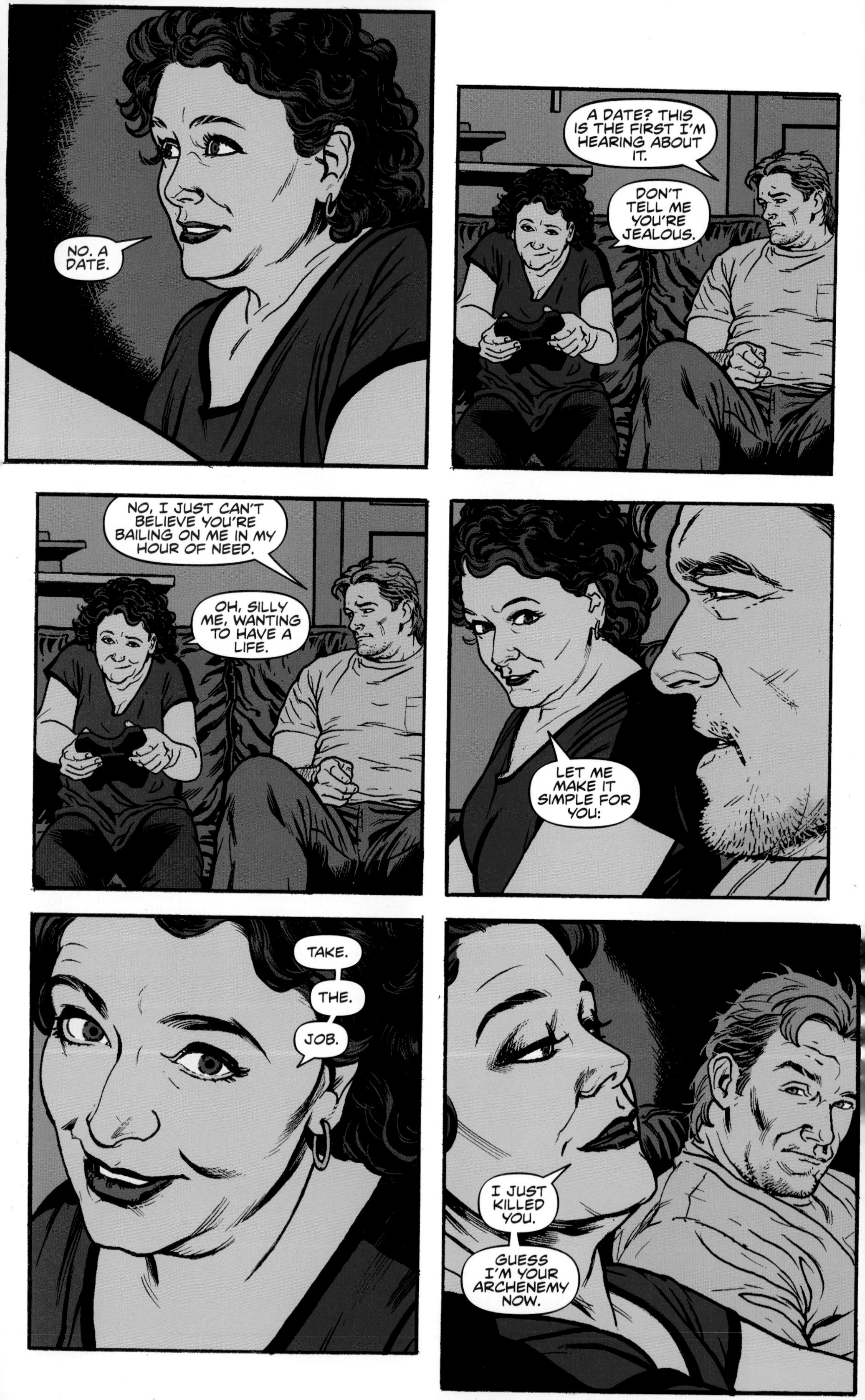
NO. A DATE.
A DATE? THIS IS THE FIRST I'M HEARING ABOUT IT.
DON'T TELL ME YOU'RE JEALOUS.
NO, I JUST CAN'T BELIEVE YOU'RE BAILING ON ME IN MY HOUR OF NEED.
OH, SILLY ME, WANTING TO HAVE A LIFE.
LET ME MAKE IT SIMPLE FOR YOU:
TAKE.
THE.
JOB.
I JUST KILLED YOU.
GUESS I'M YOUR ARCHENEMY NOW.

NICKY, MY MAN!

OH GREAT.

TWO MORE, BARTENDER.

HOW WAS THE MEETING WITH MORGANFELD?

DON'T WORRY ABOUT IT, HUDSON.

I'M YOUR BUSINESS MANAGER. I'M SUPPOSED TO NEGOTIATE YOUR DEALS.

YOU ARE NOT MY BUSINESS MANAGER.

YOU'RE JUST A PARASITE.

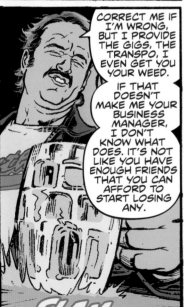

CORRECT ME IF I'M WRONG, BUT I PROVIDE THE GIGS, THE TRANSPO, I EVEN GET YOU YOUR WEED.

IF THAT DOESN'T MAKE ME YOUR BUSINESS MANAGER, I DON'T KNOW WHAT DOES. IT'S NOT LIKE YOU HAVE ENOUGH FRIENDS THAT YOU CAN AFFORD TO START LOSING ANY.

SLAM

WHICH IS IT? ARE YOU MY BUSINESS MANAGER OR MY FRIEND?

NEITHER. I'M OUTTA HERE.

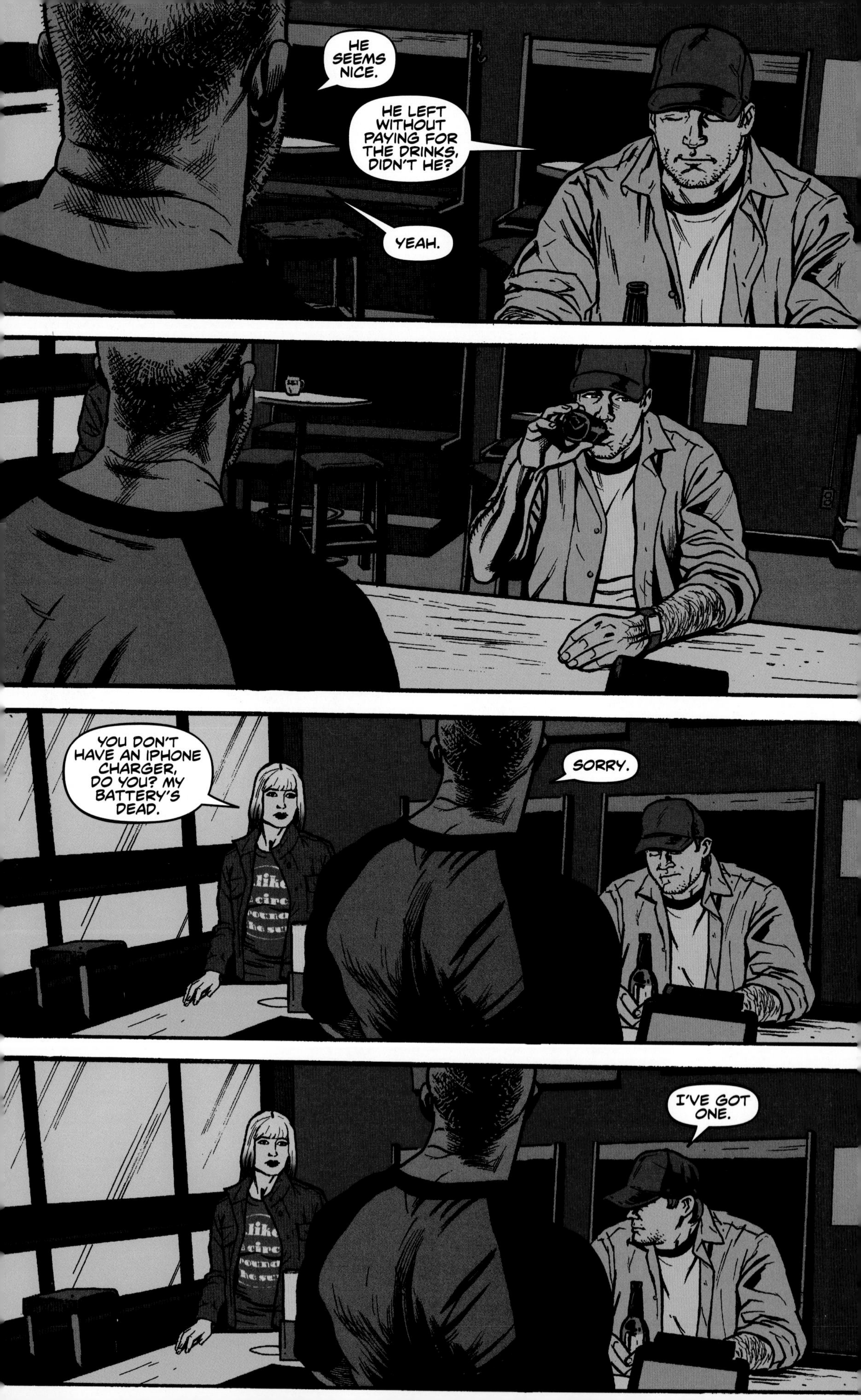
HE SEEMS NICE.
HE LEFT WITHOUT PAYING FOR THE DRINKS, DIDN'T HE?
YEAH.
YOU DON'T HAVE AN IPHONE CHARGER, DO YOU? MY BATTERY'S DEAD.
SORRY.
I'VE GOT ONE.

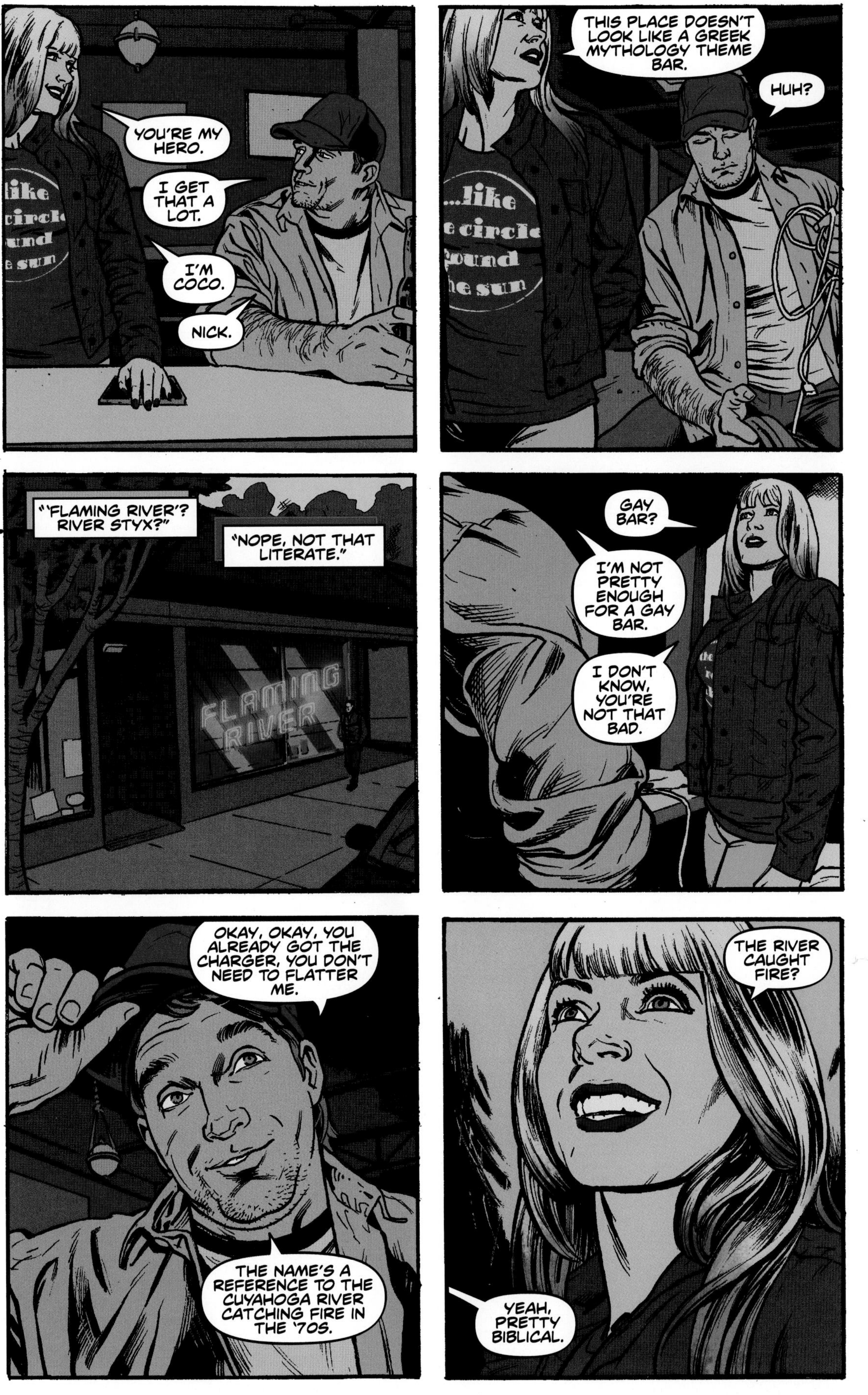
YOU'RE MY HERO.
I GET THAT A LOT.
I'M COCO.
NICK.
...like the circle round the sun
THIS PLACE DOESN'T LOOK LIKE A GREEK MYTHOLOGY THEME BAR.
HUH?
"'FLAMING RIVER'? RIVER STYX?"
"NOPE, NOT THAT LITERATE."
FLAMING RIVER
GAY BAR?
I'M NOT PRETTY ENOUGH FOR A GAY BAR.
I DON'T KNOW, YOU'RE NOT THAT BAD.
OKAY, OKAY, YOU ALREADY GOT THE CHARGER, YOU DON'T NEED TO FLATTER ME.
THE NAME'S A REFERENCE TO THE CUYAHOGA RIVER CATCHING FIRE IN THE '70S.
THE RIVER CAUGHT FIRE?
YEAH, PRETTY BIBLICAL.

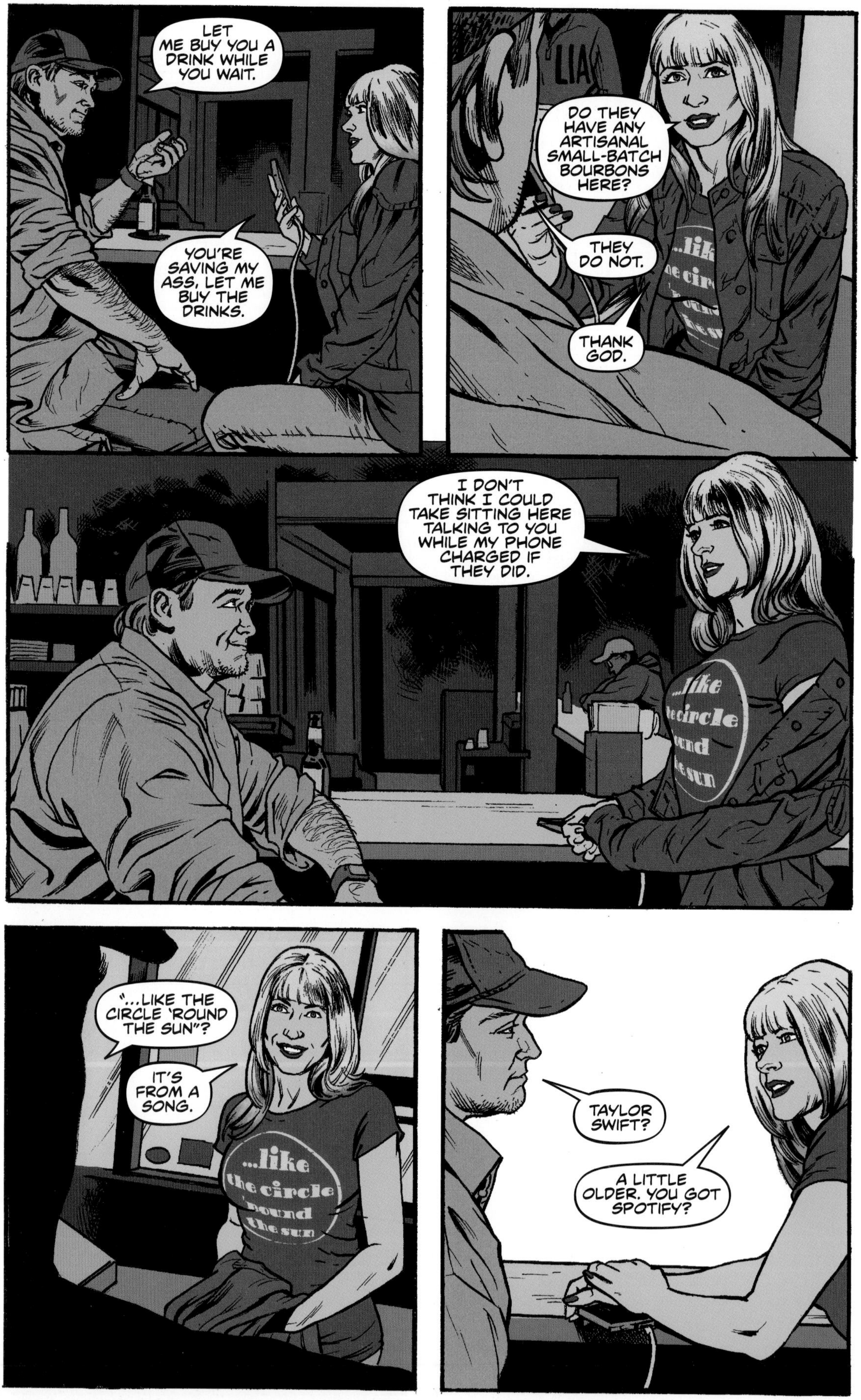
LET ME BUY YOU A DRINK WHILE YOU WAIT.
YOU'RE SAVING MY ASS, LET ME BUY THE DRINKS.
LIA
DO THEY HAVE ANY ARTISANAL SMALL-BATCH BOURBONS HERE?
THEY DO NOT.
THANK GOD.
I DON'T THINK I COULD TAKE SITTING HERE TALKING TO YOU WHILE MY PHONE CHARGED IF THEY DID.
...like the circle 'round the sun
"...LIKE THE CIRCLE 'ROUND THE SUN"?
IT'S FROM A SONG.
TAYLOR SWIFT?
A LITTLE OLDER. YOU GOT SPOTIFY?

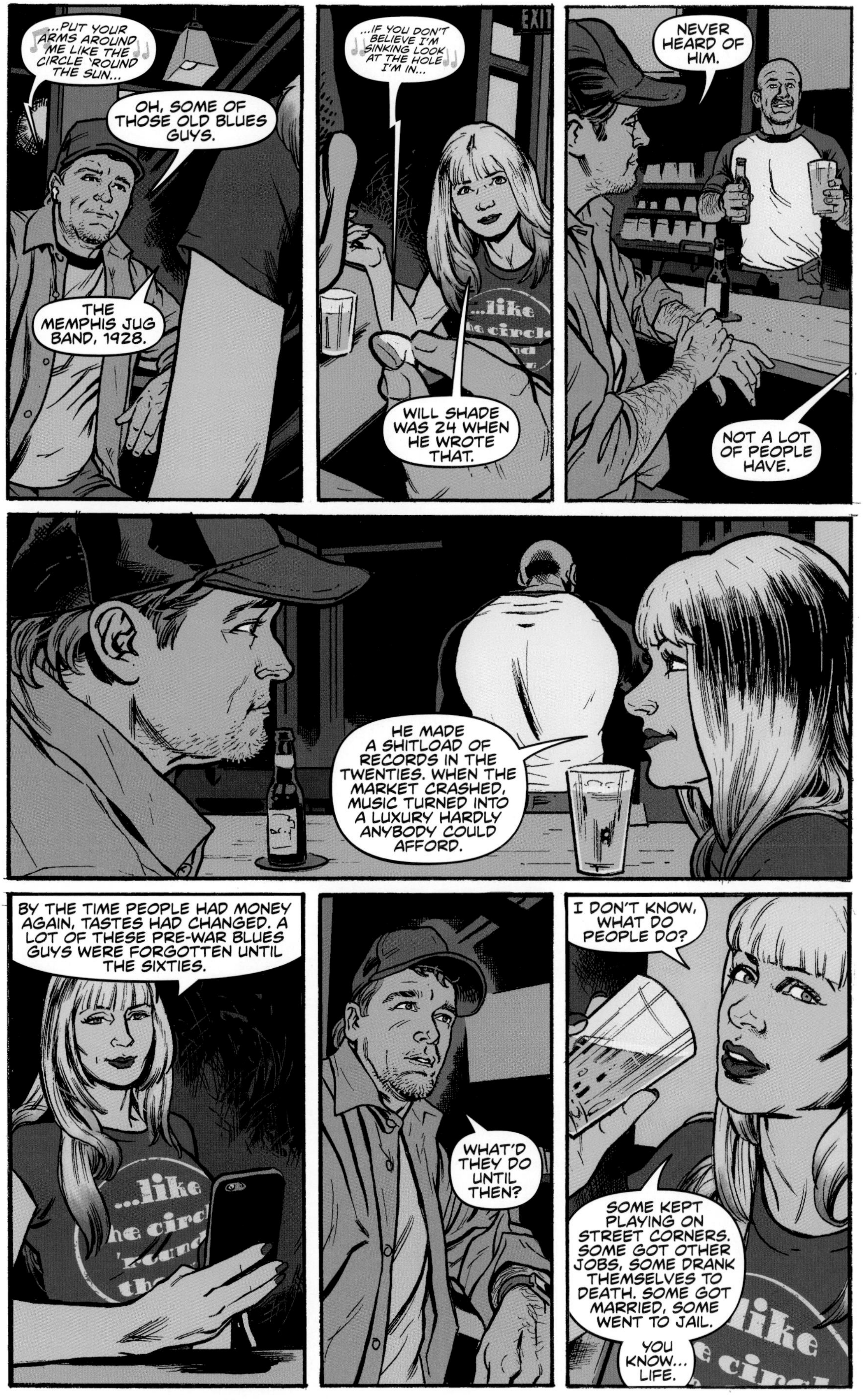
...PUT YOUR ARMS AROUND ME LIKE THE CIRCLE 'ROUND THE SUN...
OH, SOME OF THOSE OLD BLUES GUYS.
THE MEMPHIS JUG BAND, 1928.
...IF YOU DON'T BELIEVE I'M SINKING LOOK AT THE HOLE I'M IN...
WILL SHADE WAS 24 WHEN HE WROTE THAT.
NEVER HEARD OF HIM.
NOT A LOT OF PEOPLE HAVE.
HE MADE A SHITLOAD OF RECORDS IN THE TWENTIES. WHEN THE MARKET CRASHED, MUSIC TURNED INTO A LUXURY HARDLY ANYBODY COULD AFFORD.
BY THE TIME PEOPLE HAD MONEY AGAIN, TASTES HAD CHANGED. A LOT OF THESE PRE-WAR BLUES GUYS WERE FORGOTTEN UNTIL THE SIXTIES.
WHAT'D THEY DO UNTIL THEN?
I DON'T KNOW, WHAT DO PEOPLE DO?
SOME KEPT PLAYING ON STREET CORNERS. SOME GOT OTHER JOBS, SOME DRANK THEMSELVES TO DEATH. SOME GOT MARRIED, SOME WENT TO JAIL.
YOU KNOW... LIFE.

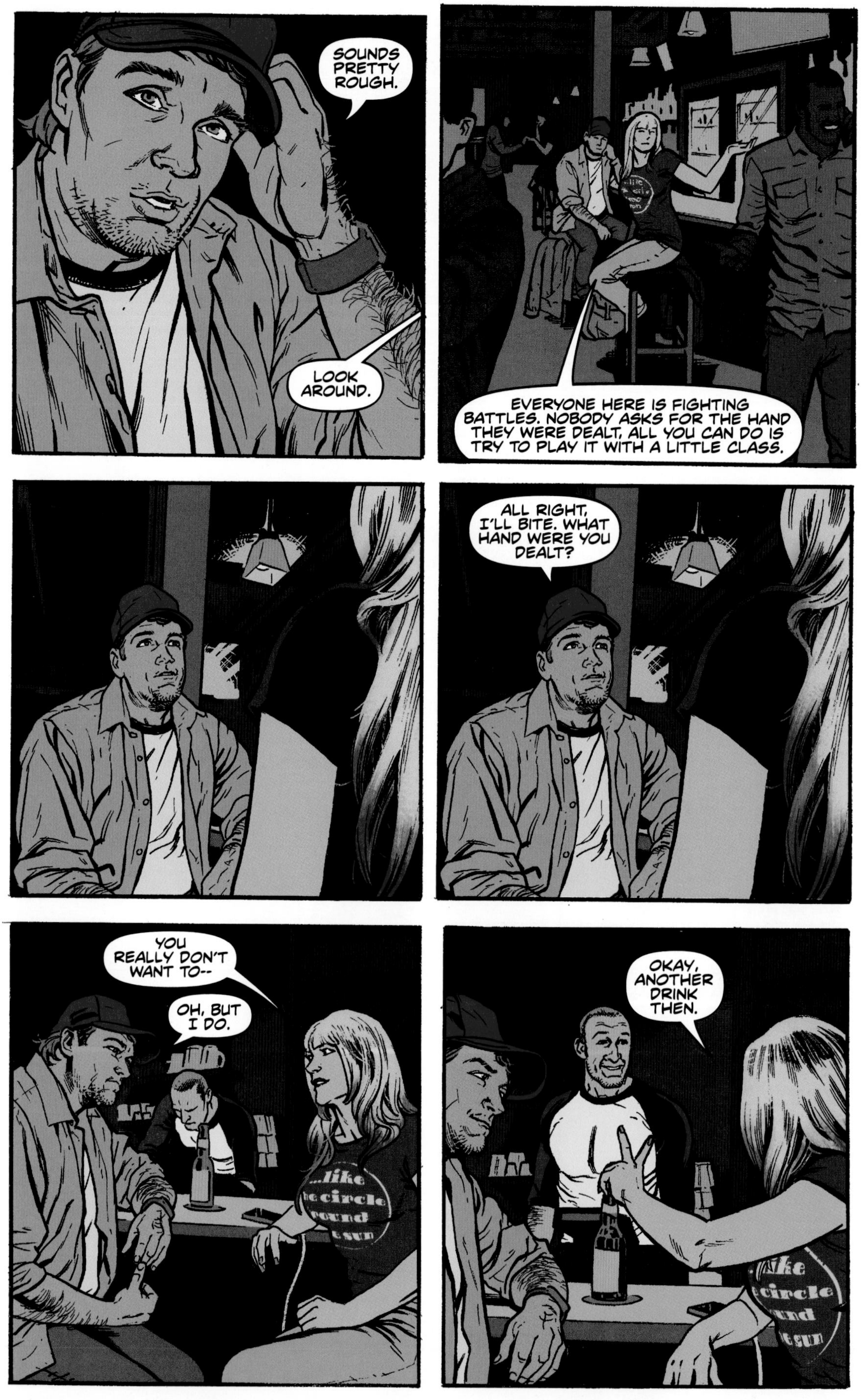
SOUNDS PRETTY ROUGH.
LOOK AROUND.
EVERYONE HERE IS FIGHTING BATTLES. NOBODY ASKS FOR THE HAND THEY WERE DEALT, ALL YOU CAN DO IS TRY TO PLAY IT WITH A LITTLE CLASS.
ALL RIGHT, I'LL BITE. WHAT HAND WERE YOU DEALT?
YOU REALLY DON'T WANT TO--
OH, BUT I DO.
OKAY, ANOTHER DRINK THEN.

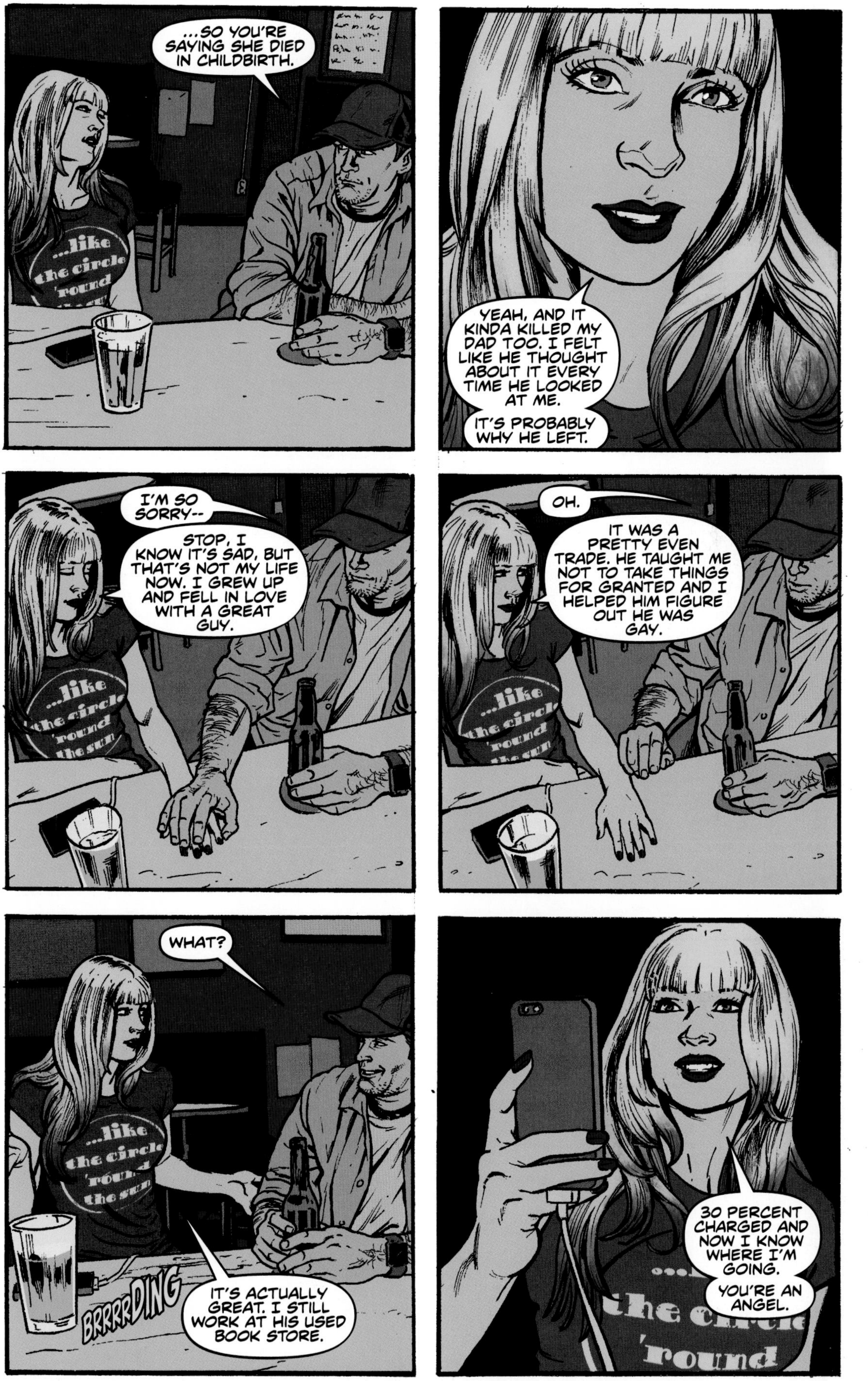
...SO YOU'RE SAYING SHE DIED IN CHILDBIRTH.
...like the circle 'round
YEAH, AND IT KINDA KILLED MY DAD TOO. I FELT LIKE HE THOUGHT ABOUT IT EVERY TIME HE LOOKED AT ME.
IT'S PROBABLY WHY HE LEFT.
I'M SO SORRY--
STOP, I KNOW IT'S SAD, BUT THAT'S NOT MY LIFE NOW. I GREW UP AND FELL IN LOVE WITH A GREAT GUY.
...like the circle 'round the sun
OH.
IT WAS A PRETTY EVEN TRADE. HE TAUGHT ME NOT TO TAKE THINGS FOR GRANTED AND I HELPED HIM FIGURE OUT HE WAS GAY.
...like the circle 'round the sun
WHAT?
...like the circle 'round the sun
IT'S ACTUALLY GREAT. I STILL WORK AT HIS USED BOOK STORE.
BRRRRDING
30 PERCENT CHARGED AND NOW I KNOW WHERE I'M GOING.
YOU'RE AN ANGEL.
the circle 'round

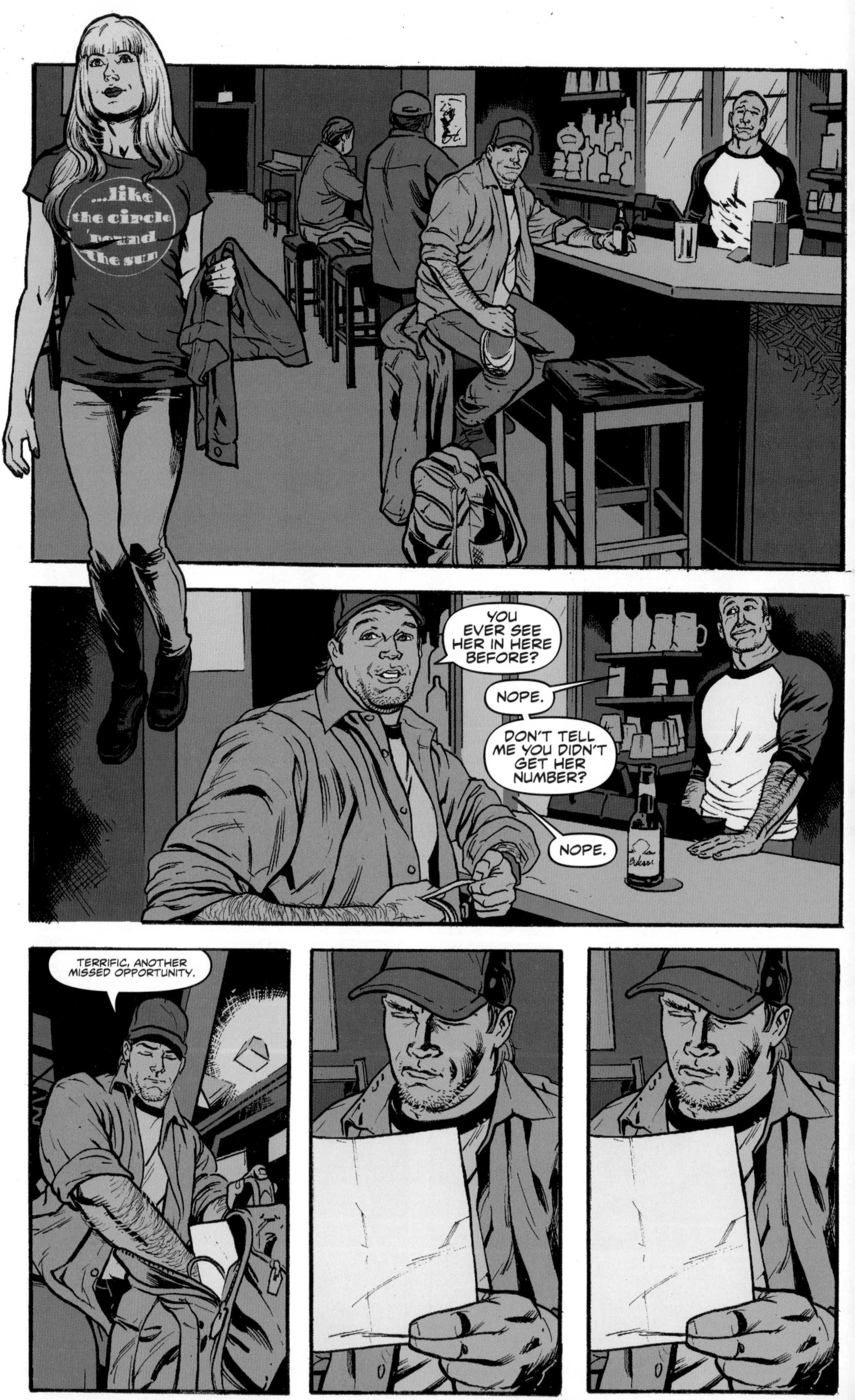
...like the circle 'round the sun
YOU EVER SEE HER IN HERE BEFORE?
NOPE.
DON'T TELL ME YOU DIDN'T GET HER NUMBER?
NOPE.
TERRIFIC, ANOTHER MISSED OPPORTUNITY.

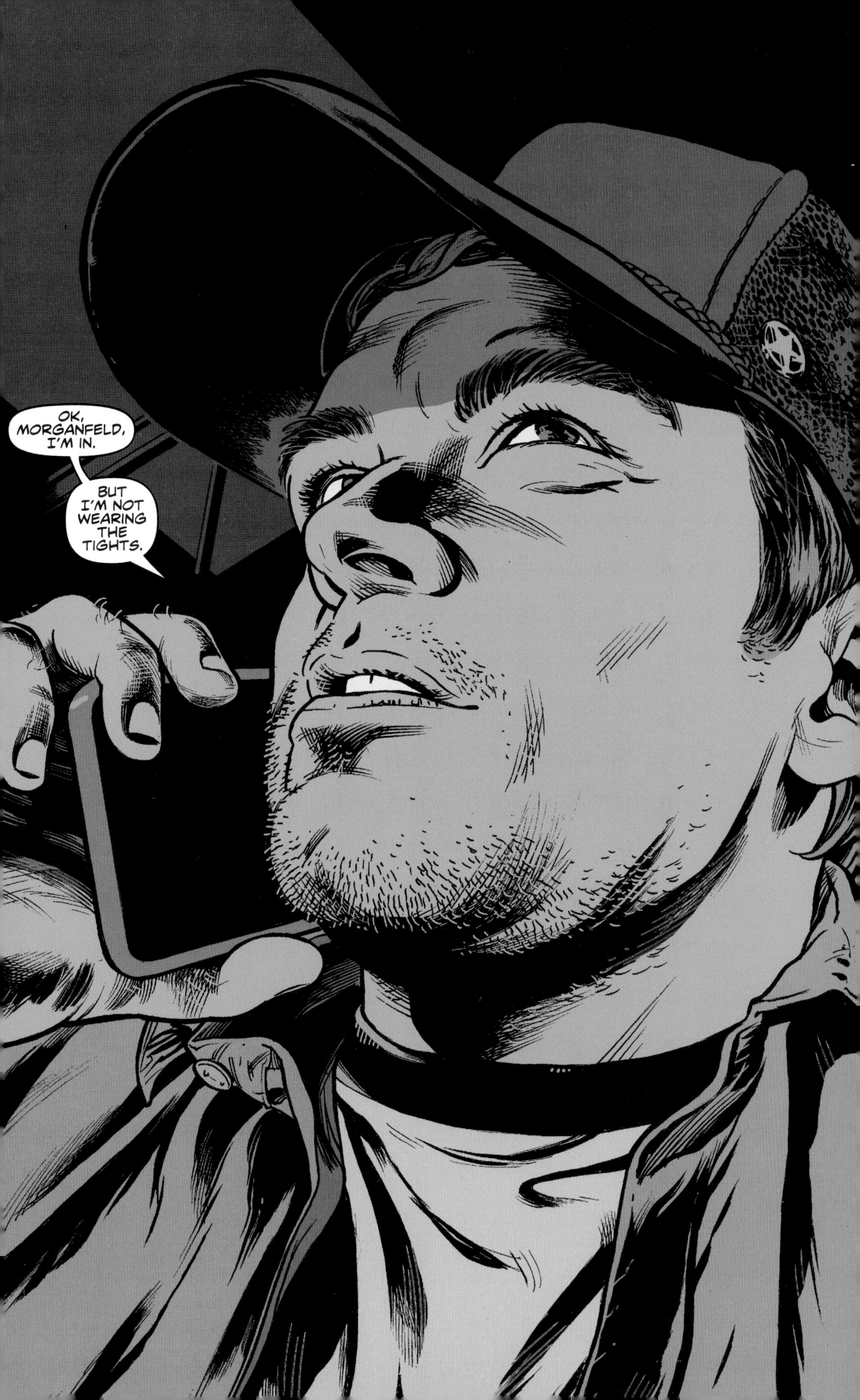
OK, MORGANFELD, I'M IN.
BUT I'M NOT WEARING THE TIGHTS.

Dear Reader—

First and foremost, thanks for reading "**The Further Adventures of Nick Wilson.**" I know you have lots of choices out there and I'm glad you opted to spend time and money with us. And, since this is appearing in issue two, we are especially happy to welcome you back.

I have a real love/hate relationship with text pages or anywhere authors or artists interact with their audience. It's not born out of any kind of snobbery. On the contrary, I think the reader is smart and imaginative. Because of that, I hesitate to limit their perspective by pointing them towards signposts that are personal or might have been influential in the writing, but are unimportant to the finished product. A bad bowl of curry may have inspired a story but that shouldn't keep *you* away from curry.

The danger with too much interaction between artist and audience is it can render a work mundane, merely representational and eliminate what may be my favorite part in any creative work, the application in one's own life. We all may be curious who inspired Carly Simon's "You're So Vain" but once we know who is so vain can we still use it as effectively to describe someone in our own lives?

But the rub is, we create to communicate so the temptation to parse and examine, and at times reduce the work to its core ingredients, is always there. Like I said, a love/hate relationship.

The Memphis Jug Band

My esteemed co-author Marc Andreyko, knowing my love of music, suggested I use the text pages to make a playlist of songs to listen to while reading this book. Rather than a list, troublesome in this age of immediate downloads making a world of instant experts, I thought I'd offer a handful of songs and try to give them some context. Because we don't need more experts and I'd rather talk to a person who really truly loves one song than someone who kinda knows a hundred.

So, here are a handful of songs that have something to do with this book—

"*On The Road Again*" by **The Memphis Jug Band**, **The Grateful Dead**, **Nas**

In this issue, Coco turns Nick onto a record by the **Memphis Jug Band**. She tells a bit of their story there and talks about Will Shade's lyrics. "*On The Road Again*" is another Shade composition recorded by the Memphis Jug Band.

I love blues records from the twenties and thirties. Some people think they all sound the same, but I contend that all music sounds the same until you take the time to hear the nuance. That's why small-minded people say all hip-hop sounds the same or all jazz sounds alike. When I start listening to any different type of music—tango, bossa nova, high-life — it all seems the same until I find some way to unlock it. It's not that the music changes, I have to find my way in.

Jug band music is particularly fun—infectious and rhythmic with lyrics full of braggadocio and surprising poetry. The structure of the groups was not unlike the old minstrel shows with a lead vocalist taking up the role of the Interlocutor, inspiring call and response from endmen called "Tambo and Bones" (named after their tambourine and castanets, respectively).

I used to tell people that I could hear a connection between groups like that and the early hip-hop bands that were coming out then—this was back in the eighties. This past year, **Nas** gave credence to my theory, recording The Memphis Jug Band's "*On The Road Again*" drawing a straight line from their recording in 1928.

The Grateful Dead also recorded the same song in 1966. I used to hate the Grateful Dead. I still hate their long jammy stuff—spare me your vitriol, it's my opinion, yours is just as worthy and correct. I was slave to the wrong haircut for a long time, a punk in a time of hippies, and refused to hear the beauty and wonder in some of the Dead's work. Fortunately, I was patient enough to go back and rediscover a couple dozen songs that have touched my heart as much as any songs have. Their sixties cover of Will Shade, though interesting, is not one of them.

"*Superman*" by **Larry Wald**

Here's a great example of context. If I was asked to name favorite soul songs, this wouldn't be in my top thousand. Actually it's closer to horn-rock like Chase or the Ides of March. And it wasn't even made in the States. It's the flip side of Larry's 1971 single "*Love Train.*" And it's kinda hokey.

But it works perfectly in relation to the subject at hand here. In this book, Nick Wilson has been impotent since he lost his powers. He feels like every woman he meets still expects a super-powered lover and he knows he can't deliver.

Larry Wald has no such inhibitions. In this track, he implores potential romantic partners to hop inside his phone booth to watch him change into their super-man. And it's amazing that he uses *"Great Caesar's Ghost"* as a cry of passion, especially surprising as it sounds like Larry is not singing in his native language. No surprise there as this is just one of a handful of records Mister Wald released in his native Spain.

Curious listeners may have a hard time finding the original single but thanks to the good folks at the mighty *Vampisoul* label, it is available on their "Sensacional Soul" reissue series.

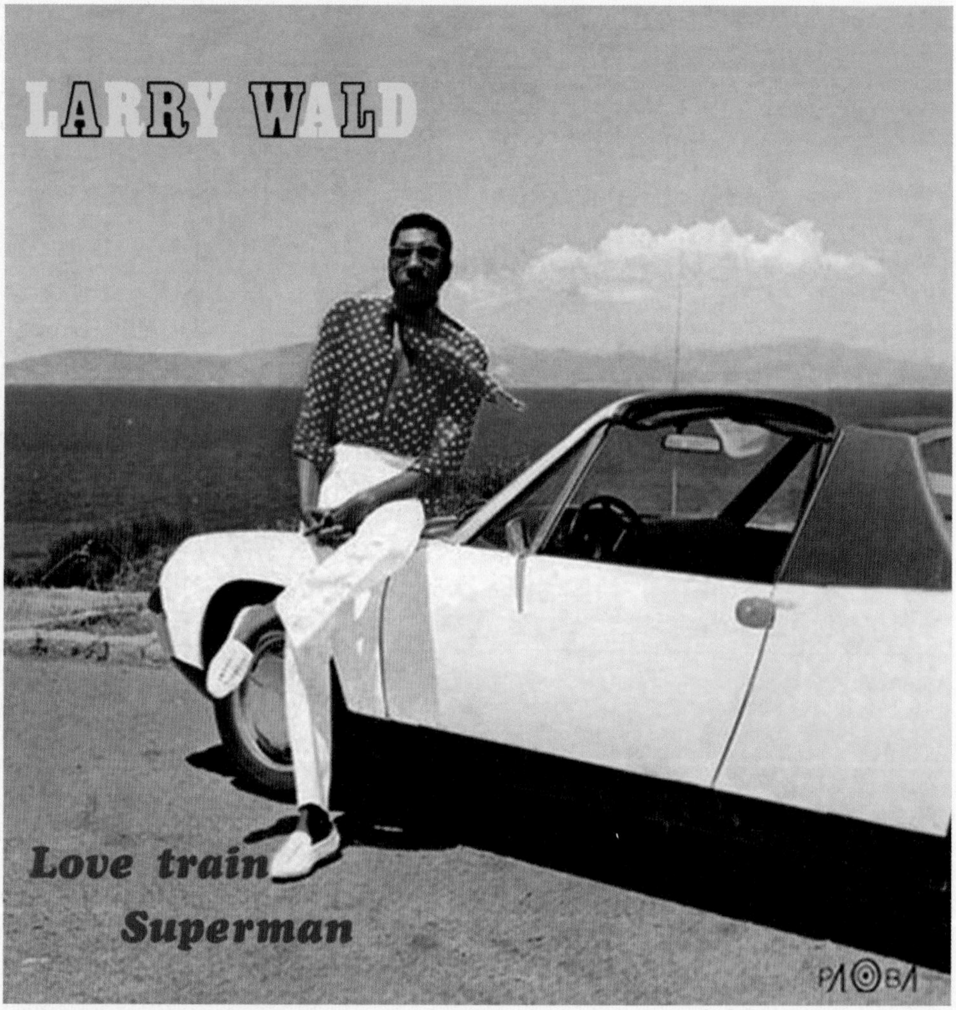
LARRY WALD
Love train
Superman

"***Mississippi***" by **Bob Dylan**

Look, I have no problem with anyone who doesn't like **Bob Dylan**. That's a matter of taste. But anyone who doesn't recognize the breadth and importance of his body of work reveals more to me than they might wish. You can knock him all you want, but when push comes to shove, there are songs that can still break my heart. Bob's so badass that he recorded killer versions of *"Mississippi"* a couple of years and albums before the one he eventually released. Those versions were terrific but didn't satisfy him for some reason.

Photo: David Gahr

Bob Dylan

And part of being an artist is deciding where to put the frame around the thing you made. That's the artist's decision, no matter how much we want to second-guess.

I could spend too much of your time picking Bob Dylan songs but I went with *"Mississippi"* because the lyric:

> Well the emptiness is endless, cold as the clay
> You can always come back, but you can't come back all the way

was pretty central to Nick's dilemma.

"Rise Up With Fists!!" by **Jenny Lewis with the Watson Twins**

I had a very specific thing in mind for Coco in this issue. I wanted her to love music and she had to have her own vibe. It's hard to convey that in just a couple of panels. I sent Stephen Sadowski pictures of **Jenny Lewis** and a few of her friends from one of her myriad side projects, *"Nice as Fuck"* (hello, Tennessee). For my money, Jenny is one of,

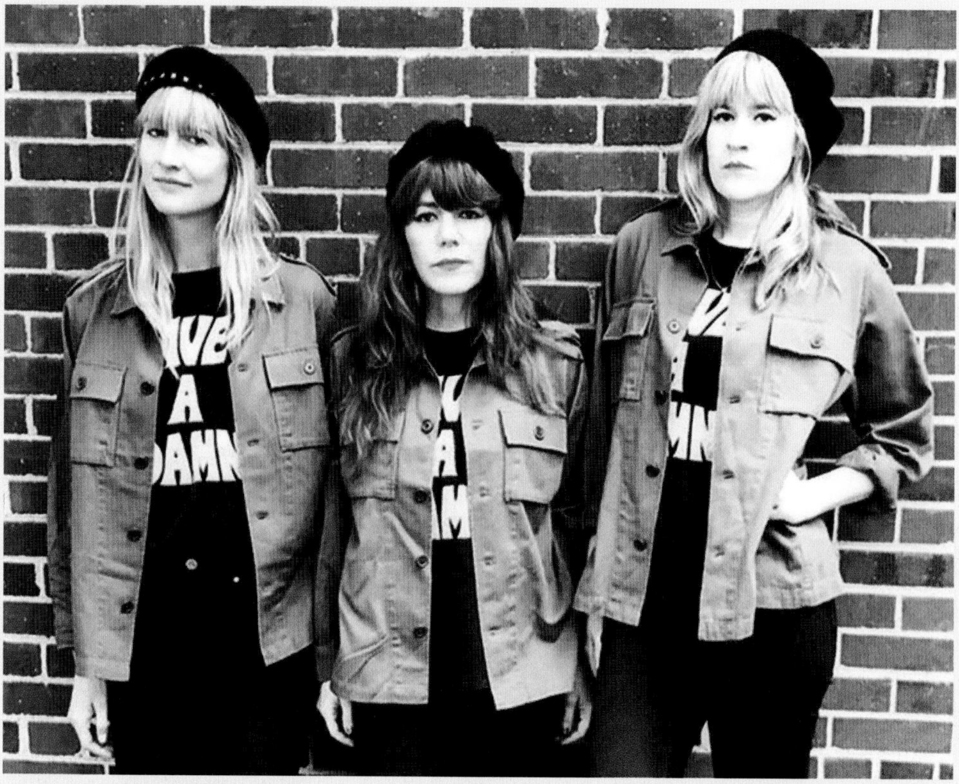
A
A

Photo: Love's Way

Jenny Lewis / NAF

if not *the* best, singers and songwriters out there. Her music is full of melody and heart and her lyrics are sly and surprising with honesty and enough left turns to stymie any kind of cookie-cutter sentiment. Her love for many kinds of music comes through, not in terms of slavish genre-hopping imitation but through canny use of detail utilizing a bag of tricks big enough to encompass country & western, electronica, hip-hop, power-pop, Americana, psychedelia and lots more. She made a perfect template for Coco.

It's hard to single out one of her fine compositions as an example but this melancholy anthem from *"Rabbit Fur Coat"* makes a fine entry point.

To tell you the truth, there are so many more songs just in the pages of the first two issues I could could go on forever, but I fear I may have already worn out my welcome. But if there's room, I'll come back and talk about a few more songs in a later issue.

In the meantime, thanks again for reading. And remember, there are no mistakes in taste, stand by the things that move you, but don't be afraid to open your eyes and ears to something new.

See you soon.
eddie
los feliz, 2018

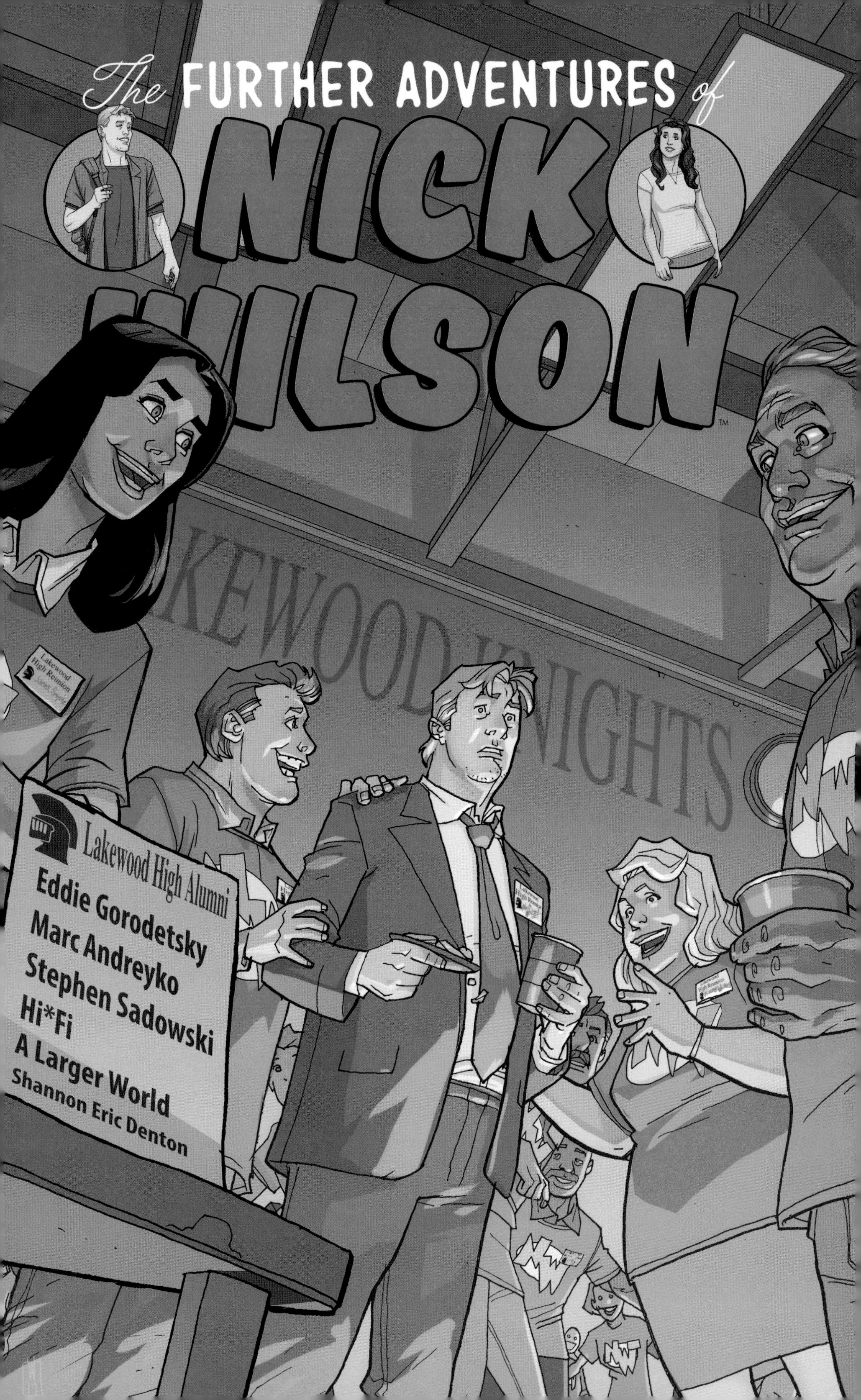
The FURTHER ADVENTURES of
NICK WILSON™
LAKEWOOD KNIGHTS
Lakewood High Alumni
Eddie Gorodetsky
Marc Andreyko
Stephen Sadowski
Hi*Fi
A Larger World
Shannon Eric Denton

The FURTHER ADVENTURES of NICK WILSON

Stephanie S... ...Jennifer ... ...rene

Phillip McCl... ...Sa... Swe... ...er Wi... ...ary ...ooks

Brenda Hanrahan

Edward Gorodetsky

Nicholas Wilson

Marc Andreyko

Shannon E. Denton

Jane Jenkins

Stephen Sadowski

Ian Churchill

Priyanka Patel

Brian Miller

Kristy Miller

Jason Woods

Lakewood High School

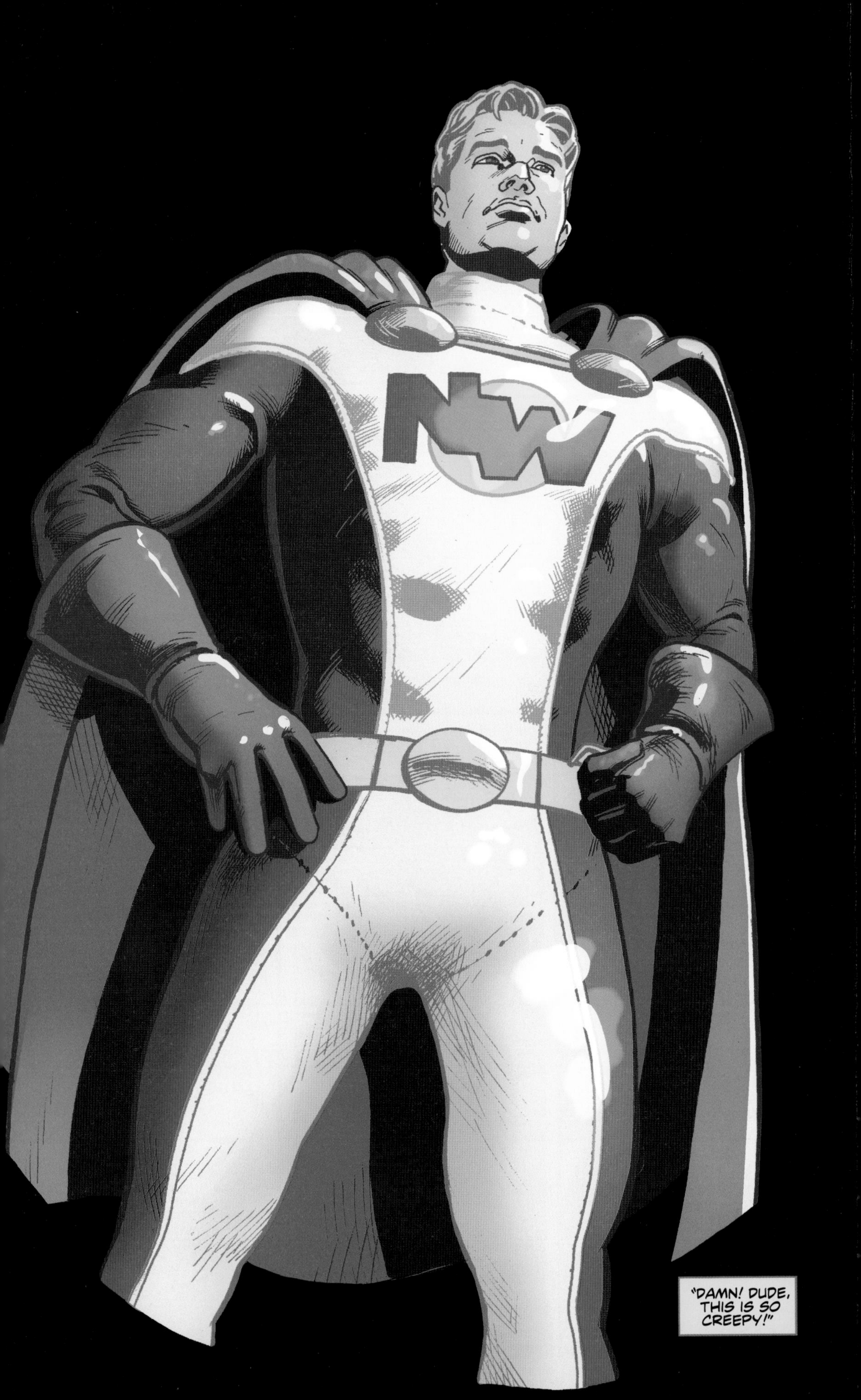
"DAMN! DUDE, THIS IS SO CREEPY!"

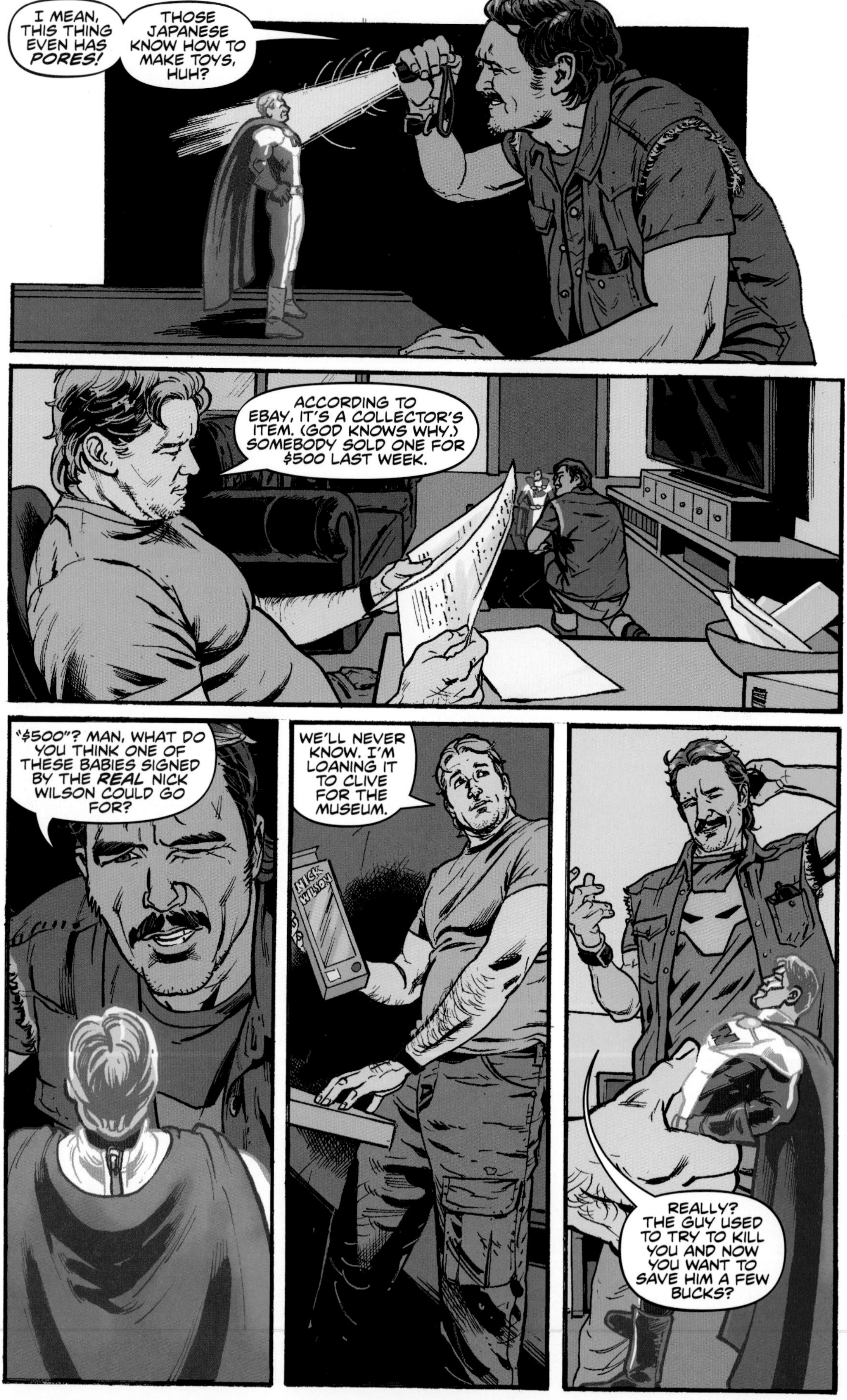
I MEAN, THIS THING EVEN HAS *PORES!*
THOSE JAPANESE KNOW HOW TO MAKE TOYS, HUH?
ACCORDING TO EBAY, IT'S A COLLECTOR'S ITEM. (GOD KNOWS WHY.) SOMEBODY SOLD ONE FOR $500 LAST WEEK.
"$500"? MAN, WHAT DO YOU THINK ONE OF THESE BABIES SIGNED BY THE *REAL* NICK WILSON COULD GO FOR?
WE'LL NEVER KNOW. I'M LOANING IT TO CLIVE FOR THE MUSEUM.
NICK WILSON
REALLY? THE GUY USED TO TRY TO KILL YOU AND NOW YOU WANT TO SAVE HIM A FEW BUCKS?

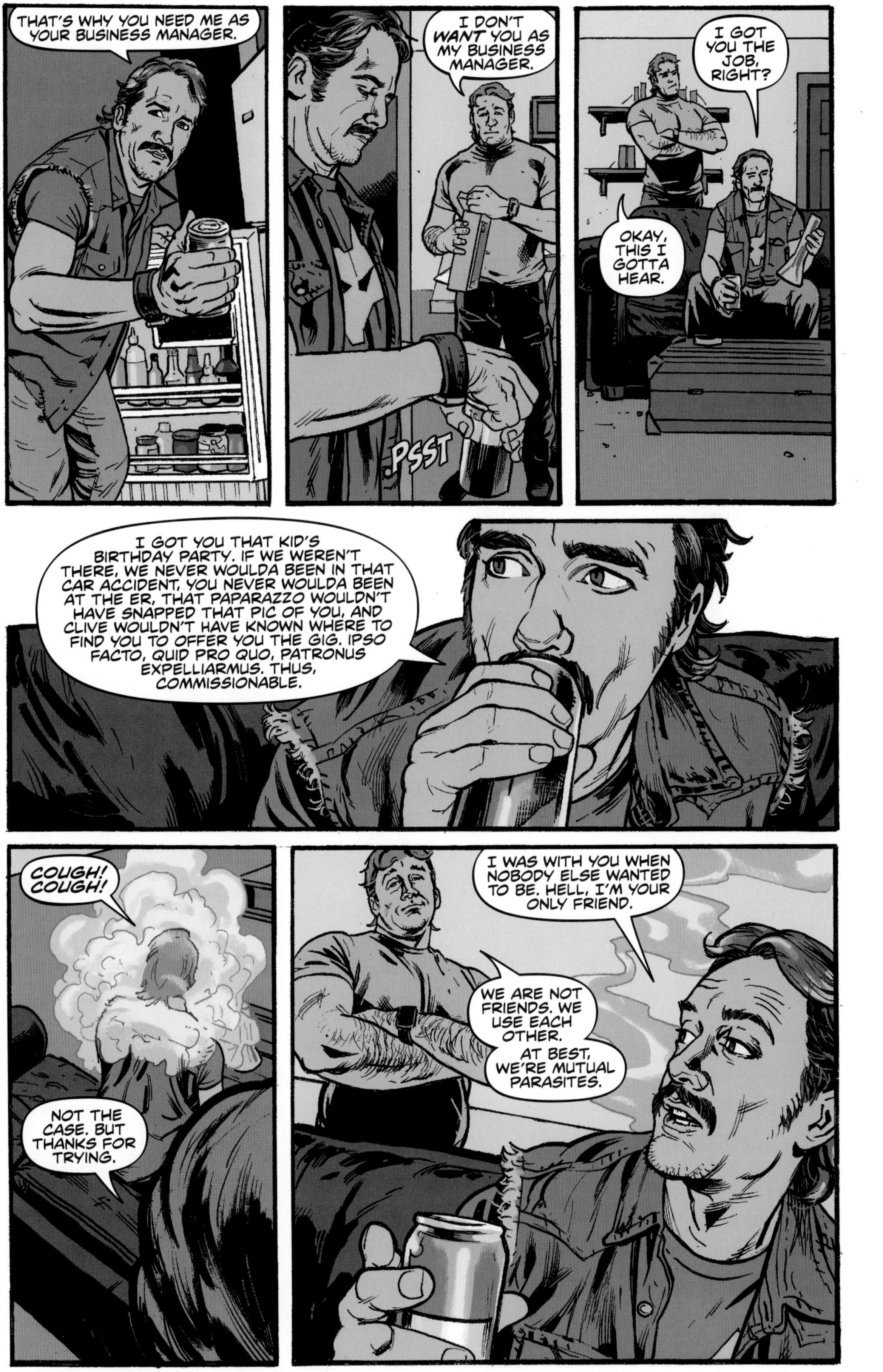
THAT'S WHY YOU NEED ME AS YOUR BUSINESS MANAGER.
I DON'T *WANT* YOU AS MY BUSINESS MANAGER.
PSST
I GOT YOU THE JOB, RIGHT?
OKAY, THIS I GOTTA HEAR.
I GOT YOU THAT KID'S BIRTHDAY PARTY. IF WE WEREN'T THERE, WE NEVER WOULDA BEEN IN THAT CAR ACCIDENT, YOU NEVER WOULDA BEEN AT THE ER, THAT PAPARAZZO WOULDN'T HAVE SNAPPED THAT PIC OF YOU, AND CLIVE WOULDN'T HAVE KNOWN WHERE TO FIND YOU TO OFFER YOU THE GIG. IPSO FACTO, QUID PRO QUO, PATRONUS EXPELLIARMUS. THUS, COMMISSIONABLE.
COUGH! COUGH!
NOT THE CASE. BUT THANKS FOR TRYING.
I WAS WITH YOU WHEN NOBODY ELSE WANTED TO BE. HELL, I'M YOUR ONLY FRIEND.
WE ARE NOT FRIENDS. WE USE EACH OTHER.
AT BEST, WE'RE MUTUAL PARASITES.

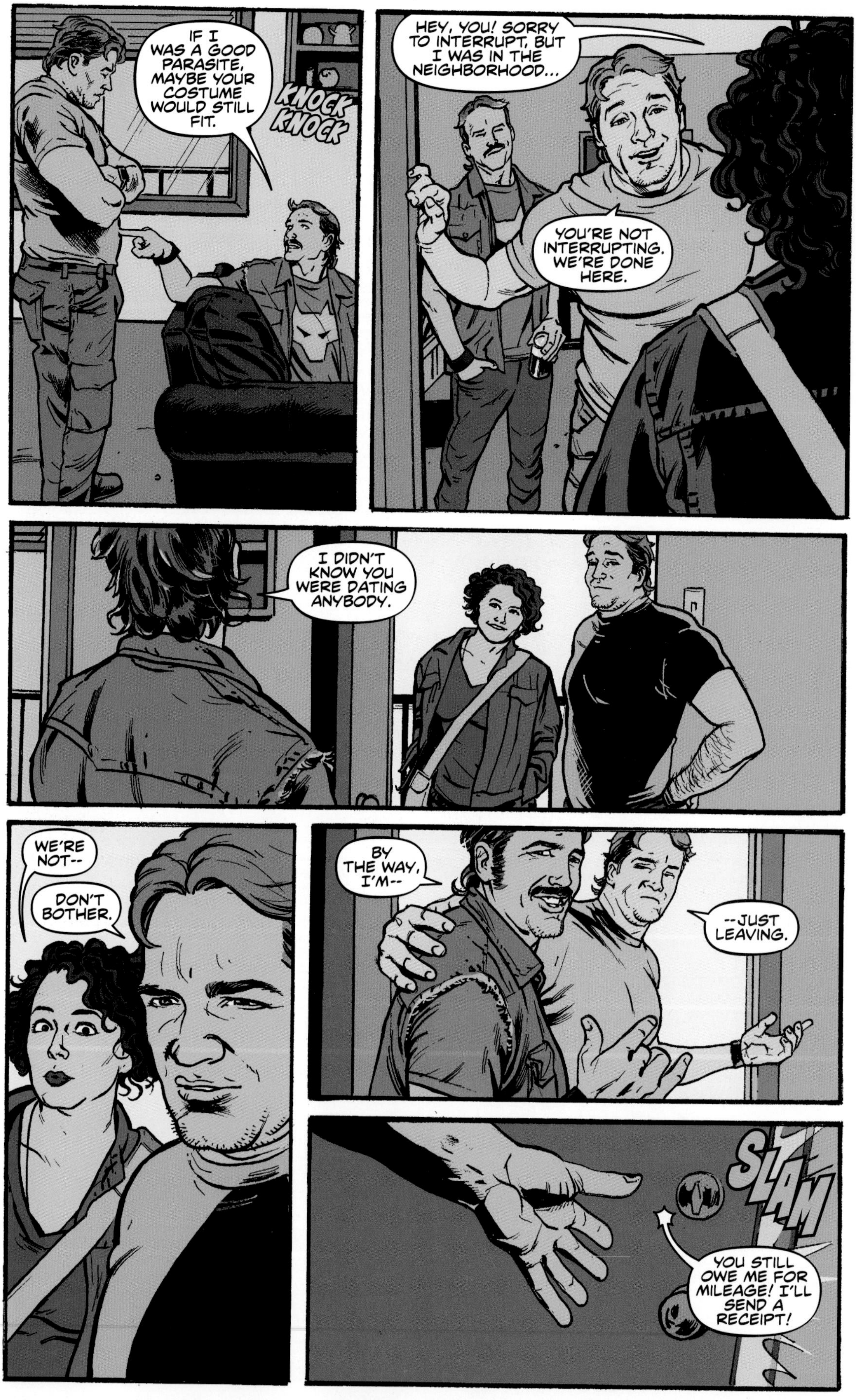
IF I WAS A GOOD PARASITE, MAYBE YOUR COSTUME WOULD STILL FIT.
KNOCK KNOCK
HEY, YOU! SORRY TO INTERRUPT, BUT I WAS IN THE NEIGHBORHOOD...
YOU'RE NOT INTERRUPTING. WE'RE DONE HERE.
I DIDN'T KNOW YOU WERE DATING ANYBODY.
WE'RE NOT--
DON'T BOTHER.
BY THE WAY, I'M--
--JUST LEAVING.
SLAM
YOU STILL OWE ME FOR MILEAGE! I'LL SEND A RECEIPT!

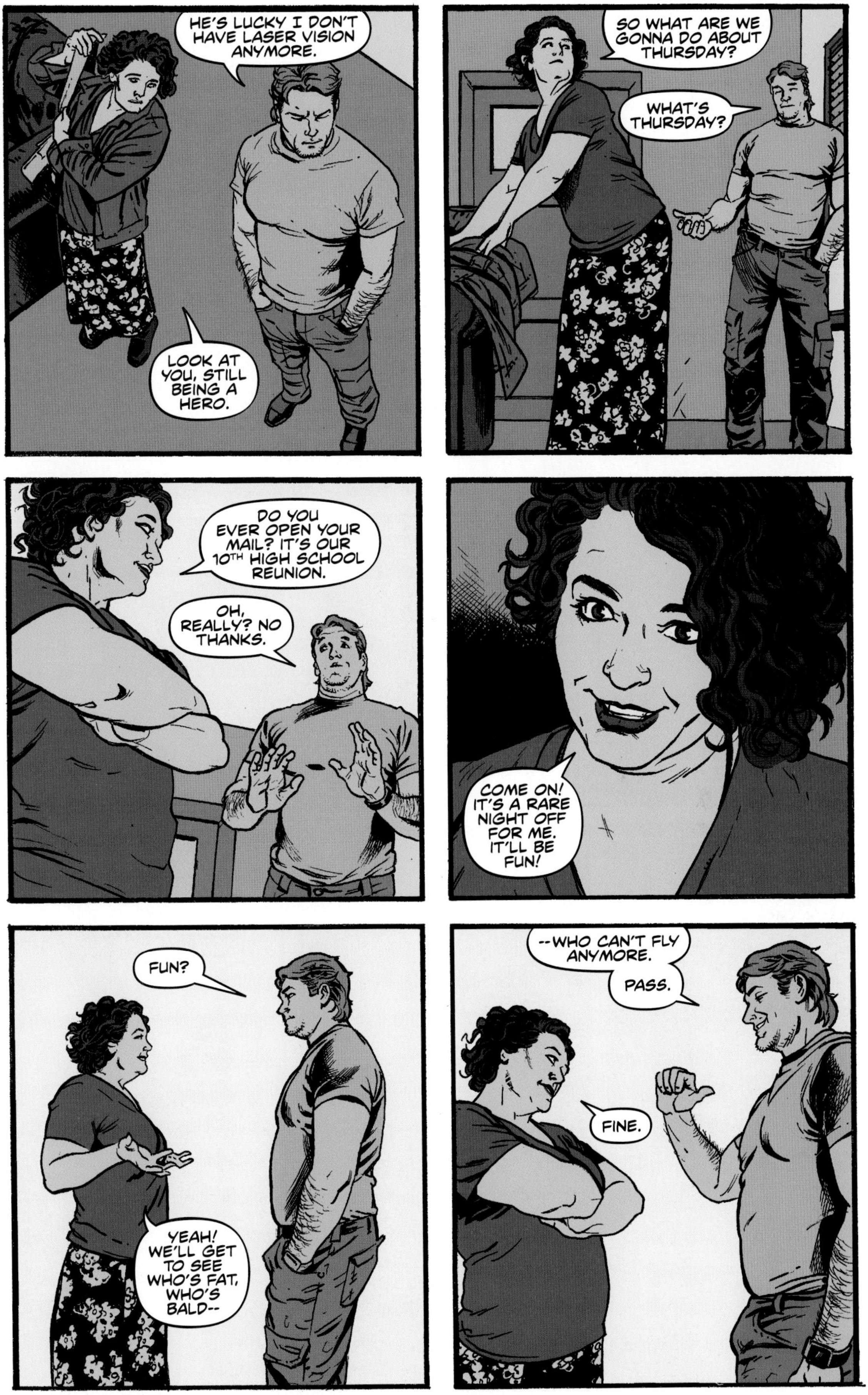

HE'S LUCKY I DON'T HAVE LASER VISION ANYMORE.
LOOK AT YOU, STILL BEING A HERO.
SO WHAT ARE WE GONNA DO ABOUT THURSDAY?
WHAT'S THURSDAY?
DO YOU EVER OPEN YOUR MAIL? IT'S OUR 10TH HIGH SCHOOL REUNION.
OH, REALLY? NO THANKS.
COME ON! IT'S A RARE NIGHT OFF FOR ME. IT'LL BE FUN!
FUN?
YEAH! WE'LL GET TO SEE WHO'S FAT, WHO'S BALD--
--WHO CAN'T FLY ANYMORE.
PASS.
FINE.

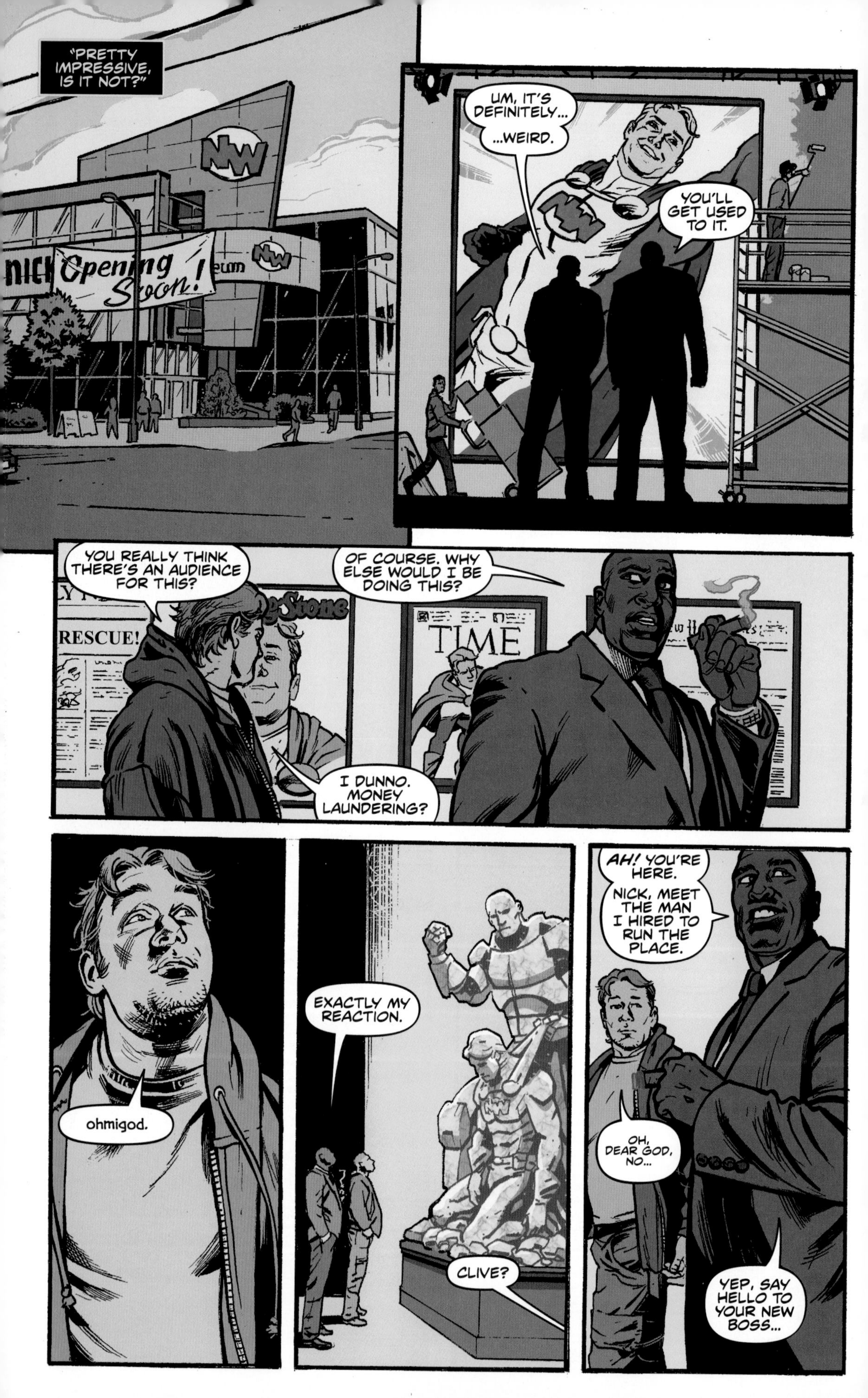

"PRETTY IMPRESSIVE, IS IT NOT?"
NICK
Opening Soon!
UM, IT'S DEFINITELY...
...WEIRD.
YOU'LL GET USED TO IT.
YOU REALLY THINK THERE'S AN AUDIENCE FOR THIS?
OF COURSE. WHY ELSE WOULD I BE DOING THIS?
I DUNNO. MONEY LAUNDERING?
RESCUE!
TIME
ohmigod.
EXACTLY MY REACTION.
CLIVE?
AH! YOU'RE HERE.
NICK, MEET THE MAN I HIRED TO RUN THE PLACE.
OH, DEAR GOD, NO...
YEP, SAY HELLO TO YOUR NEW BOSS...

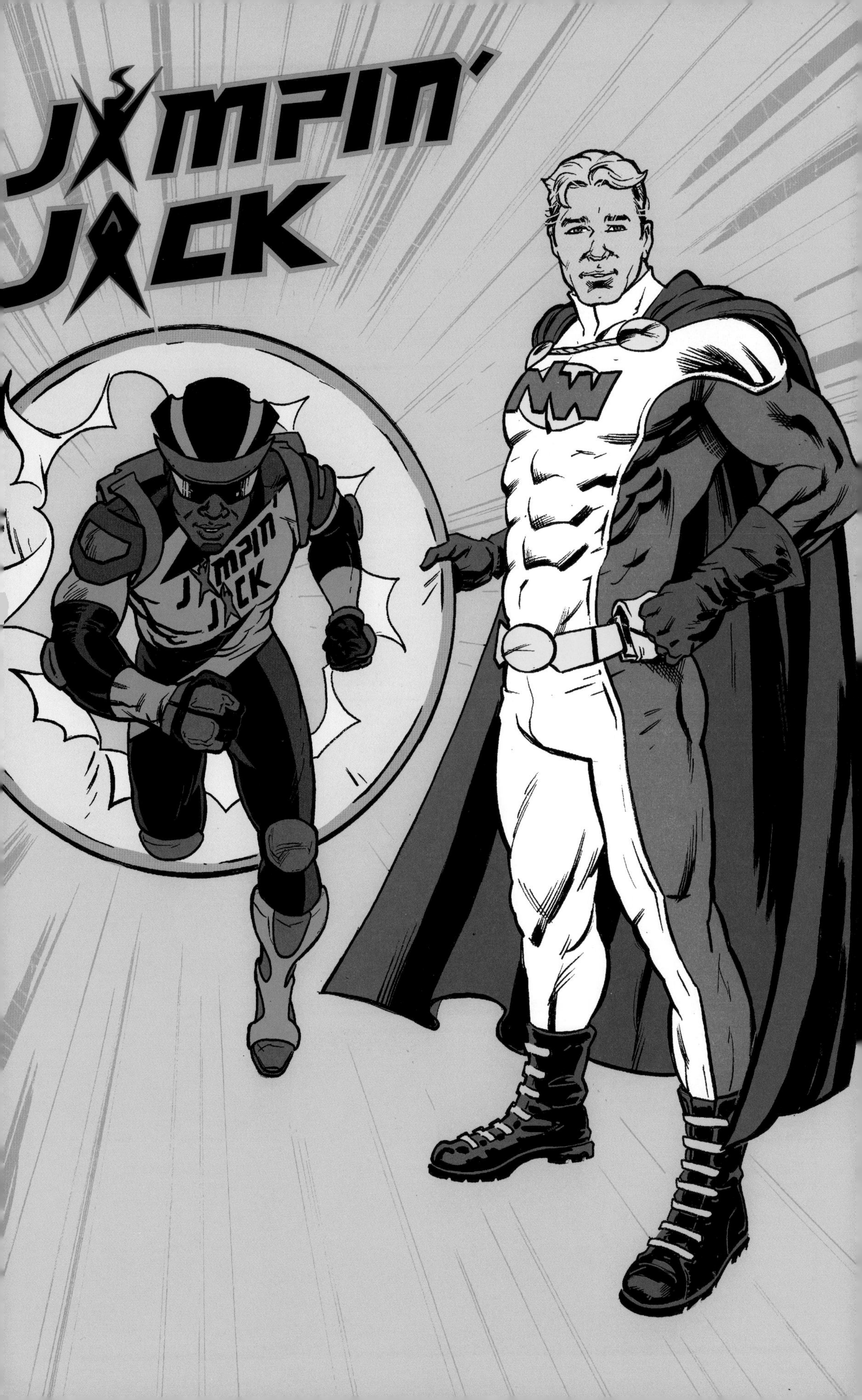
JUMPIN' JACK
NW

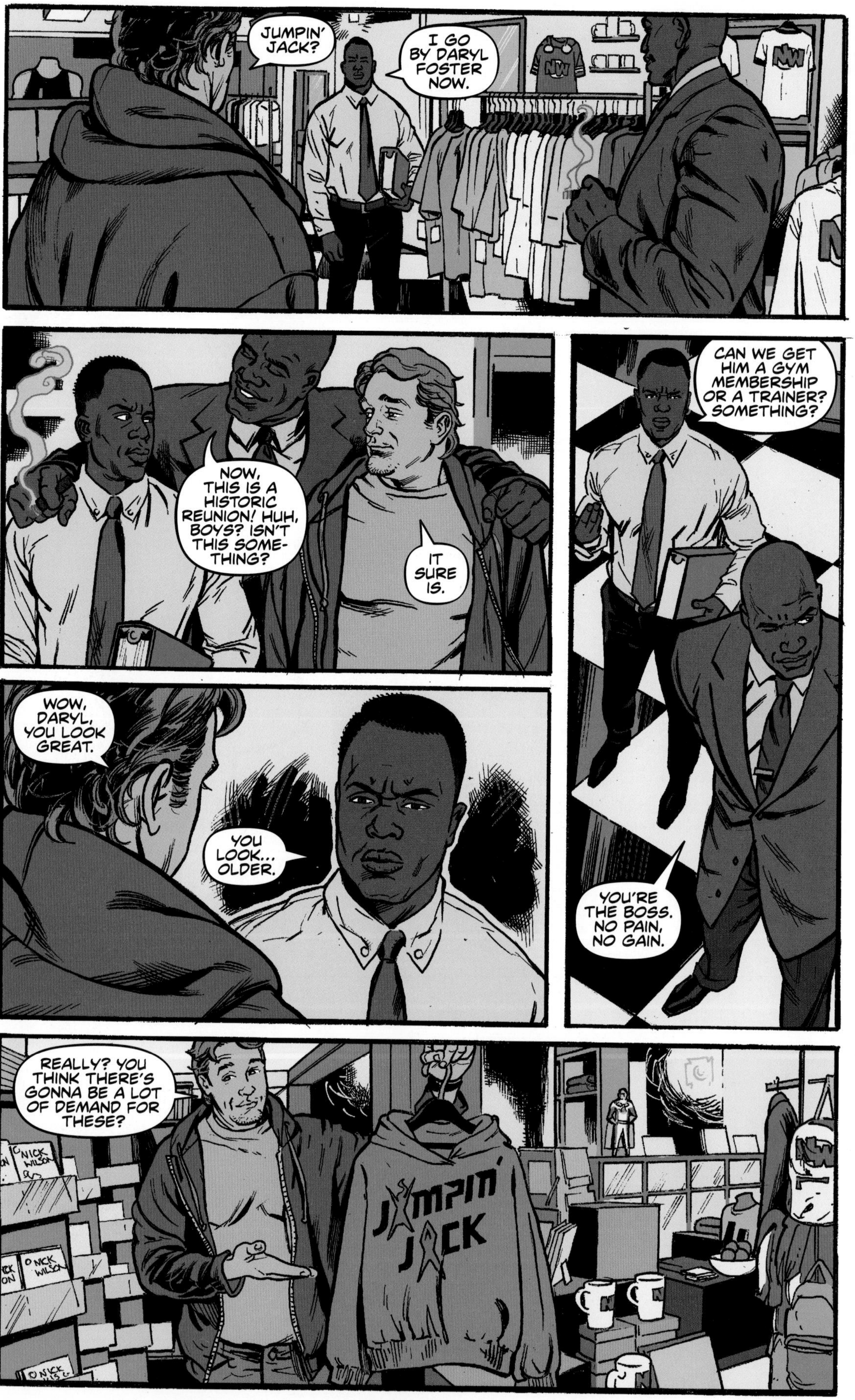
JUMPIN' JACK?
I GO BY DARYL FOSTER NOW.
NOW, THIS IS A HISTORIC REUNION! HUH, BOYS? ISN'T THIS SOME-THING?
IT SURE IS.
CAN WE GET HIM A GYM MEMBERSHIP OR A TRAINER? SOMETHING?
WOW, DARYL, YOU LOOK GREAT.
YOU LOOK... OLDER.
YOU'RE THE BOSS. NO PAIN, NO GAIN.
REALLY? YOU THINK THERE'S GONNA BE A LOT OF DEMAND FOR THESE?
JUMPIN' JACK
NICK WILSON

YOU'D BE SURPRISED.

HERE. THIS IS YOUR EMPLOYEE HANDBOOK.

GOOD GOD. HOW MANY PAGES DO YOU NEED TO EXPLAIN "SAY 'HI' TO GUESTS" AND "SMILE FOR PICTURES"?

STANDARD REQUIREMENT FOR EMPLOYEES OF MORGAN-CORP.

WOW. SOMEBODY TAKES THEIR JOB SERIOUSLY.

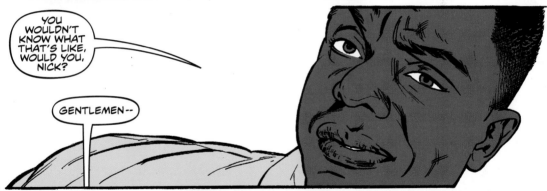

YOU WOULDN'T KNOW WHAT THAT'S LIKE, WOULD YOU, NICK?

GENTLEMEN--

I TRUST EVERYTHING IS GOING WELL?

I WORK FOR YOUR FATHER, XAVIER, NOT FOR YOU.

READ THE MANUAL, NICK. AND BRING SOME URINE FOR HR.

WHAT AN ASSHOLE.

AMEN, SISTER.

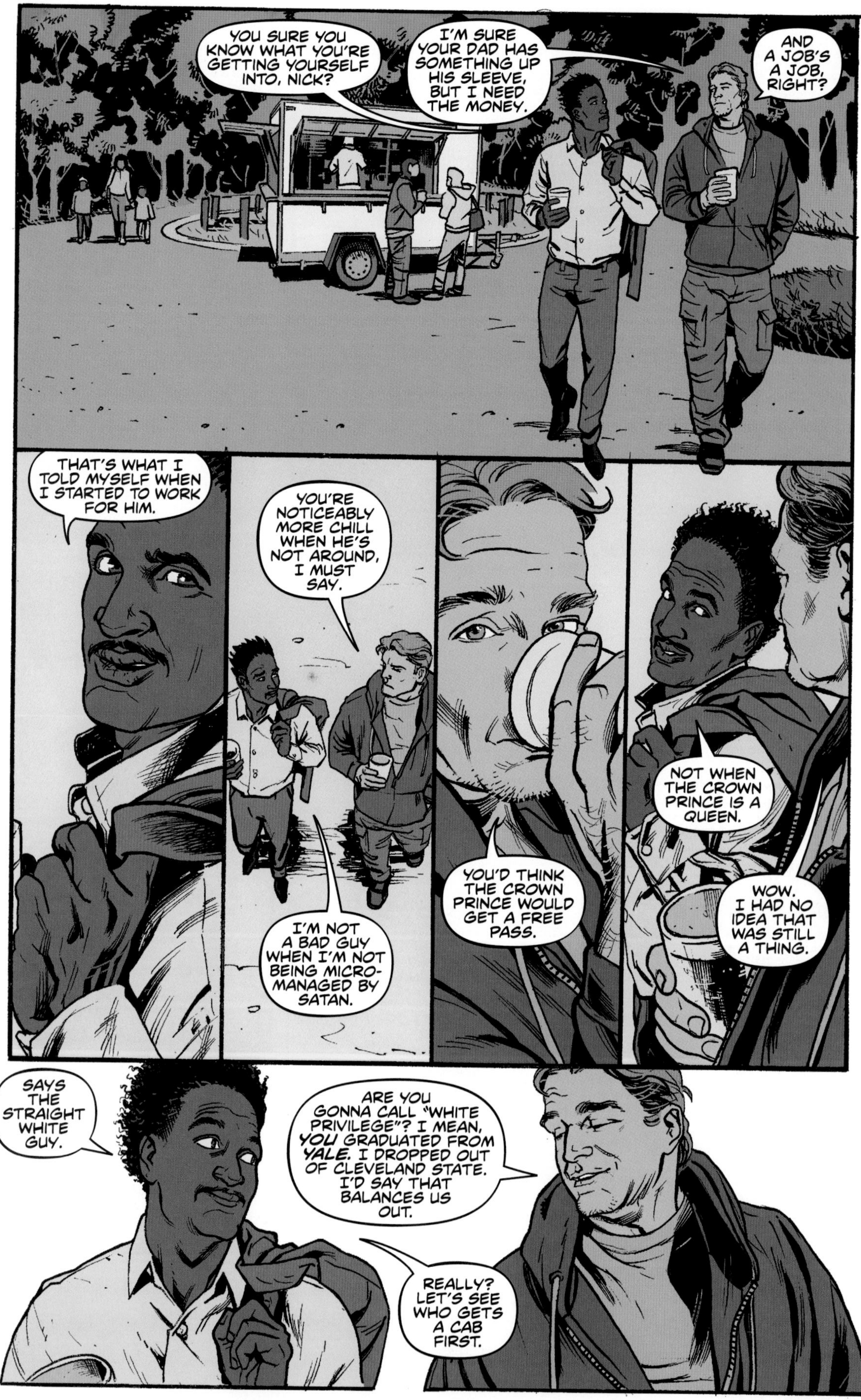
YOU SURE YOU KNOW WHAT YOU'RE GETTING YOURSELF INTO, NICK?
I'M SURE YOUR DAD HAS SOMETHING UP HIS SLEEVE, BUT I NEED THE MONEY.
AND A JOB'S A JOB, RIGHT?
THAT'S WHAT I TOLD MYSELF WHEN I STARTED TO WORK FOR HIM.
YOU'RE NOTICEABLY MORE CHILL WHEN HE'S NOT AROUND, I MUST SAY.
I'M NOT A BAD GUY WHEN I'M NOT BEING MICRO-MANAGED BY SATAN.
YOU'D THINK THE CROWN PRINCE WOULD GET A FREE PASS.
NOT WHEN THE CROWN PRINCE IS A QUEEN.
WOW. I HAD NO IDEA THAT WAS STILL A THING.
SAYS THE STRAIGHT WHITE GUY.
ARE YOU GONNA CALL "WHITE PRIVILEGE"? I MEAN, YOU GRADUATED FROM YALE. I DROPPED OUT OF CLEVELAND STATE. I'D SAY THAT BALANCES US OUT.
REALLY? LET'S SEE WHO GETS A CAB FIRST.

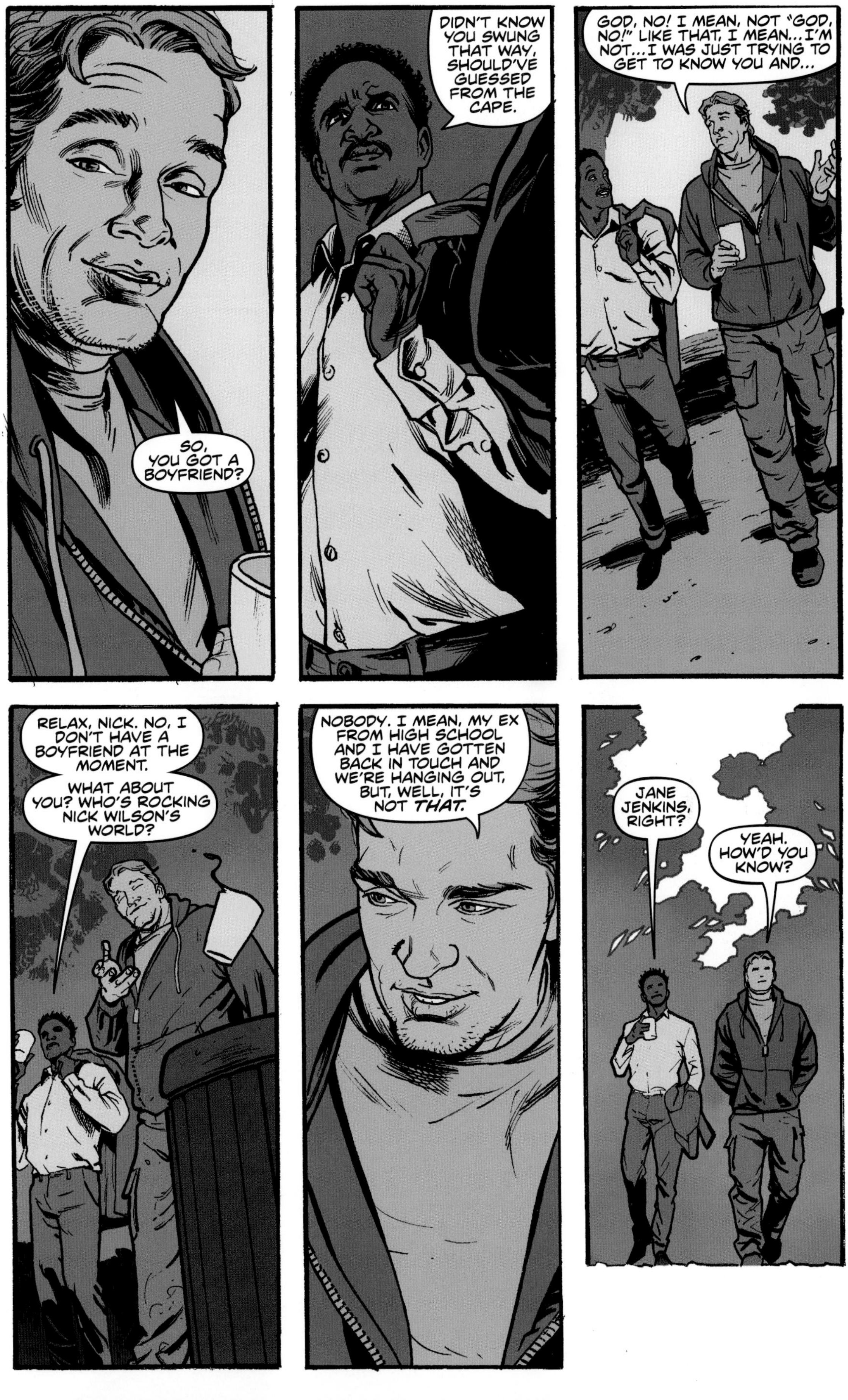
SO, YOU GOT A BOYFRIEND?
DIDN'T KNOW YOU SWUNG THAT WAY, SHOULD'VE GUESSED FROM THE CAPE.
GOD, NO! I MEAN, NOT "GOD, NO!" LIKE THAT, I MEAN...I'M NOT...I WAS JUST TRYING TO GET TO KNOW YOU AND...
RELAX, NICK. NO, I DON'T HAVE A BOYFRIEND AT THE MOMENT.
WHAT ABOUT YOU? WHO'S ROCKING NICK WILSON'S WORLD?
NOBODY. I MEAN, MY EX FROM HIGH SCHOOL AND I HAVE GOTTEN BACK IN TOUCH AND WE'RE HANGING OUT, BUT, WELL, IT'S NOT *THAT.*
JANE JENKINS, RIGHT?
YEAH. HOW'D YOU KNOW?

I HAVE TO GET HER TO GRANT US USE OF HER LIKENESS.

SHE'S NOT MY "TRUE LOVE."

IRRELEVANT FOR THE NARRATIVE OF THE MUSEUM.

AND YOU'LL PAY HER FOR THAT?

CERTAINLY.

OTHERWISE, YOUR "TRUE LOVE" IS GOING TO BE SOME DEAD-EYED STOCK PHOTO MODEL.

I'M REALLY LOOKING FORWARD TO THURSDAY.

WAIT, YOU'RE GOING TO MY REUNION?

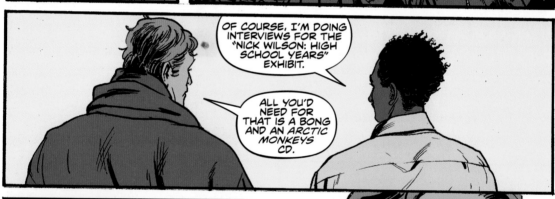

OF COURSE, I'M DOING INTERVIEWS FOR THE "NICK WILSON: HIGH SCHOOL YEARS" EXHIBIT.

ALL YOU'D NEED FOR THAT IS A BONG AND AN ARCTIC MONKEYS CD.

DO YOU WANT ME TO PICK YOU UP?

I REALLY DON'T WANT TO GO.

TECHNICALLY IT'S A WORK OUTING, SO YOU'LL BE MAKING TIME AND A HALF.

HOW'S EIGHT O'CLOCK?

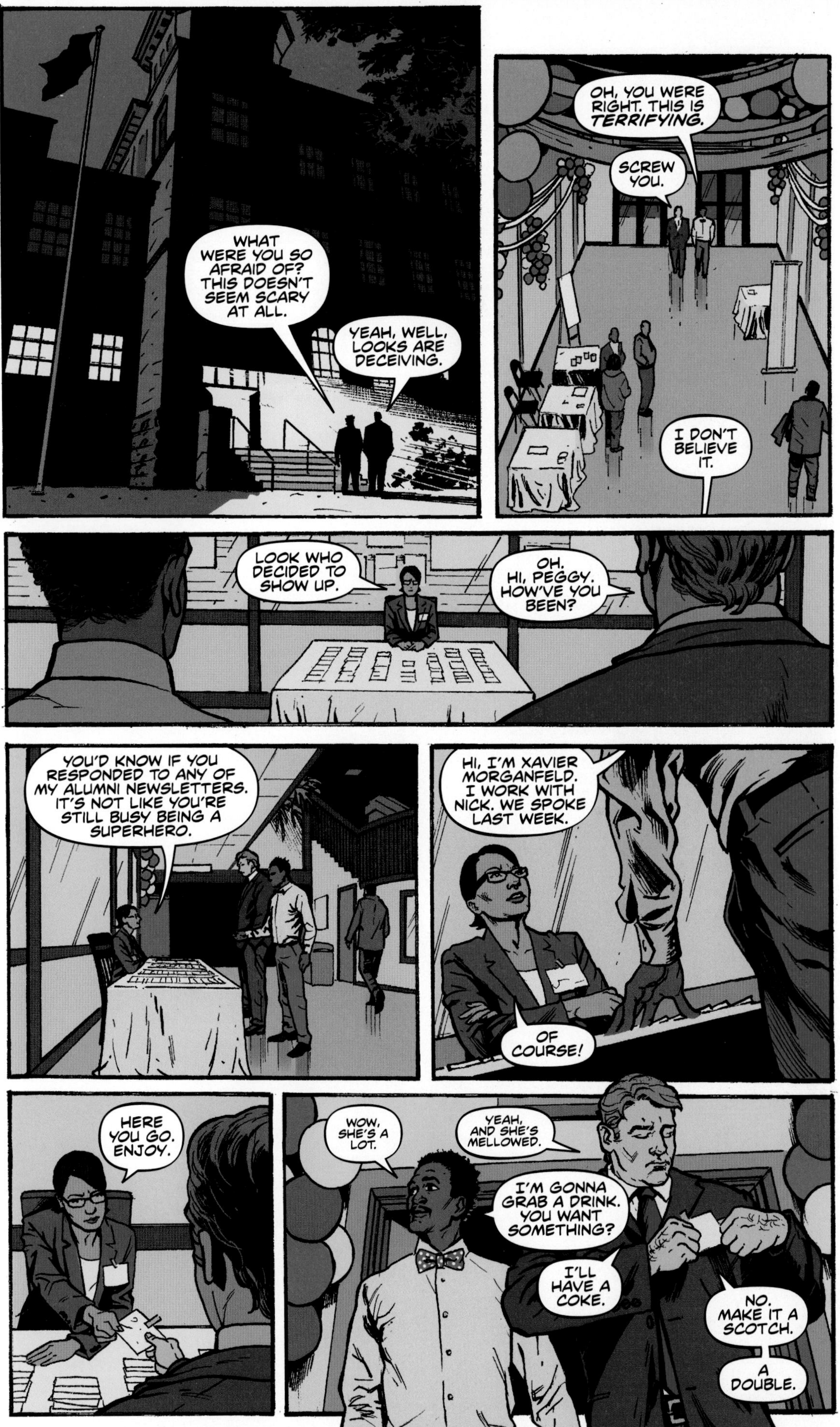
WHAT WERE YOU SO AFRAID OF? THIS DOESN'T SEEM SCARY AT ALL.
YEAH, WELL, LOOKS ARE DECEIVING.
OH, YOU WERE RIGHT. THIS IS *TERRIFYING.*
SCREW YOU.
I DON'T BELIEVE IT.
LOOK WHO DECIDED TO SHOW UP.
OH. HI, PEGGY. HOW'VE YOU BEEN?
YOU'D KNOW IF YOU RESPONDED TO ANY OF MY ALUMNI NEWSLETTERS. IT'S NOT LIKE YOU'RE STILL BUSY BEING A SUPERHERO.
HI, I'M XAVIER MORGANFELD. I WORK WITH NICK. WE SPOKE LAST WEEK.
OF COURSE!
HERE YOU GO. ENJOY.
WOW, SHE'S A LOT.
YEAH, AND SHE'S MELLOWED.
I'M GONNA GRAB A DRINK. YOU WANT SOMETHING?
I'LL HAVE A COKE.
NO. MAKE IT A SCOTCH.
A DOUBLE.

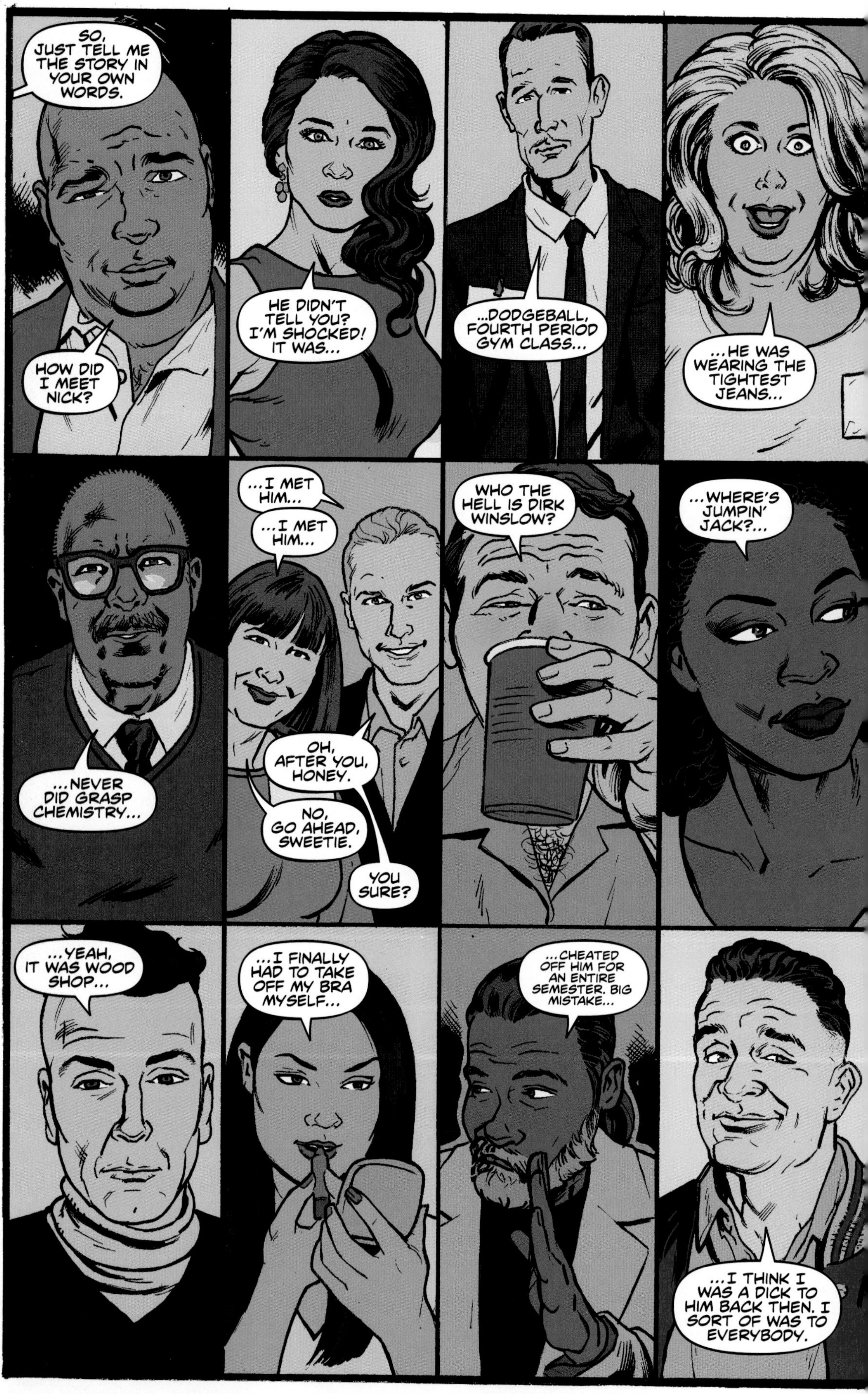
SO, JUST TELL ME THE STORY IN YOUR OWN WORDS.
HOW DID I MEET NICK?
HE DIDN'T TELL YOU? I'M SHOCKED! IT WAS...
...DODGEBALL, FOURTH PERIOD GYM CLASS...
...HE WAS WEARING THE TIGHTEST JEANS...
...NEVER DID GRASP CHEMISTRY...
...I MET HIM...
...I MET HIM...
OH, AFTER YOU, HONEY.
NO, GO AHEAD, SWEETIE.
YOU SURE?
WHO THE HELL IS DIRK WINSLOW?
...WHERE'S JUMPIN' JACK?...
...YEAH, IT WAS WOOD SHOP...
...I FINALLY HAD TO TAKE OFF MY BRA MYSELF...
...CHEATED OFF HIM FOR AN ENTIRE SEMESTER. BIG MISTAKE...
...I THINK I WAS A DICK TO HIM BACK THEN. I SORT OF WAS TO EVERYBODY.

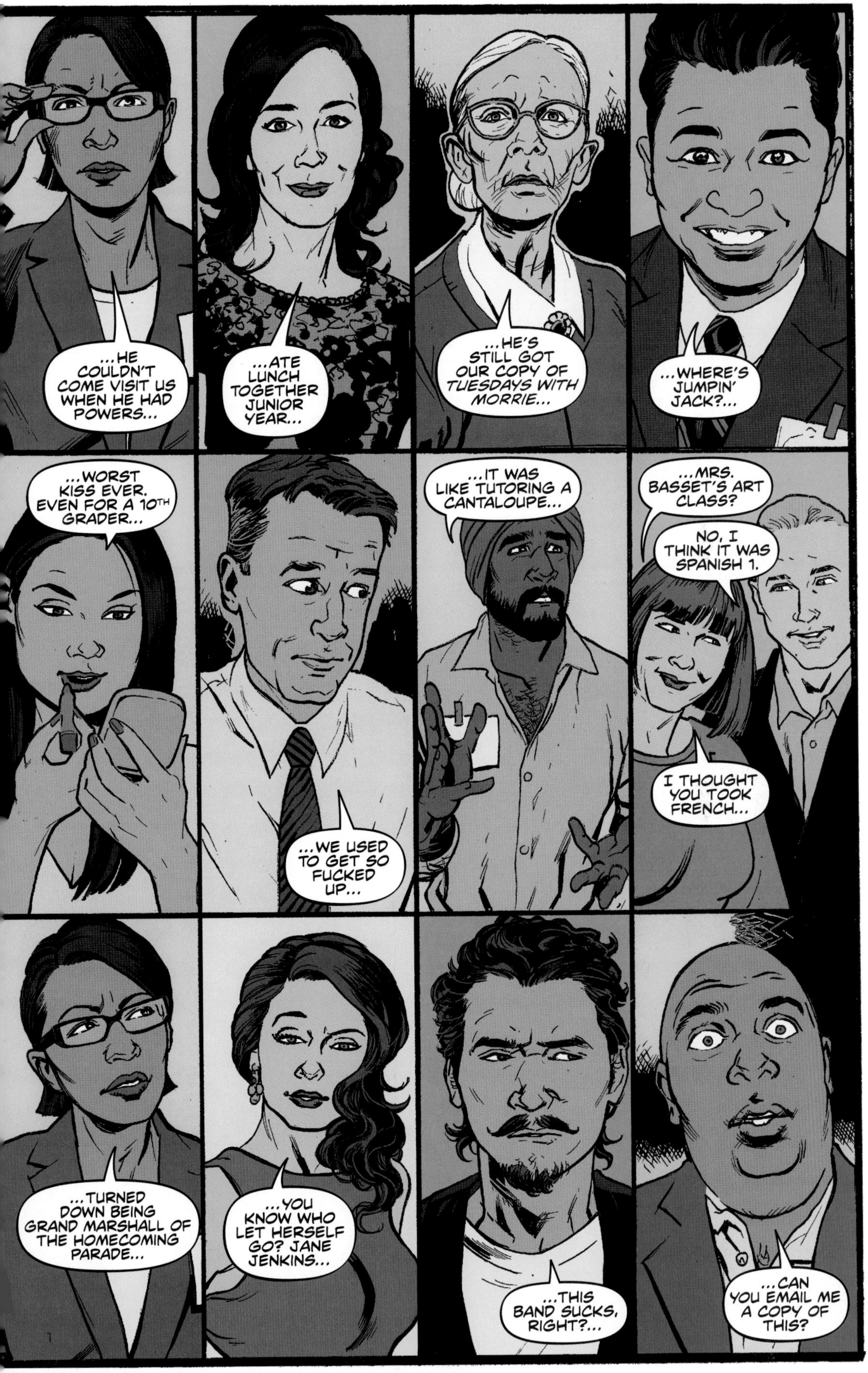
...HE COULDN'T COME VISIT US WHEN HE HAD POWERS...
...ATE LUNCH TOGETHER JUNIOR YEAR...
...HE'S STILL GOT OUR COPY OF *TUESDAYS WITH MORRIE*...
...WHERE'S JUMPIN' JACK?...
...WORST KISS EVER. EVEN FOR A 10TH GRADER...
...WE USED TO GET SO FUCKED UP...
...IT WAS LIKE TUTORING A CANTALOUPE...
...MRS. BASSET'S ART CLASS?
NO, I THINK IT WAS SPANISH 1.
I THOUGHT YOU TOOK FRENCH...
...TURNED DOWN BEING GRAND MARSHALL OF THE HOMECOMING PARADE...
...YOU KNOW WHO LET HERSELF GO? JANE JENKINS...
...THIS BAND SUCKS, RIGHT?...
...CAN YOU EMAIL ME A COPY OF THIS?

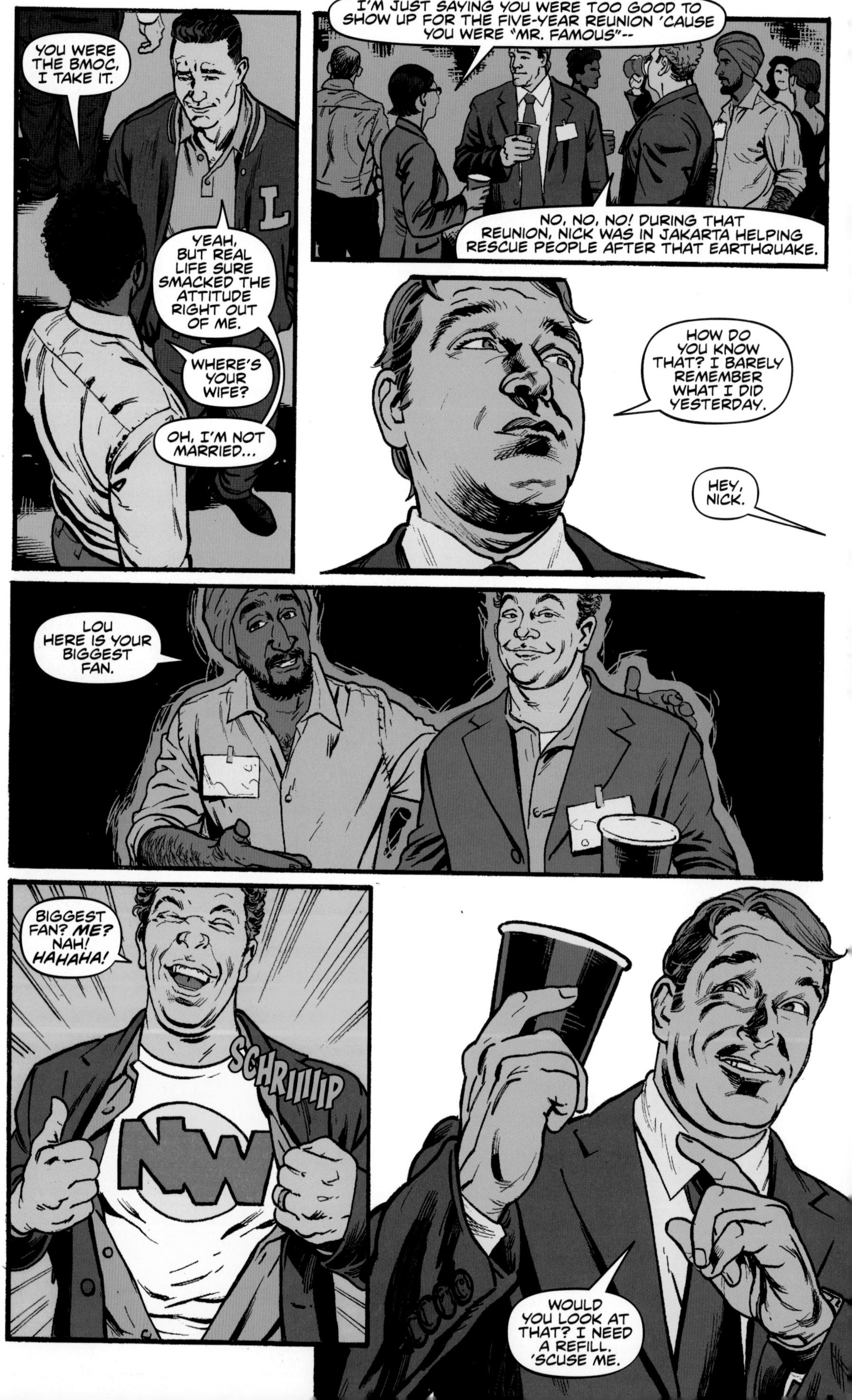
YOU WERE THE BMOC, I TAKE IT.
YEAH, BUT REAL LIFE SURE SMACKED THE ATTITUDE RIGHT OUT OF ME.
WHERE'S YOUR WIFE?
OH, I'M NOT MARRIED...
I'M JUST SAYING YOU WERE TOO GOOD TO SHOW UP FOR THE FIVE-YEAR REUNION 'CAUSE YOU WERE "MR. FAMOUS"--
NO, NO, NO! DURING THAT REUNION, NICK WAS IN JAKARTA HELPING RESCUE PEOPLE AFTER THAT EARTHQUAKE.
HOW DO YOU KNOW THAT? I BARELY REMEMBER WHAT I DID YESTERDAY.
HEY, NICK.
LOU HERE IS YOUR BIGGEST FAN.
BIGGEST FAN? ME? NAH! HAHAHA!
SCHRIIIIIP
NW
WOULD YOU LOOK AT THAT? I NEED A REFILL. 'SCUSE ME.

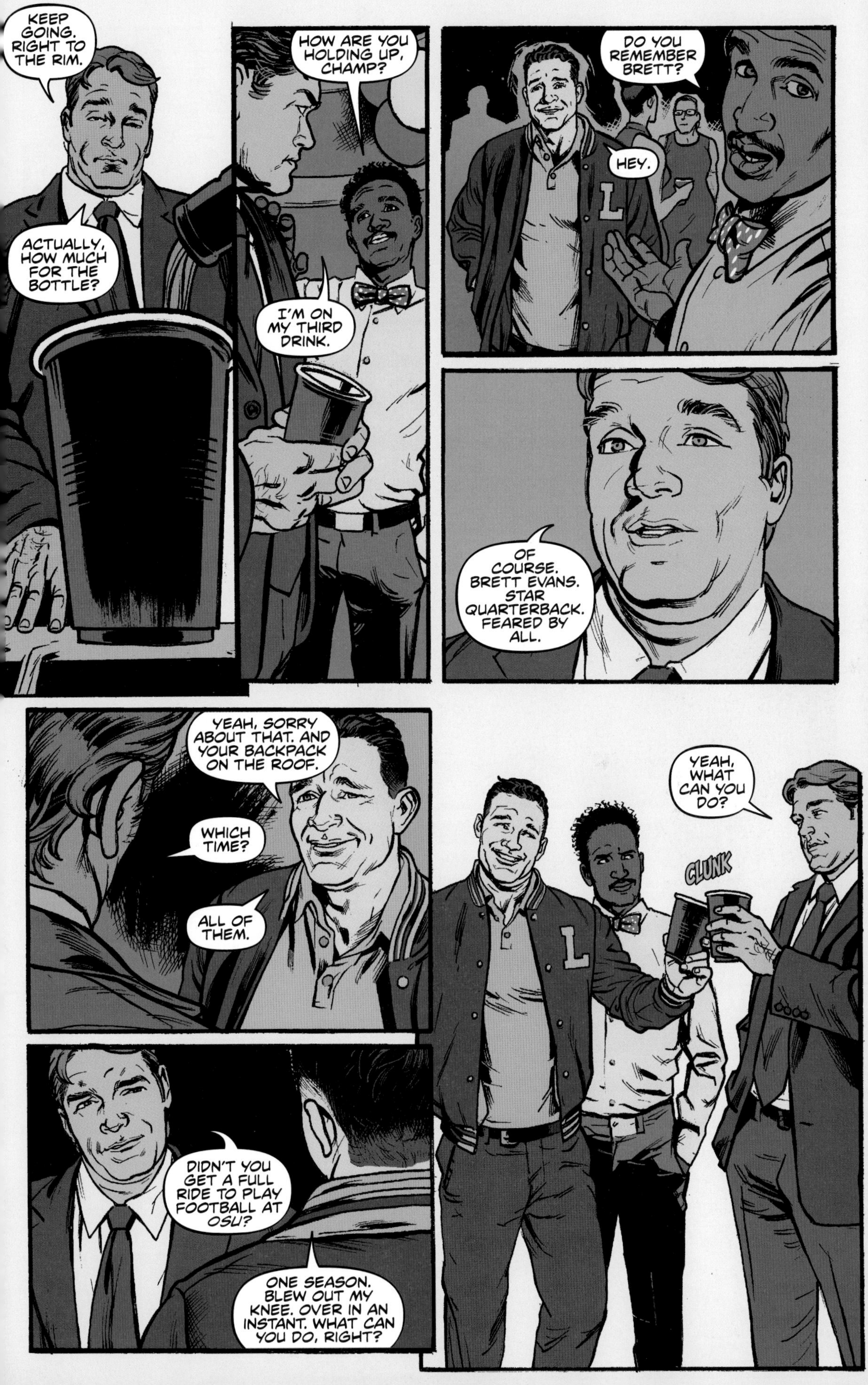
KEEP GOING. RIGHT TO THE RIM.
ACTUALLY, HOW MUCH FOR THE BOTTLE?
HOW ARE YOU HOLDING UP, CHAMP?
I'M ON MY THIRD DRINK.
DO YOU REMEMBER BRETT?
HEY.
OF COURSE. BRETT EVANS. STAR QUARTERBACK. FEARED BY ALL.
YEAH, SORRY ABOUT THAT. AND YOUR BACKPACK ON THE ROOF.
WHICH TIME?
ALL OF THEM.
DIDN'T YOU GET A FULL RIDE TO PLAY FOOTBALL AT OSU?
ONE SEASON. BLEW OUT MY KNEE. OVER IN AN INSTANT. WHAT CAN YOU DO, RIGHT?
YEAH, WHAT CAN YOU DO?
CLUNK

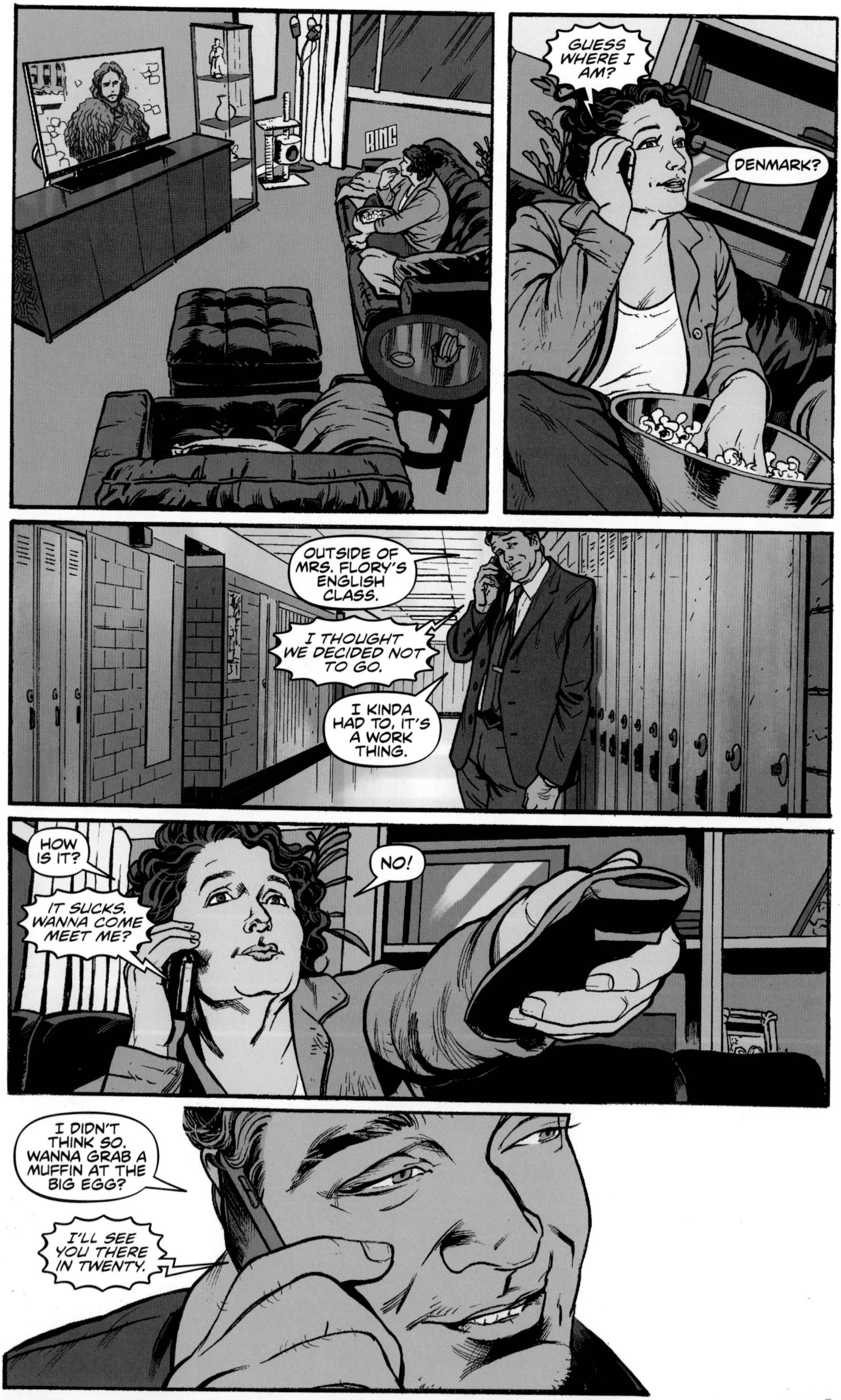
RING
GUESS WHERE I AM?
DENMARK?
OUTSIDE OF MRS. FLORY'S ENGLISH CLASS.
I THOUGHT WE DECIDED NOT TO GO.
I KINDA HAD TO, IT'S A WORK THING.
HOW IS IT?
IT SUCKS. WANNA COME MEET ME?
NO!
I DIDN'T THINK SO. WANNA GRAB A MUFFIN AT THE BIG EGG?
I'LL SEE YOU THERE IN TWENTY.

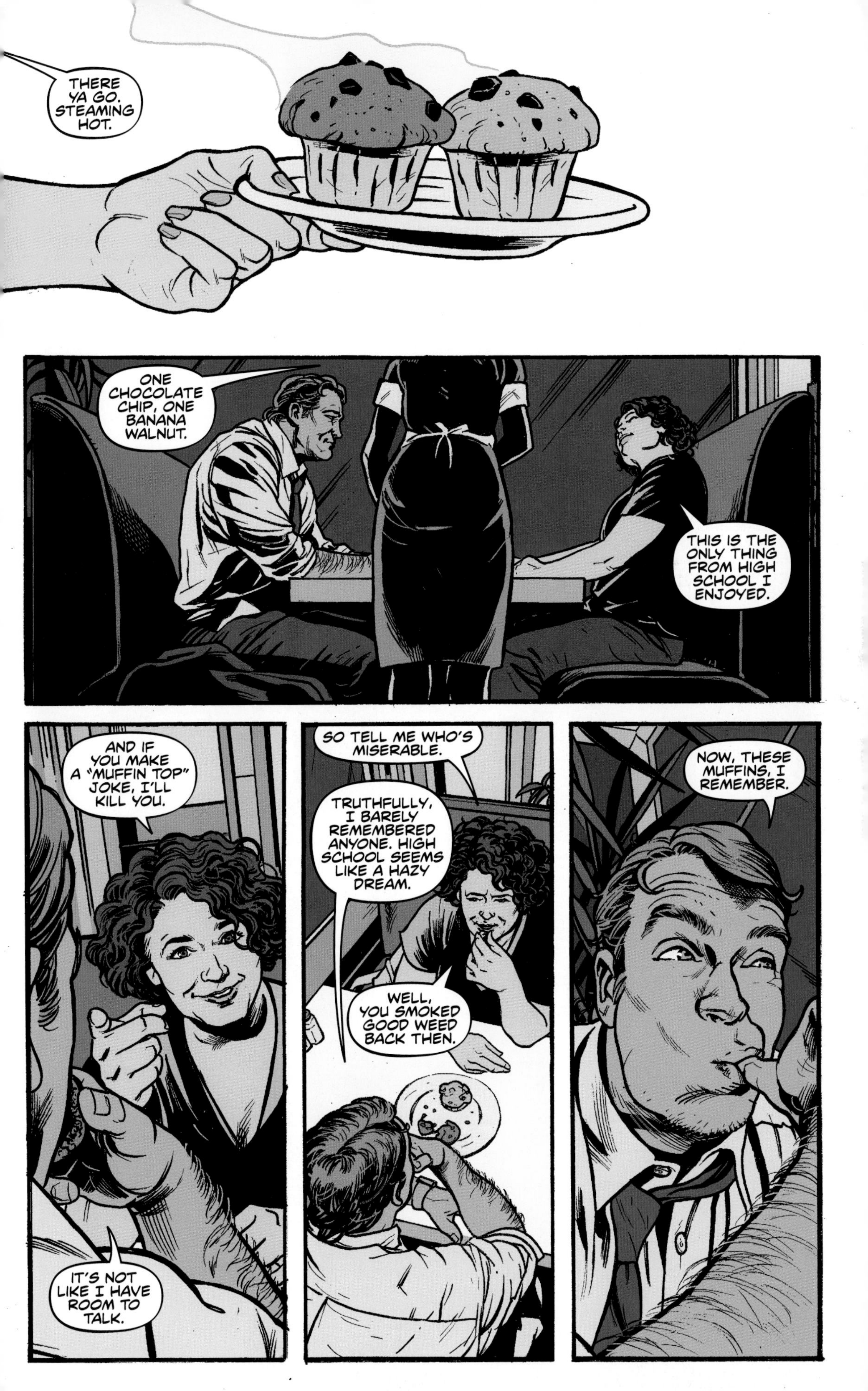
THERE YA GO. STEAMING HOT.
ONE CHOCOLATE CHIP, ONE BANANA WALNUT.
THIS IS THE ONLY THING FROM HIGH SCHOOL I ENJOYED.
AND IF YOU MAKE A "MUFFIN TOP" JOKE, I'LL KILL YOU.
IT'S NOT LIKE I HAVE ROOM TO TALK.
SO TELL ME WHO'S MISERABLE.
TRUTHFULLY, I BARELY REMEMBERED ANYONE. HIGH SCHOOL SEEMS LIKE A HAZY DREAM.
WELL, YOU SMOKED GOOD WEED BACK THEN.
NOW, THESE MUFFINS, I REMEMBER.

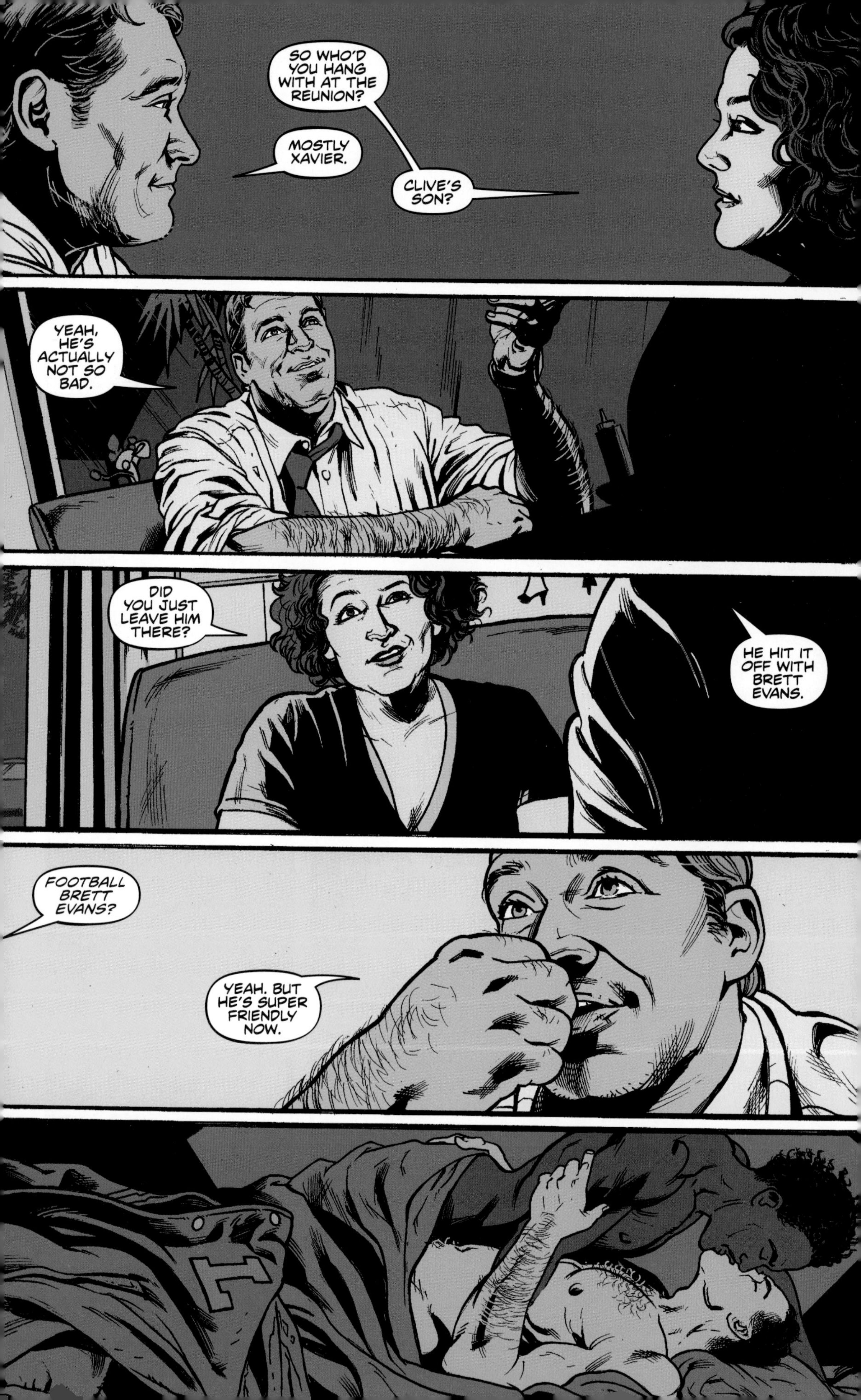
SO WHO'D YOU HANG WITH AT THE REUNION?
MOSTLY XAVIER.
CLIVE'S SON?
YEAH, HE'S ACTUALLY NOT SO BAD.
DID YOU JUST LEAVE HIM THERE?
HE HIT IT OFF WITH BRETT EVANS.
FOOTBALL BRETT EVANS?
YEAH. BUT HE'S SUPER FRIENDLY NOW.

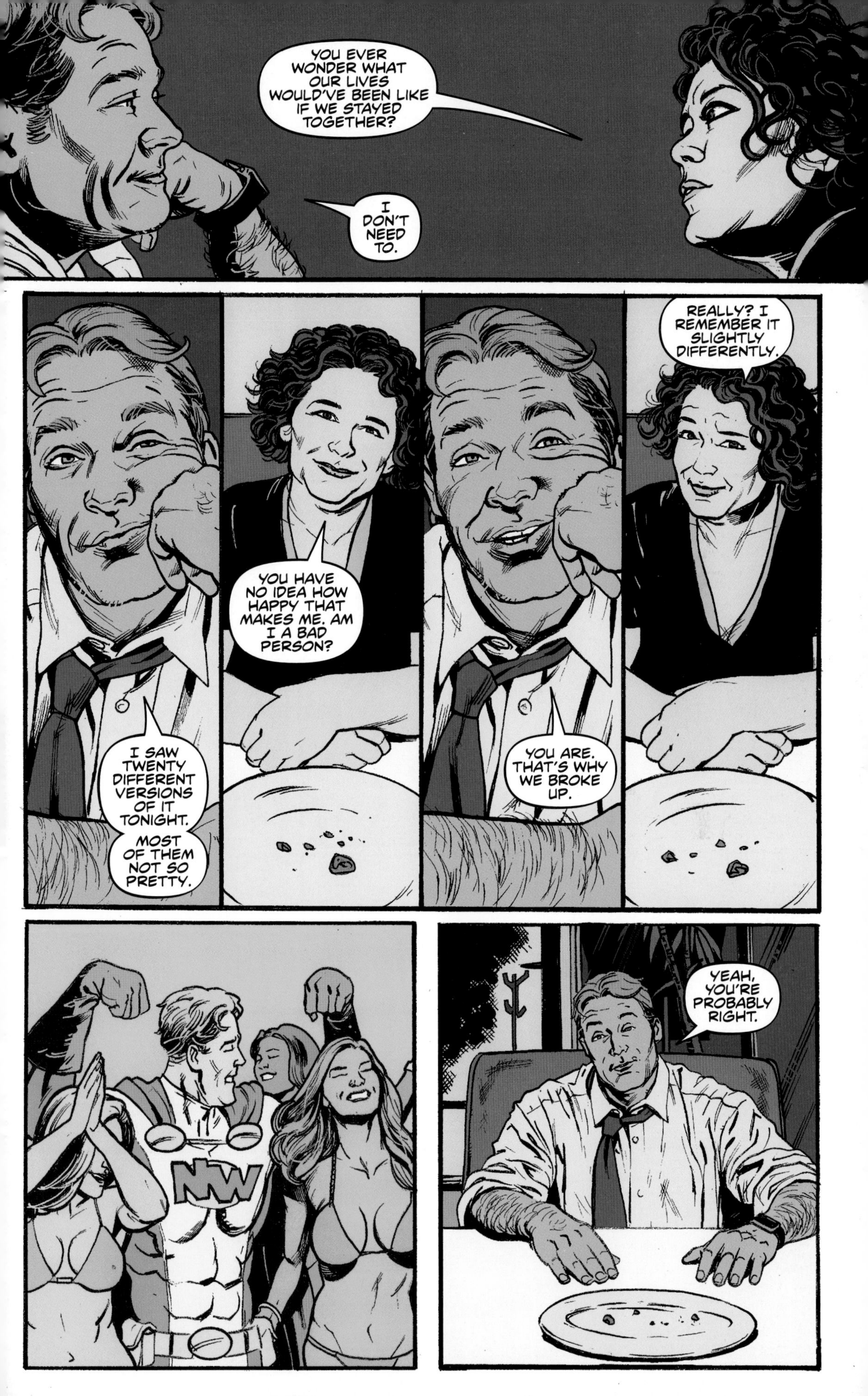

YOU EVER WONDER WHAT OUR LIVES WOULD'VE BEEN LIKE IF WE STAYED TOGETHER?
I DON'T NEED TO.
I SAW TWENTY DIFFERENT VERSIONS OF IT TONIGHT.
MOST OF THEM NOT SO PRETTY.
YOU HAVE NO IDEA HOW HAPPY THAT MAKES ME. AM I A BAD PERSON?
YOU ARE. THAT'S WHY WE BROKE UP.
REALLY? I REMEMBER IT SLIGHTLY DIFFERENTLY.
NW
YEAH, YOU'RE PROBABLY RIGHT.

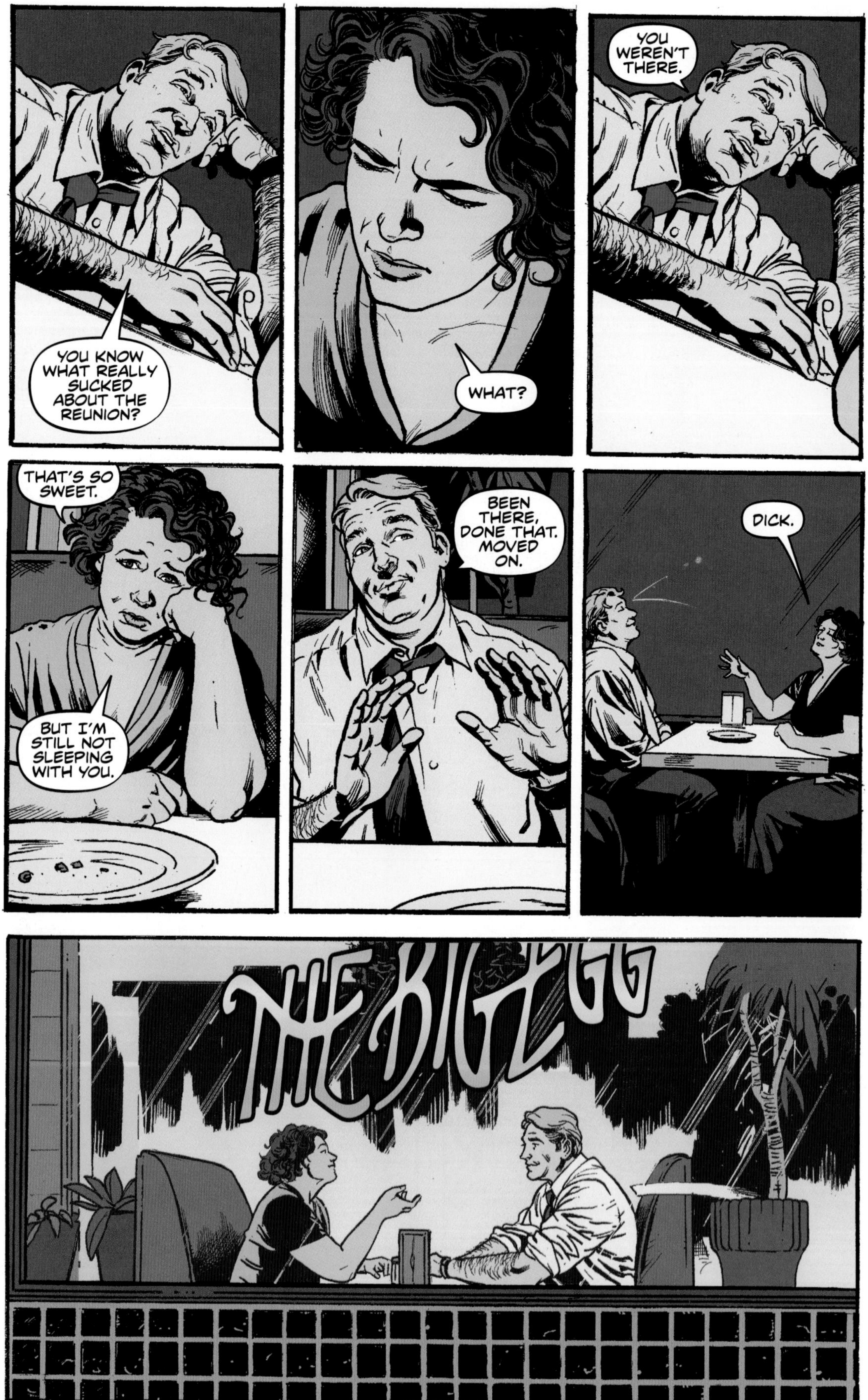
YOU KNOW WHAT REALLY SUCKED ABOUT THE REUNION?
WHAT?
YOU WEREN'T THERE.
THAT'S SO SWEET.
BUT I'M STILL NOT SLEEPING WITH YOU.
BEEN THERE, DONE THAT. MOVED ON.
DICK.
THE BIG EGG

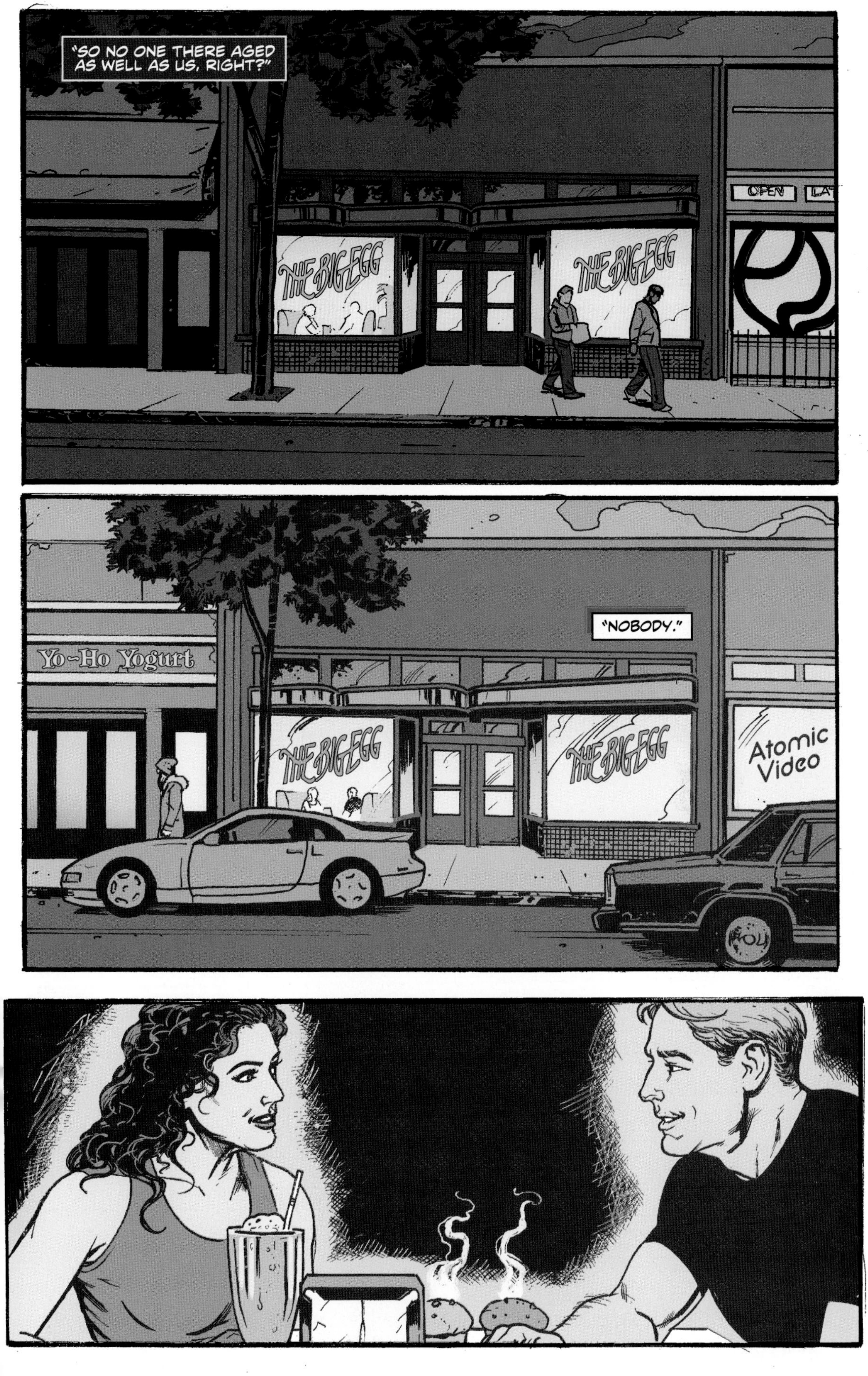
"SO NO ONE THERE AGED AS WELL AS US, RIGHT?"
OPEN
THE BIG EGG
THE BIG EGG
Yo-Ho Yogurt
"NOBODY."
THE BIG EGG
THE BIG EGG
Atomic Video

HIGH SCHOOL.

Those words either make you smile with nostalgia or make you twitch with teenaged PTSD.

And while writing this issue, I felt a mixture of both. You see, growing up in Mentor, Ohio (about 40 minutes outside of Cleveland) I was neither popular nor a total outcast. I kept my head down, tried to dodge any bullies looking for new prey, and longed for the days when I would be free to be who I knew I was.

Sure, there were some good times, some lifelong friends, and some indelible memories but, for me at least, I romanticized what I wanted high school to be and not what it was.

I blame John Hughes.

Even the geekiest of geeks (see Anthony Michael Hall circa 1984) was kinda cool in Hughes' films. I wanted that. I wanted a cool OMD/Simple Minds/ New Order soundtrack for my angsty teen years. I wanted my wit to disarm the popular jocks and make them adopt me as their jester/mascot/ maybe even friend.

But life, as we all know if we live long enough, is NOT the movies.

So, when Eddie and I talked about Nick going to a HS reunion for issue three, I took to it so quickly that I surprised myself. Here was my chance to go through the reunion experience and finally, and literally, control the narrative. (I, as yet, have not attended any of my own actual reunions. A big one is coming up and my teeth hurt just thinking about it.)

I pitched ideas and instantly went to the stuff we all have been conditioned to expect our reunions to be. Familiar tropes and wish-fulfillment.* But Eddie sensed stuff in me that I didn't know was there. Stuff that, even though I never had superpowers, Nick and I (and lots of you readers I'd wager) shared.

It was therapeutic and (almost) made me nostalgic for those days of mix tapes, designer jeans, and lots of Redmond hair gel. Hell, and still having hair!

While I'm undecided if I'll ever actually attend one of my HS reunions, after this issue, I'm okay with it.

Now, I'm gonna go watch the Criterion blu-ray of "The Breakfast Club".

Marc Andreyko

Los Angeles, January 2018.

*Ok, so I kept in some wish-fulfillment. I never actually did get to sleep with the popular jock. Yet ☺

THE NATURE OF CLICHÉ & OTHER SUBJECTS

Frankly, when Marc suggested we make issue three of *Nick Wilson* about our hero's high school reunion I was aghast. You see, in television rewrite rooms the "high school reunion episode" is one of those dreaded tropes that are looked upon with disdain.

Or should I say, that were looked on with disdain, for I feel that may be just another sign of my age. I have had a feeling for a while now that many of the things that were the clichés of my youth are now the new "new." I first felt this when I realized that the other dreaded sit-com conventions—often called *clams* (allegedly for the stale joke of using bad clams as an excuse for stomach distress as opposed to the jazzman slang of a sour note) —were popping up in other ways.

Self-righteous sit-com writers refused to tell certain types of familiar stories but it turned out there was a demand for them and I contend that those stories almost demanded to be told and eventually bubbled up as reality shows. Let's take a look.

THE TALENT SHOW EPISODE—an excuse to show the other skills your cast has. Your second lead can play the banjo? Your funny neighbor is a ventriloquist? Well, give them a chance to shine in a talent show. Extra points if it's to save a beloved local business. This type of episode would be met with a special type of derision if pitched in a writers' room but people love talent shows as the accountants of everything from *American Idol* to *The Voice* to *The Four* will tell you.

THE CAMPING SHOW—even more dreaded than the Talent Show, the Camping Show would take the regular cast out of their home set and take out into nature (actually a horrible indoor set with some terrible shrubbery) and force them to confront some problem they had been avoiding inside the pressure cooker of a tent with rationed toilet paper and perhaps the threat of a bear (usually sound effects, but perhaps stock footage or a drugged up animal depending on your budget). Once people refused to do the Camping Show, *Survivor* had to fill the void.

TWO DATES TO THE PROM—How is he/she gonna choose? You can see six or seven examples on TVLand or one of the streaming services specializing in narcotizing nostalgia seven nights a week. At a certain point, writers threw up their hands and couldn't recycle the clichés anymore. But audiences wanted the stories populated by people with haircuts and clothes they might wear so *The Bachelor* and *The Bachelorette* were born.

THE STUCK IN A. . .—Sometimes you want to put a group of people in a pressure cooker that wouldn't go camping together. So you get them stuck in an elevator, or on a train, or in an airport—anywhere where they can't escape and tempers might run hot and feelings and secrets might be exposed. This eventually became *Big Brother*.

There are other examples but you get the point and so we find ourselves at the high school reunion issue and quite a good story it is I think. At first, when we discussed it I thought it might be because Nick's life was so highly attenuated that the distance he raveled from high school to the here and now made him unique but as Marc and I talked realized that that is how we all feel. We all look at our lives through a wildly warped lens hat is reflected onto an equally warped magnifying mirror. And as writers, we then make choices to describe that reflection in terms that can make you laugh or cry.

And the distance between tears and laughter is not as far as you may think. As Mel Brooks said, "tragedy is when I cut my finger, comedy is when you fall into an open sewer and die." You may laugh at that but he was dead serious.

Time is a funny thing—the adage "what's old is new again" is itself a cliché but consider Frank Ocean. Twenty years ago the thought of covering the Johnny Mercer/Henry Mancini song "Moon River" yet again would be laughable, there were enough versions to fill the halls of hell and at times it seemed they had. But Mister Ocean recently covered the song and not only did his fans enjoy it, many of them took it to be a new song he had written.

There are records and by extension, films, books, concepts that I take for granted as being in the public vernacular. I am constantly surprised what has fallen from the lexicon. Some people bemoan that fact. I don't. I think it just means I have more crayons in my box hat the public hasn't seen; more tools to use in my own work.

But the temptation is to use too may of them at once and out-clever yourself. I can be as guilty as the next writer who thinks that just because I can cleave—a fascinating word because it can mean both to separate or to adhere—half a dozen adjectives to a noun n a vaguely rhythmic and somewhat euphonious sentence I am a good writer. Often the sentences are labored and so full of curlicues so as to be incomprehensible.

But on the other side of complexity lies simplicity or as Albert Einstein said "The definition of genius is taking the complex and making it simple." I read so many modern comics and have no fucking idea what is happening, lost in maddening flow of horrible visual design and confused retro-fitting of what was a poor grasp of science to begin with that I am lost before I leave the splash page.

That's why Tom King's recent run on *Batman* was such nice surprise – crisp and direct with art in service to the story telling. He reminds me of Noah Hawley – there are things both of them have done that I had not warmed up to immediately but I have found that i s more often than not my limitation and not their work's fault. Even when I haven't liked a specific thing they have done, I have loved the sheer nerve and courage to try something outside the expectations I brought to their work. Ultimately, I came around and became a rabid fan of Hawley's first season of Legion, so different than his three seasons of *Fargo* ust as I came to embrace King's current wild run of *Mister Miracle*.

Which brings me to the thing I like the most about the ending this issue's story. It's a total ie. A bit of sleight of hand.

I know I told you last issue I didn't like talking about what was going on in the pages but an oversight on our side left us with some blank pages and it gives me a chance to tell you how much I hate nostalgia. And, yeah, at first glance it sure looks like we are being swathed in sepia tones of bullshit here. But what is really happening, Nick is finally coming o terms with what an asshole he was to Jane. Him owning it is a big step towards moving

Nostalgia on the other hand, traps people into looking at their life in the rear view mirror. A terrible side effect of that is they only connect to movies and music that were in the zeitgeist when they were young and vital. If I have to listen to another person frozen in time worse than Steve Rogers quote a swath of pages from a mediocre film just because it came out in their junior year of high school I'm gonna jump off a building. They're not Proust and *Camp Beverly Hills* is not a *Madeleine*. I don't discount the emotional resonance of art in your life but once you free yourself from the temporal tyranny of thinking your generation has the lock on quality there is a wild and wooly world of painting, literature, film, music and much more to enjoy.

But I digress, Nick and Jane take steps in this sequence towards building a new future —they move into uncharted territory – they are looking through the windshield and not the rear window and that's exciting. They revel in the past but they are not going to languish there, those days are gone and they both know it is a momentary visit, a goodbye to those days not a prolonged stay.

Nick is poking his head out of a hole—he is facing his demons. He is rebuilding, rejoining the human race. We have all had those moments—It is a universal story told against a background of capes and powers but it is not a superhero story.

It is a human story.

I hope when you read Nick Wilson you see a little bit of yourself like I always did when I read *Superman*, the outsider looking to connect and *Spider-Man*, the awkward teen learning about power and responsibility. On one of our first dates my wife said to me and I'm not even sure how we got there, "The Hulk is probably stronger but the Thing has more heart." I think I knew then I would marry her.

I know women read *Wonder Woman* and see themselves and African Americans do the same with *Black Panther*. That's a big part of what will make them endure. Nick Wilson is a smaller story – but for anyone who has had to climb up from public failure, who has had to regroup under reduced circumstances, who had to figure out how to find their way back out of a hole, this story is to show you that you are not alone. And hopefully with a few laughs along the way.

I want Nick Wilson to be a likable guy who is working to get better. Who amongst us can't identify with that.

It's a small story told in a big world and we still have some rocks to throw at him. Stick with us; I think we all have been Nick Wilson sometimes.

Thanks for being part of it.

Yer ol pal,

eddie gorodetsky
los feliz, march 2018

FROM THE CORNER

KRIKORIAN WRITES

"Nick Wilson" Comic Book May Have Saved Woman's Life, Hospital Officials Say

By MICHAEL KRIKORIAN

Ninety minutes before a fallen superhero arrived to save the night, Dr. Saji Mathai looked at the monitor above the head of emergency room patient Kate Elizabeth Green. He was stunned.

"The numbers were so astronomical I thought I was looking at the dashboard of a McLaren P1," said Mathai, head of the ER at Olympia Medical Center in Los Angeles. "At first, the blood pressure, the pulse, the vitals, they reminded me of the P1's tachometer and speedometer."

Green, 32, had been exposed to the rare and deadly syndrome known as "Proxsimus Crimsoni Scampi Gigantus," a vicious, unforgiving parasite of an unusually large red shrimp that, like a thief in the afternoon, sneaks into the air passages of humans who would never order skrimps of any kind.

Green, the storied assistant to Nancy Silverton, was at a party in Brentwood and shortly after a waiter sauntered by carrying a tray of Red Scampi Gigantic from Madagascar. Her long, slender throat began to quiver, but not in a good way. Mere seconds later, Chad Colby, former chef of Chi Spacca and long time dear friend of Green's, came up to her and said "You don't look so good." Colby did nothing to help, but did launch into a lengthy spiel about the joys of making pasta without a machine.

Meanwhile, unable to speak, Green stumbled out of the house and toward her McLaren, (a 720). Her stumbling caused no alarm as most of the Brentwood party-goers were also stumbling. She managed to drive home in Miracle Mile South, then decided she needed to go to the hospital. Fortunately, Olympia Medical Center was less than a mile away.

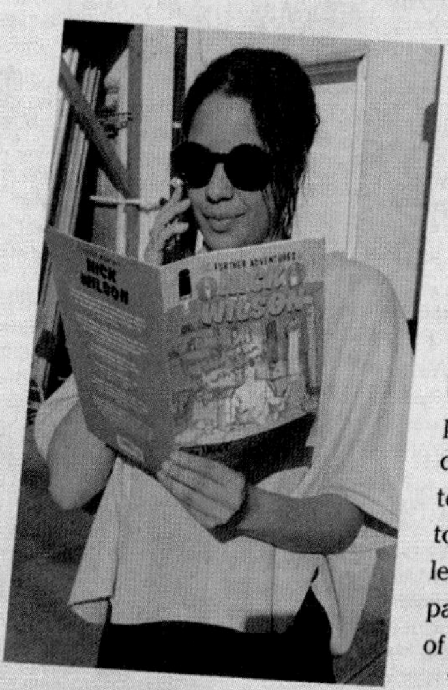
NICK WILSON

Kate Elizabeth Green

Although up to a dozen people were waiting to be seen, nurses rushed the trembling former Miss Modesto past them and began trying to lower and/or raise her vitals. Enough steroids were pumped into her to make Barry Bonds drool.

Still, nothing seemed to help. By the time an uncle arrived, Kate Green was—in the words of Neil Young—"shaking like the leaves of an old maple."

Knowing medicines were not doing the trick, the uncle resorted to the ancient practice of comfort. He pulled out a comic book he just happened to have in his coat. It was *The Further Adventures of Nick Wilson* by Eddie Gorodetsky, Marc Andreyko and Stephen Sadowski. The book tells the story of Nick Wilson, a once-mighty superhero who has lost his powers and takes refuge behind a Kona Gold-filled bong.

The comic book begins with Nick reduced to taking a gig at a boy's birthday party where he pretends to be himself in his glory days. As the uncle read the story to Kate Green, she slowly began to shake less, her forehead leaked less and her mind drifted from panic to interest in the fate, not of her, but of Nick Wilson.

The uncle would read, then show her the illustrations. Green's interest was piqued when the birthday boy's mother—an attractive light-skinned black woman—put her hand seductively on Nick Wilson's upper thigh. Within 20 minutes of that reading, Dr. Mathai released Green from the hospital. Seven minutes later, she was comfortably in her own bed.

Four days later, Green said she remembered being read *The Further Adventures of Nick Wilson,* but, in her haze at the time, couldn't remember what the story was about. When shown the panel of the lady's hand on Nick's thigh, Kate Green smiled and said, "Well, I do remember that."

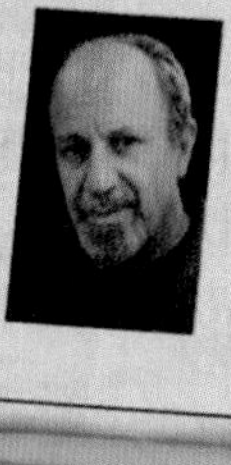

Michael Krikorian is the author of the novel Southside. *Read more at his informative website* krikorianwrites.com *or follow him on twitter* @makmak47.

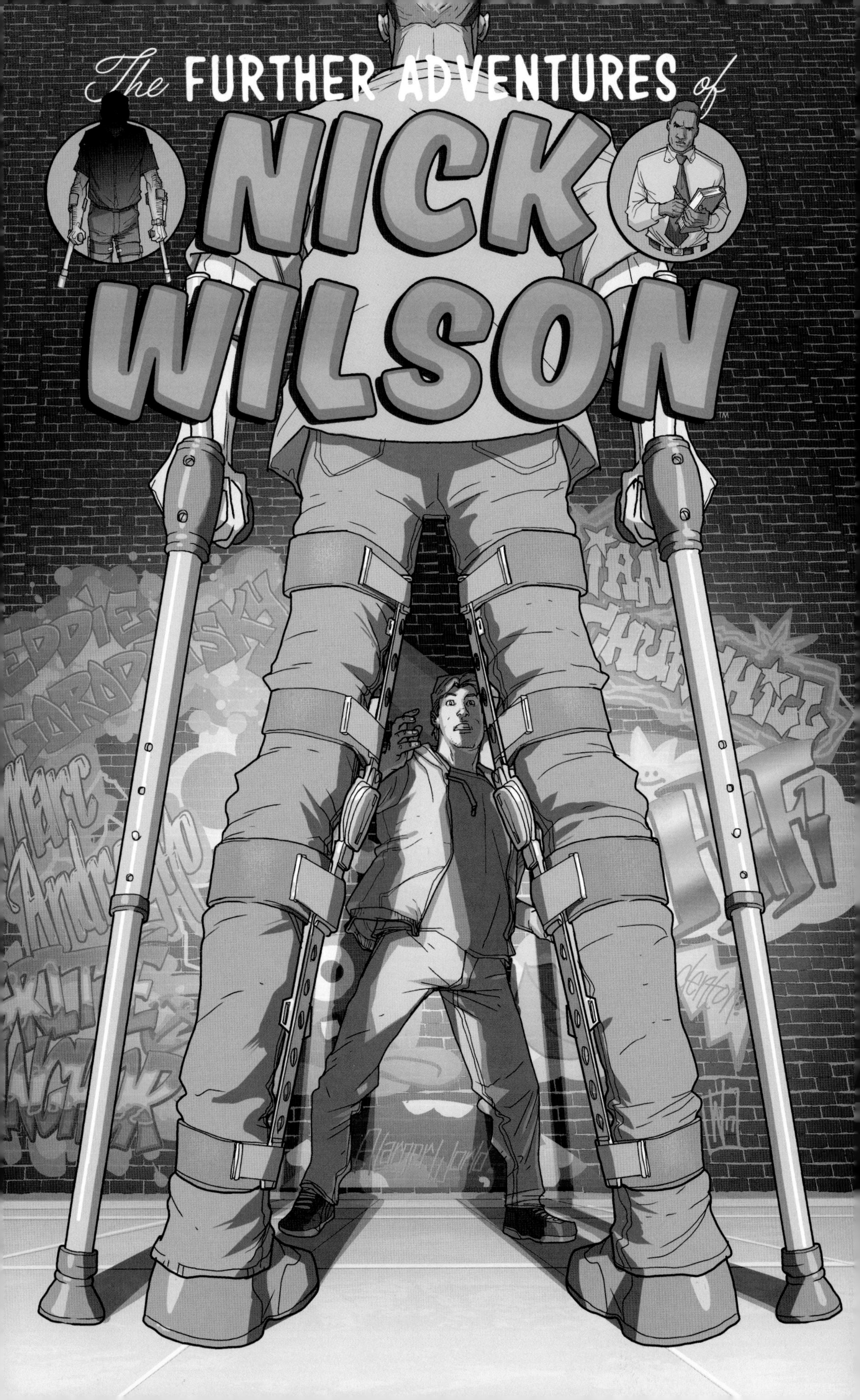

The FURTHER ADVENTURES of
NICK WILSON

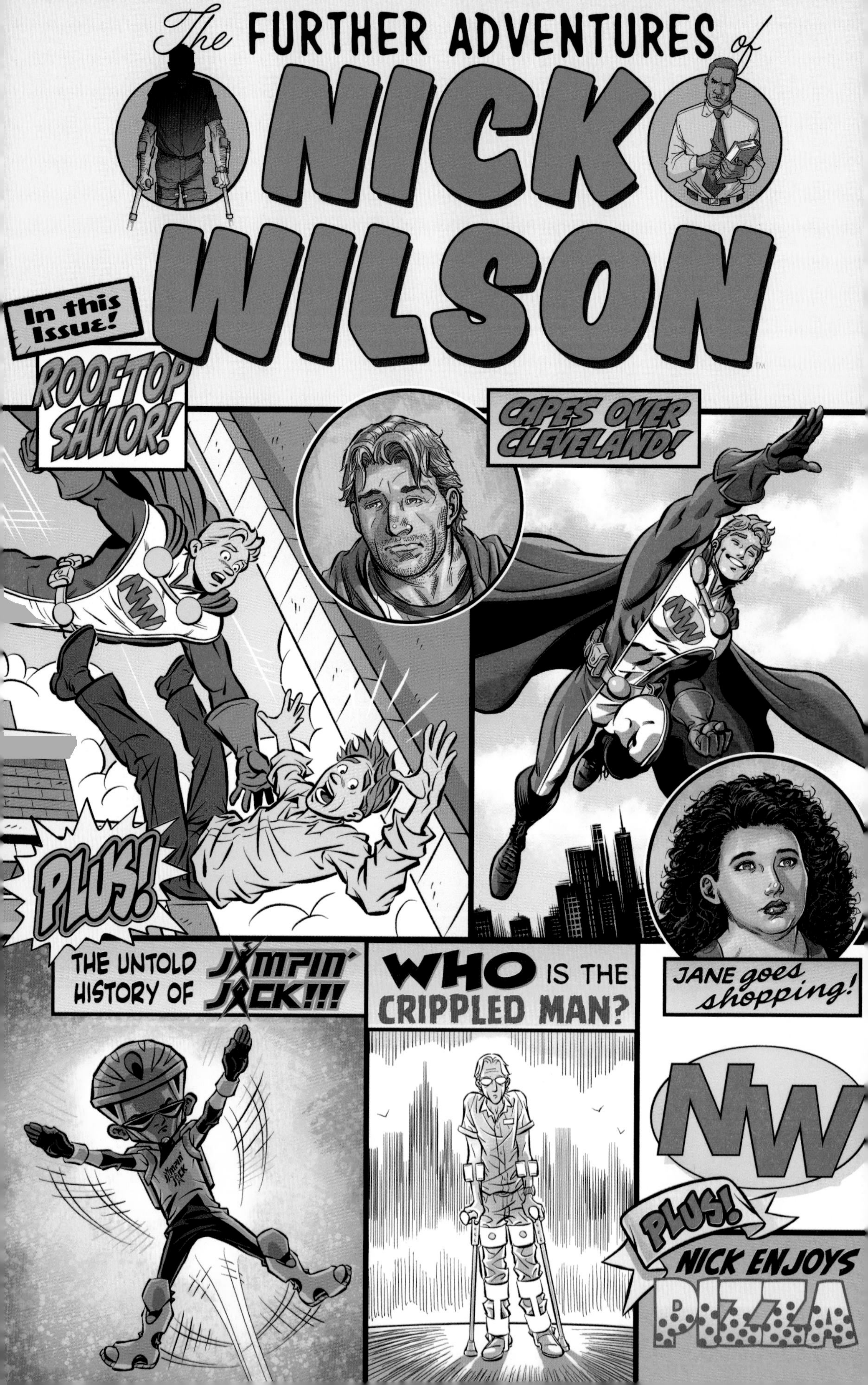

The FURTHER ADVENTURES of
NICK WILSON™
In this Issue!
ROOFTOP SAVIOR!
CAPES OVER CLEVELAND!
PLUS!
THE UNTOLD HISTORY OF JUMPIN' JACK!!!
WHO IS THE CRIPPLED MAN?
JANE goes shopping!
NW
PLUS!
NICK ENJOYS PIZZA

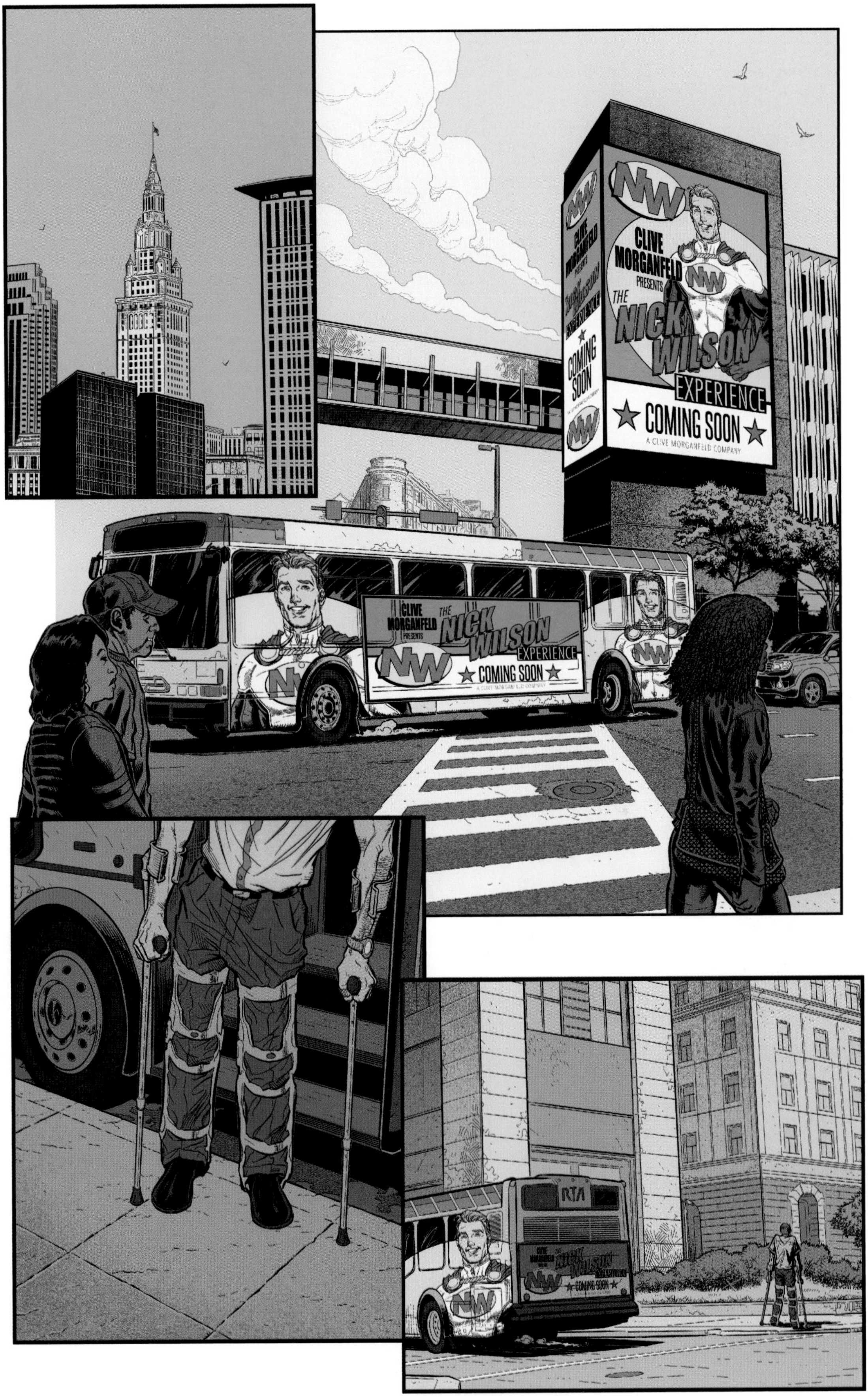

NW
CLIVE MORGANFELD PRESENTS
THE NICK WILSON
EXPERIENCE
COMING SOON
A CLIVE MORGANFELD COMPANY
NW
CLIVE MORGANFELD PRESENTS
COMING SOON
NW
CLIVE MORGANFELD PRESENTS
THE NICK WILSON
EXPERIENCE
NW
COMING SOON
NW
RTA
NW
COMING SOON

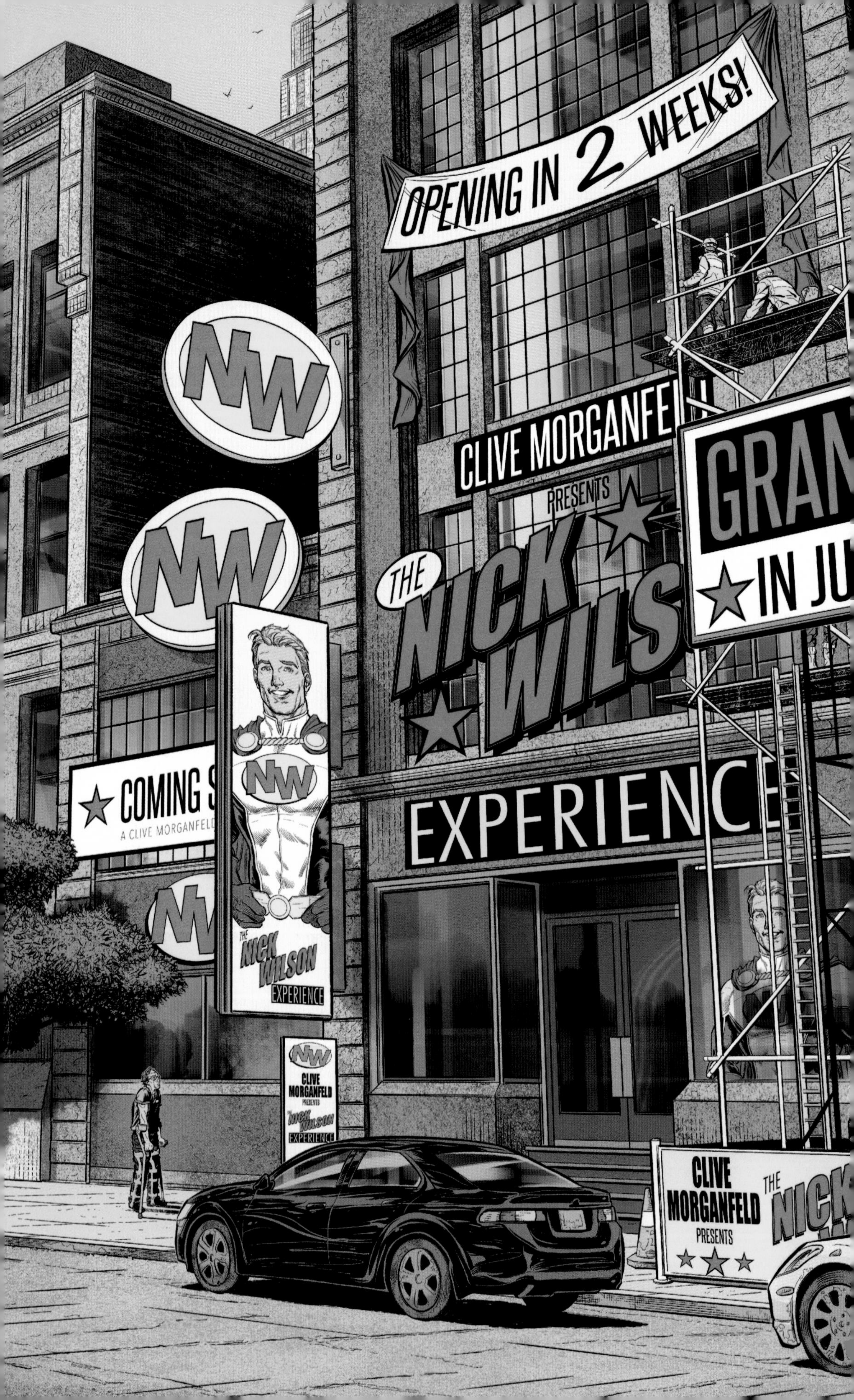

OPENING IN 2 WEEKS!
NW
CLIVE MORGANFE
PRESENTS
THE NICK WILS
GRAN
IN JU
EXPERIENC
COMING S
A CLIVE MORGANFELD
NW
THE NICK WILSON EXPERIENCE
NW
CLIVE MORGANFELD PRESENTS
THE NICK WILSON EXPERIENCE
CLIVE MORGANFELD PRESENTS
THE NICK

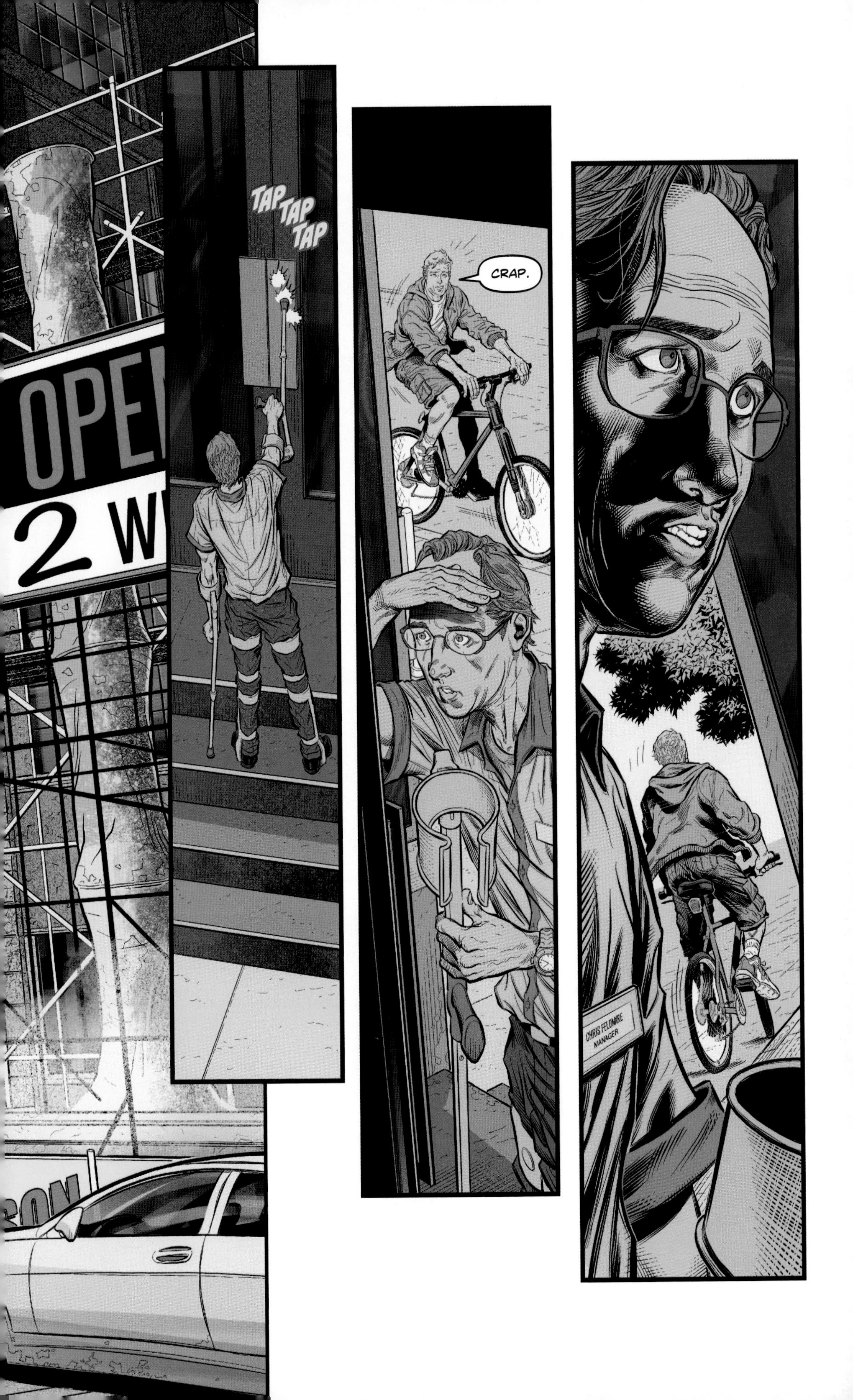
OPE
2 W
TAP TAP TAP
CRAP.
CHRIS FELOMRE
MANAGER
CON

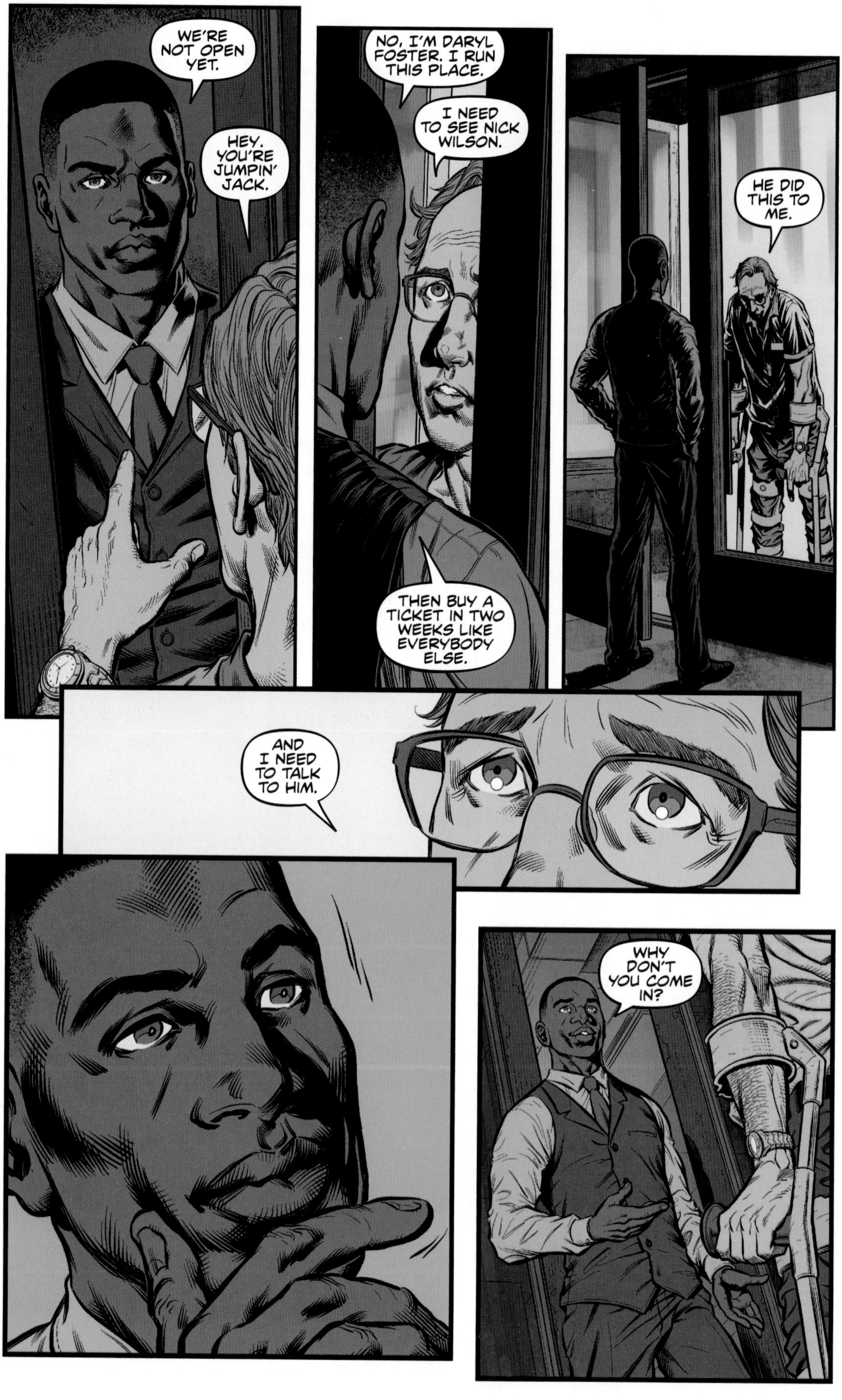
WE'RE NOT OPEN YET.
HEY. YOU'RE JUMPIN' JACK.
NO, I'M DARYL FOSTER. I RUN THIS PLACE.
I NEED TO SEE NICK WILSON.
THEN BUY A TICKET IN TWO WEEKS LIKE EVERYBODY ELSE.
HE DID THIS TO ME.
AND I NEED TO TALK TO HIM.
WHY DON'T YOU COME IN?

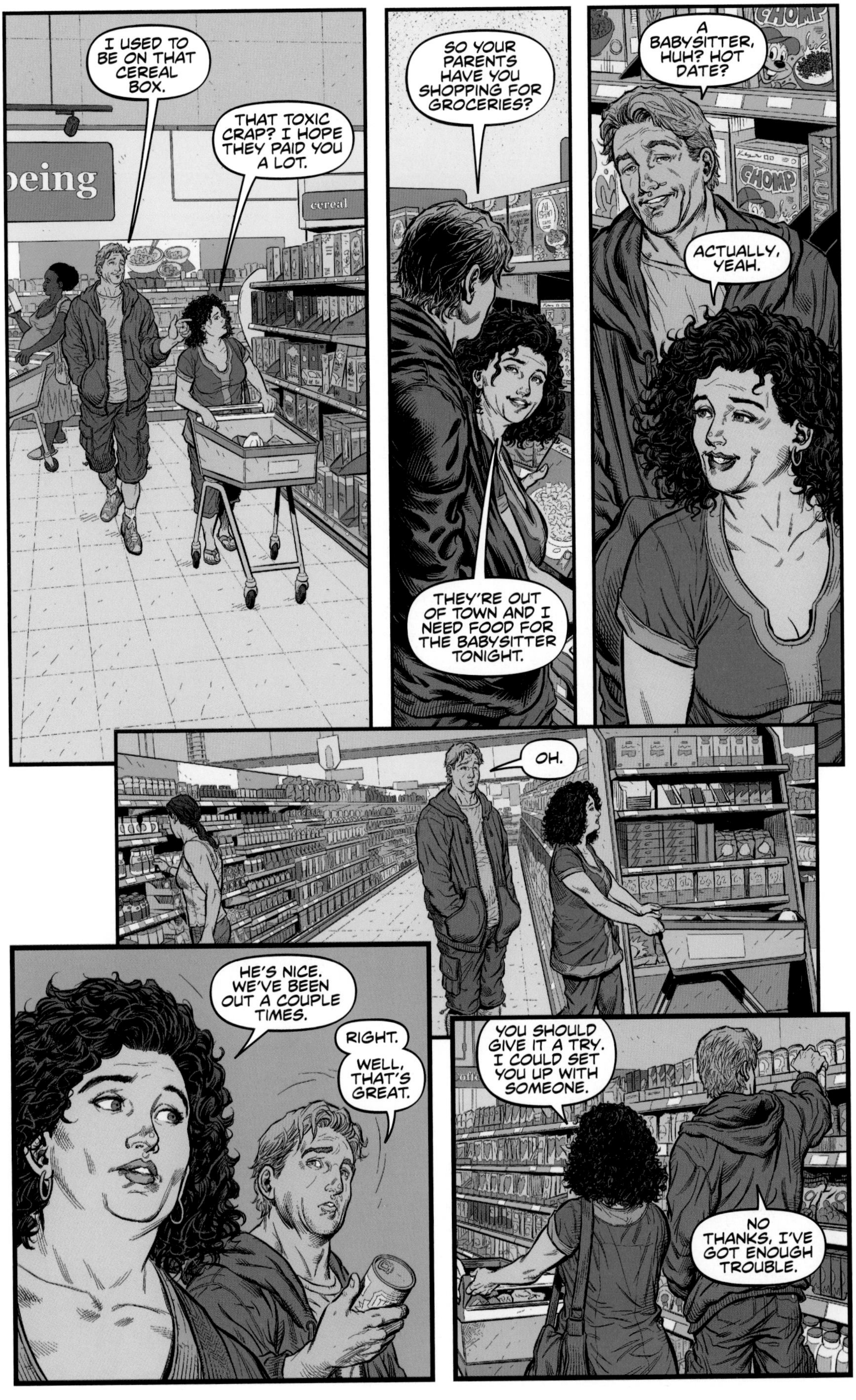
I USED TO BE ON THAT CEREAL BOX.
THAT TOXIC CRAP? I HOPE THEY PAID YOU A LOT.
eing
cereal
SO YOUR PARENTS HAVE YOU SHOPPING FOR GROCERIES?
THEY'RE OUT OF TOWN AND I NEED FOOD FOR THE BABYSITTER TONIGHT.
A BABYSITTER, HUH? HOT DATE?
CHOMP
ACTUALLY, YEAH.
OH.
HE'S NICE. WE'VE BEEN OUT A COUPLE TIMES.
RIGHT.
WELL, THAT'S GREAT.
YOU SHOULD GIVE IT A TRY. I COULD SET YOU UP WITH SOMEONE.
NO THANKS, I'VE GOT ENOUGH TROUBLE.

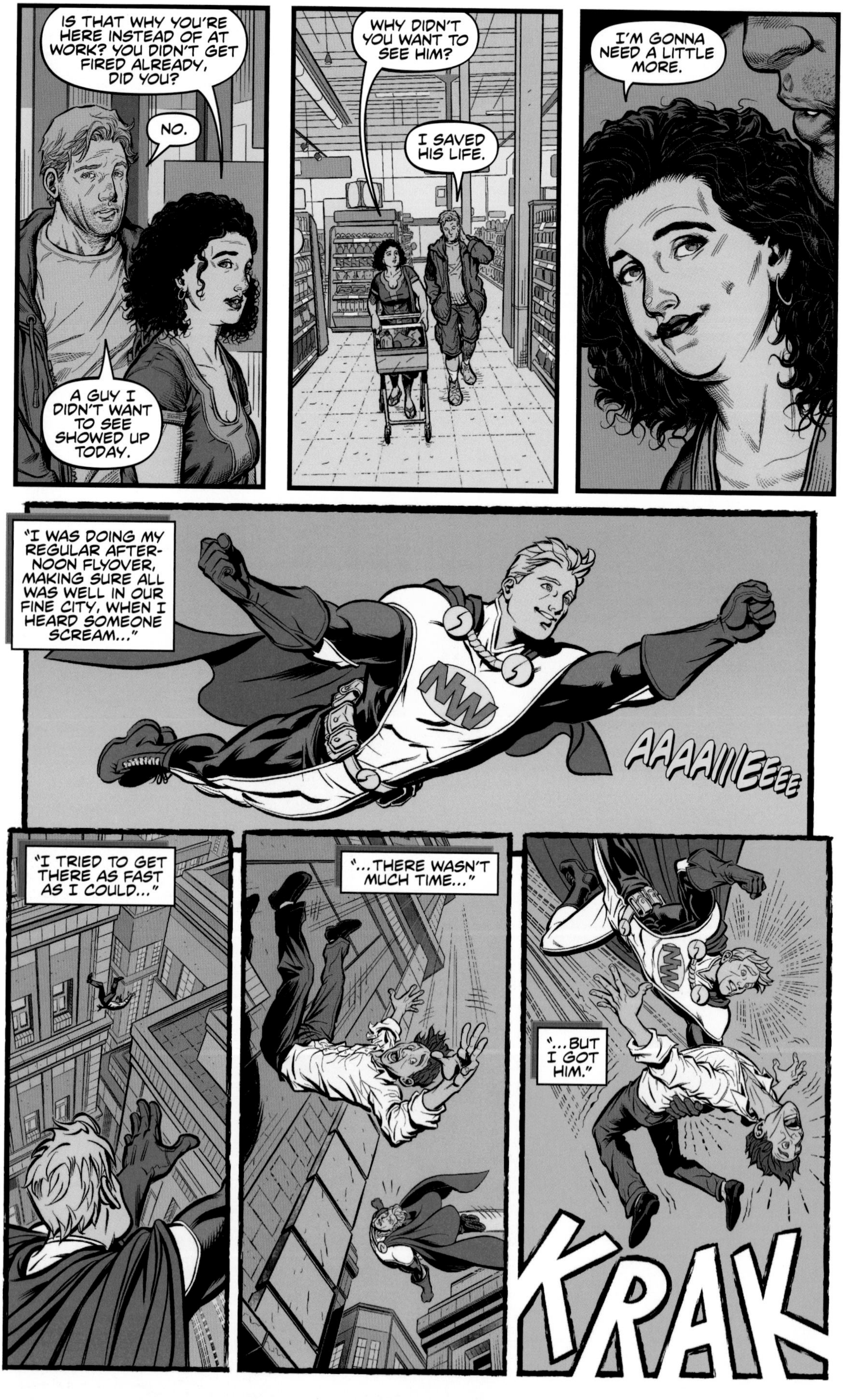

IS THAT WHY YOU'RE HERE INSTEAD OF AT WORK? YOU DIDN'T GET FIRED ALREADY, DID YOU?
NO.
A GUY I DIDN'T WANT TO SEE SHOWED UP TODAY.
WHY DIDN'T YOU WANT TO SEE HIM?
I SAVED HIS LIFE.
I'M GONNA NEED A LITTLE MORE.
"I WAS DOING MY REGULAR AFTER-NOON FLYOVER, MAKING SURE ALL WAS WELL IN OUR FINE CITY, WHEN I HEARD SOMEONE SCREAM..."
NW
AAAAIIIEEEE
"I TRIED TO GET THERE AS FAST AS I COULD..."
"...THERE WASN'T MUCH TIME..."
"...BUT I GOT HIM."
KRAK

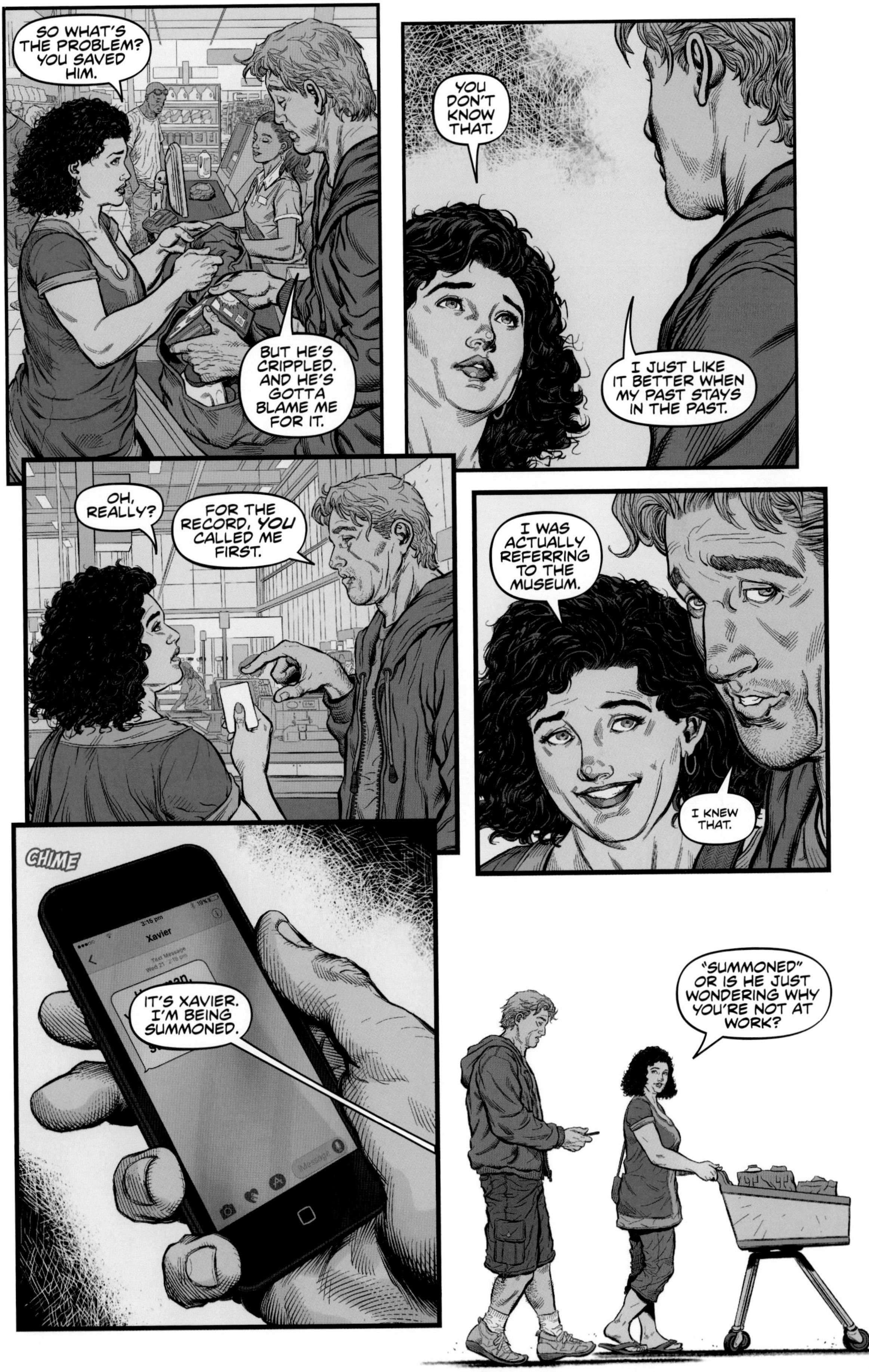
SO WHAT'S THE PROBLEM? YOU SAVED HIM.
BUT HE'S CRIPPLED. AND HE'S GOTTA BLAME ME FOR IT.
YOU DON'T KNOW THAT.
I JUST LIKE IT BETTER WHEN MY PAST STAYS IN THE PAST.
OH, REALLY?
FOR THE RECORD, *YOU* CALLED ME FIRST.
I WAS ACTUALLY REFERRING TO THE MUSEUM.
I KNEW THAT.
CHIME
Xavier
IT'S XAVIER. I'M BEING SUMMONED.
"SUMMONED" OR IS HE JUST WONDERING WHY YOU'RE NOT AT WORK?

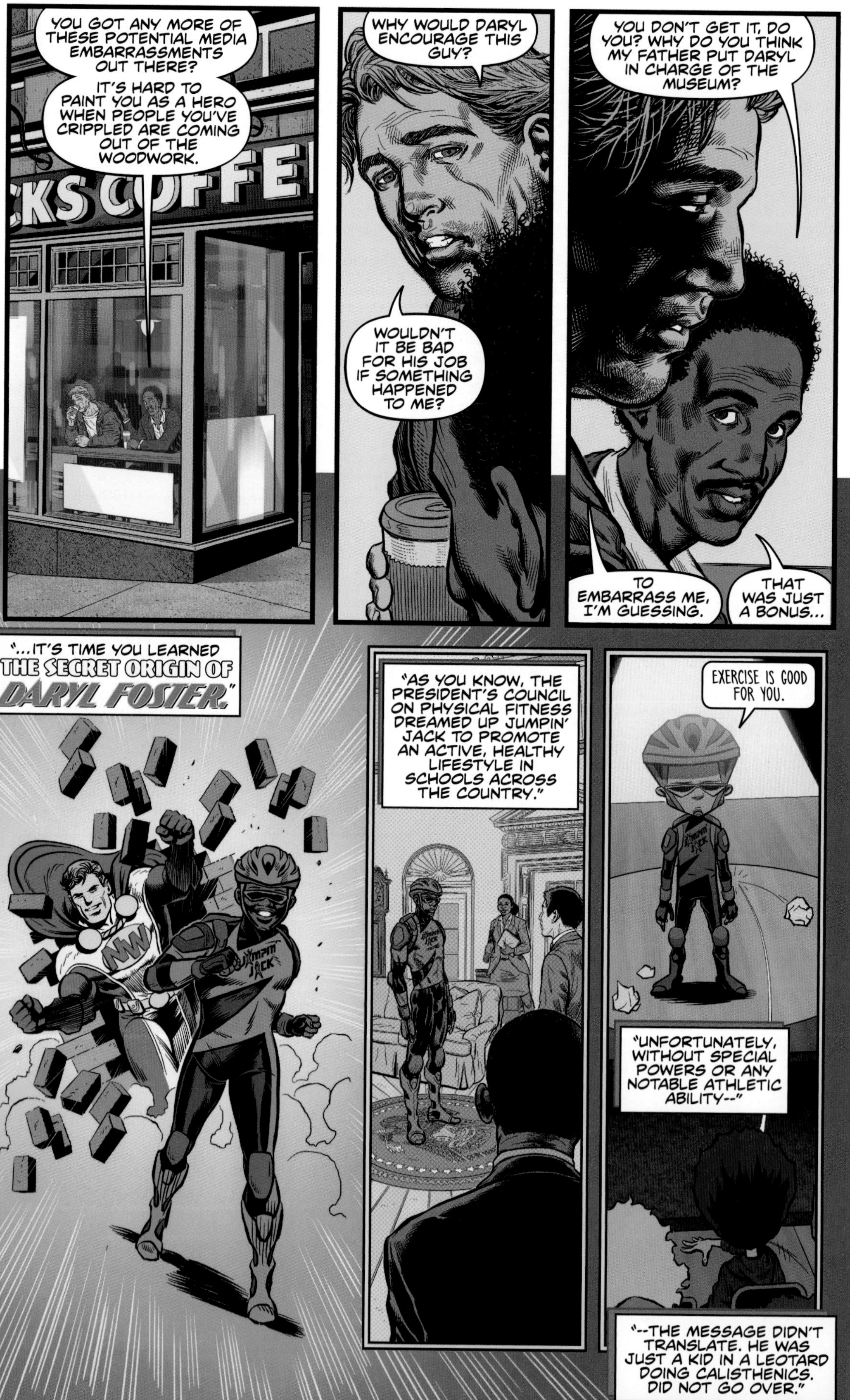
YOU GOT ANY MORE OF THESE POTENTIAL MEDIA EMBARRASSMENTS OUT THERE?
IT'S HARD TO PAINT YOU AS A HERO WHEN PEOPLE YOU'VE CRIPPLED ARE COMING OUT OF THE WOODWORK.
CKS COFFE
WHY WOULD DARYL ENCOURAGE THIS GUY?
WOULDN'T IT BE BAD FOR HIS JOB IF SOMETHING HAPPENED TO ME?
YOU DON'T GET IT, DO YOU? WHY DO YOU THINK MY FATHER PUT DARYL IN CHARGE OF THE MUSEUM?
TO EMBARRASS ME, I'M GUESSING.
THAT WAS JUST A BONUS...
"...IT'S TIME YOU LEARNED THE SECRET ORIGIN OF DARYL FOSTER."
"AS YOU KNOW, THE PRESIDENT'S COUNCIL ON PHYSICAL FITNESS DREAMED UP JUMPIN' JACK TO PROMOTE AN ACTIVE, HEALTHY LIFESTYLE IN SCHOOLS ACROSS THE COUNTRY."
EXERCISE IS GOOD FOR YOU.
"UNFORTUNATELY, WITHOUT SPECIAL POWERS OR ANY NOTABLE ATHLETIC ABILITY--"
"--THE MESSAGE DIDN'T TRANSLATE. HE WAS JUST A KID IN A LEOTARD DOING CALISTHENICS. DID NOT GO OVER."

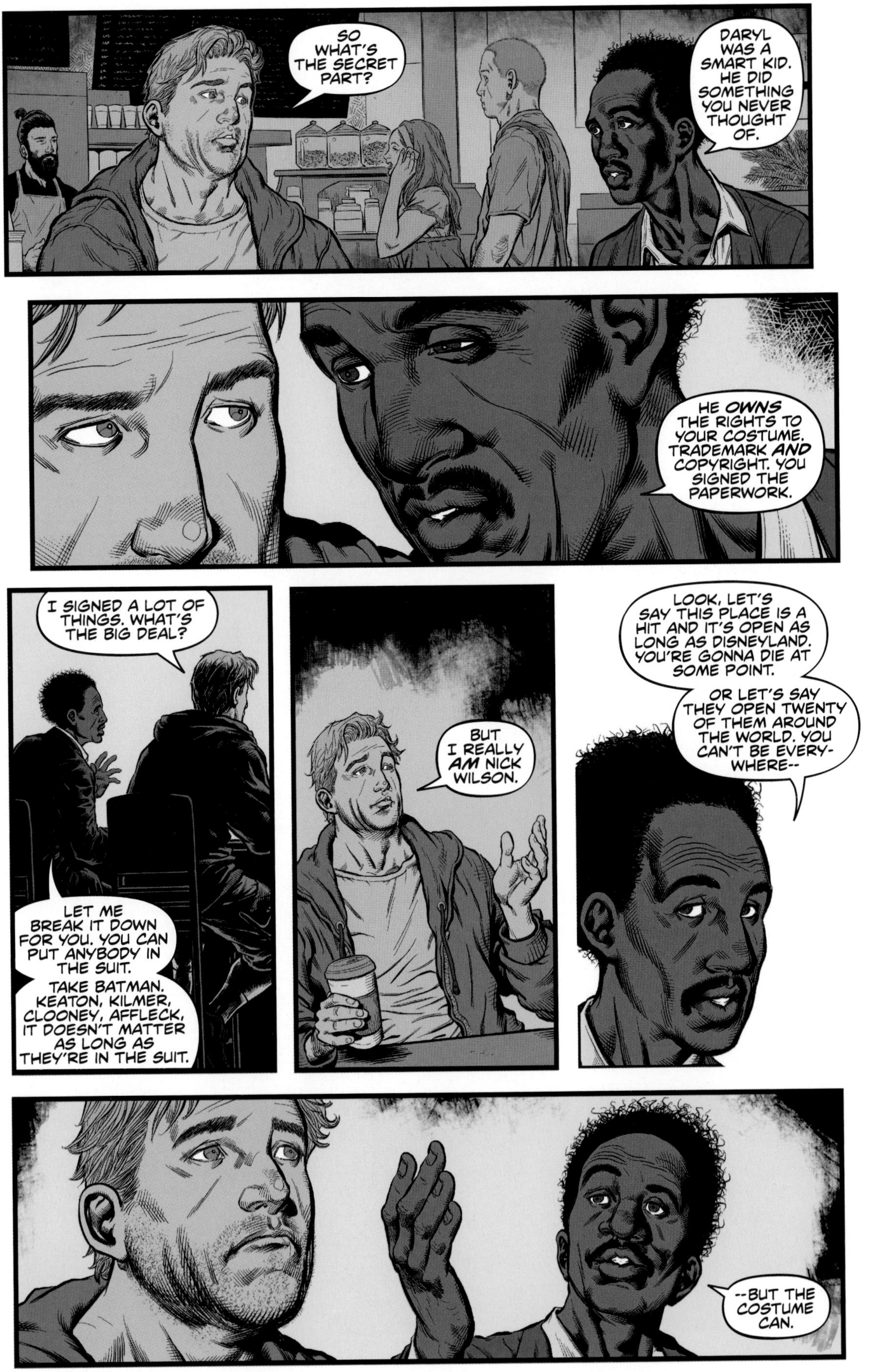

SO WHAT'S THE SECRET PART?
DARYL WAS A SMART KID. HE DID SOMETHING YOU NEVER THOUGHT OF.
HE OWNS THE RIGHTS TO YOUR COSTUME. TRADEMARK AND COPYRIGHT. YOU SIGNED THE PAPERWORK.
I SIGNED A LOT OF THINGS. WHAT'S THE BIG DEAL?
LET ME BREAK IT DOWN FOR YOU. YOU CAN PUT ANYBODY IN THE SUIT.
TAKE BATMAN. KEATON, KILMER, CLOONEY, AFFLECK, IT DOESN'T MATTER AS LONG AS THEY'RE IN THE SUIT.
BUT I REALLY AM NICK WILSON.
LOOK, LET'S SAY THIS PLACE IS A HIT AND IT'S OPEN AS LONG AS DISNEYLAND. YOU'RE GONNA DIE AT SOME POINT.
OR LET'S SAY THEY OPEN TWENTY OF THEM AROUND THE WORLD. YOU CAN'T BE EVERY-WHERE--
--BUT THE COSTUME CAN.

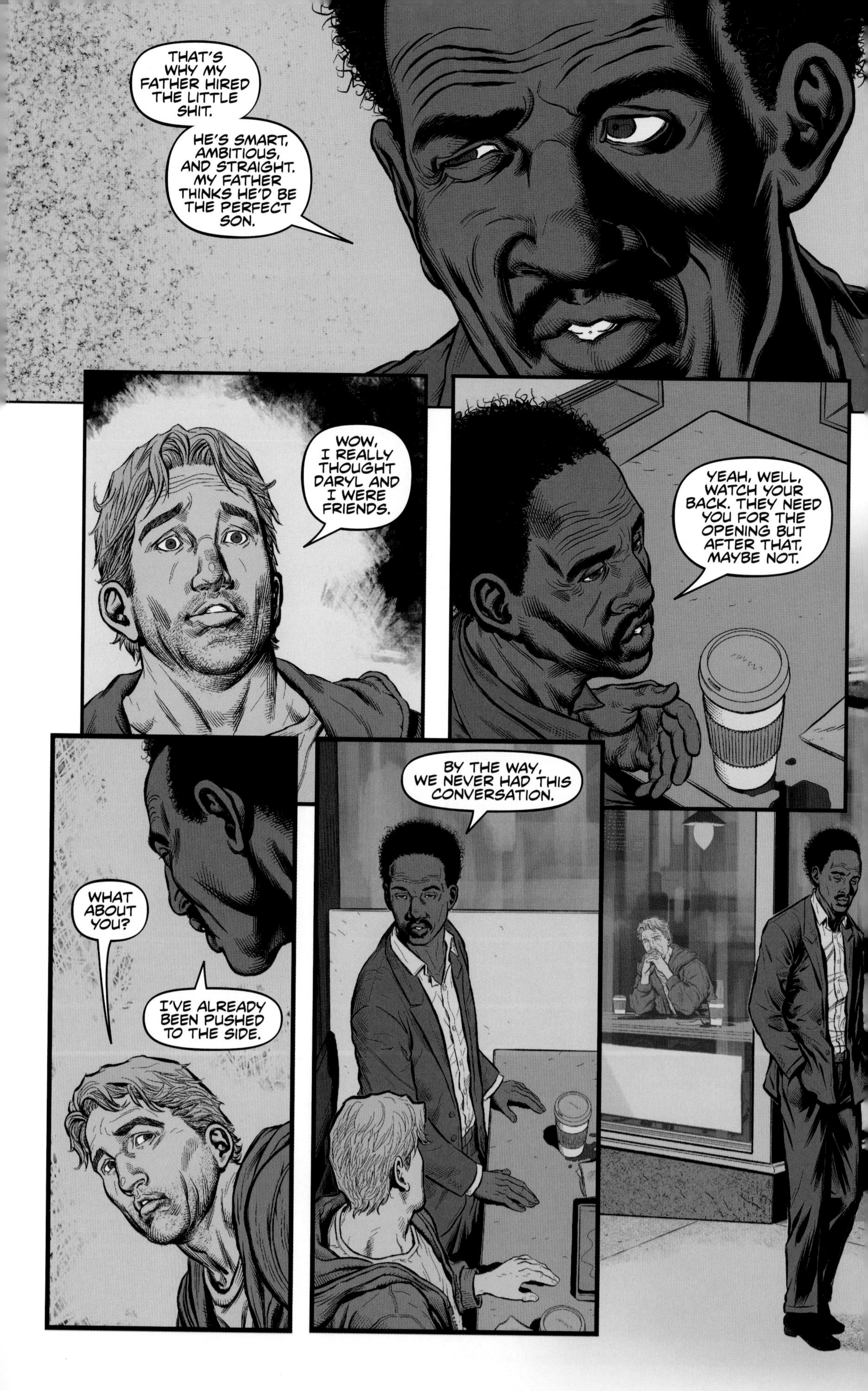
THAT'S WHY MY FATHER HIRED THE LITTLE SHIT.
HE'S SMART, AMBITIOUS, AND STRAIGHT. MY FATHER THINKS HE'D BE THE PERFECT SON.
WOW, I REALLY THOUGHT DARYL AND I WERE FRIENDS.
YEAH, WELL, WATCH YOUR BACK. THEY NEED YOU FOR THE OPENING BUT AFTER THAT, MAYBE NOT.
WHAT ABOUT YOU?
I'VE ALREADY BEEN PUSHED TO THE SIDE.
BY THE WAY, WE NEVER HAD THIS CONVERSATION.

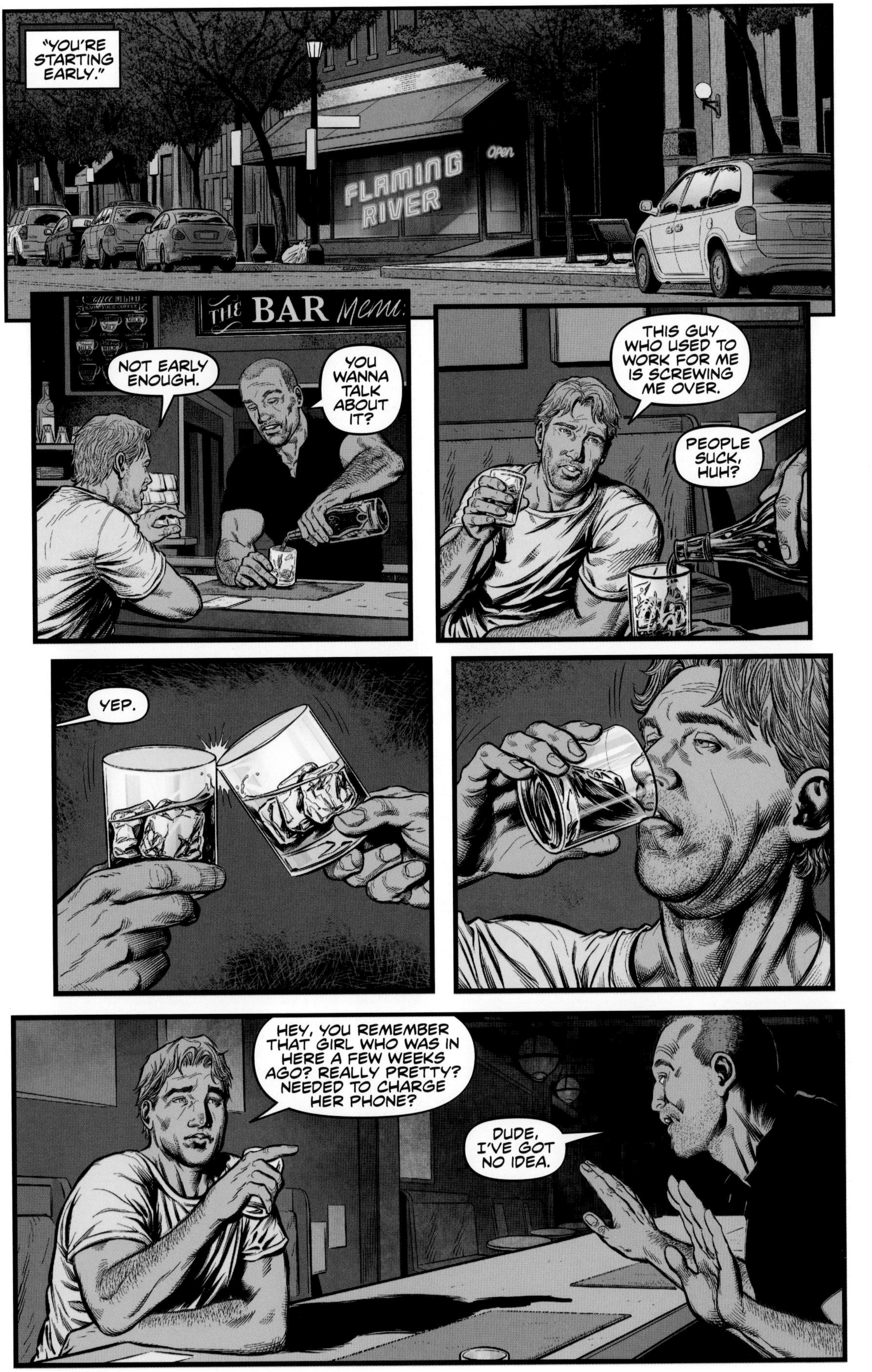
"YOU'RE STARTING EARLY."
FLAMING RIVER
OPEN
THE BAR Menu
NOT EARLY ENOUGH.
YOU WANNA TALK ABOUT IT?
THIS GUY WHO USED TO WORK FOR ME IS SCREWING ME OVER.
PEOPLE SUCK, HUH?
YEP.
HEY, YOU REMEMBER THAT GIRL WHO WAS IN HERE A FEW WEEKS AGO? REALLY PRETTY? NEEDED TO CHARGE HER PHONE?
DUDE, I'VE GOT NO IDEA.

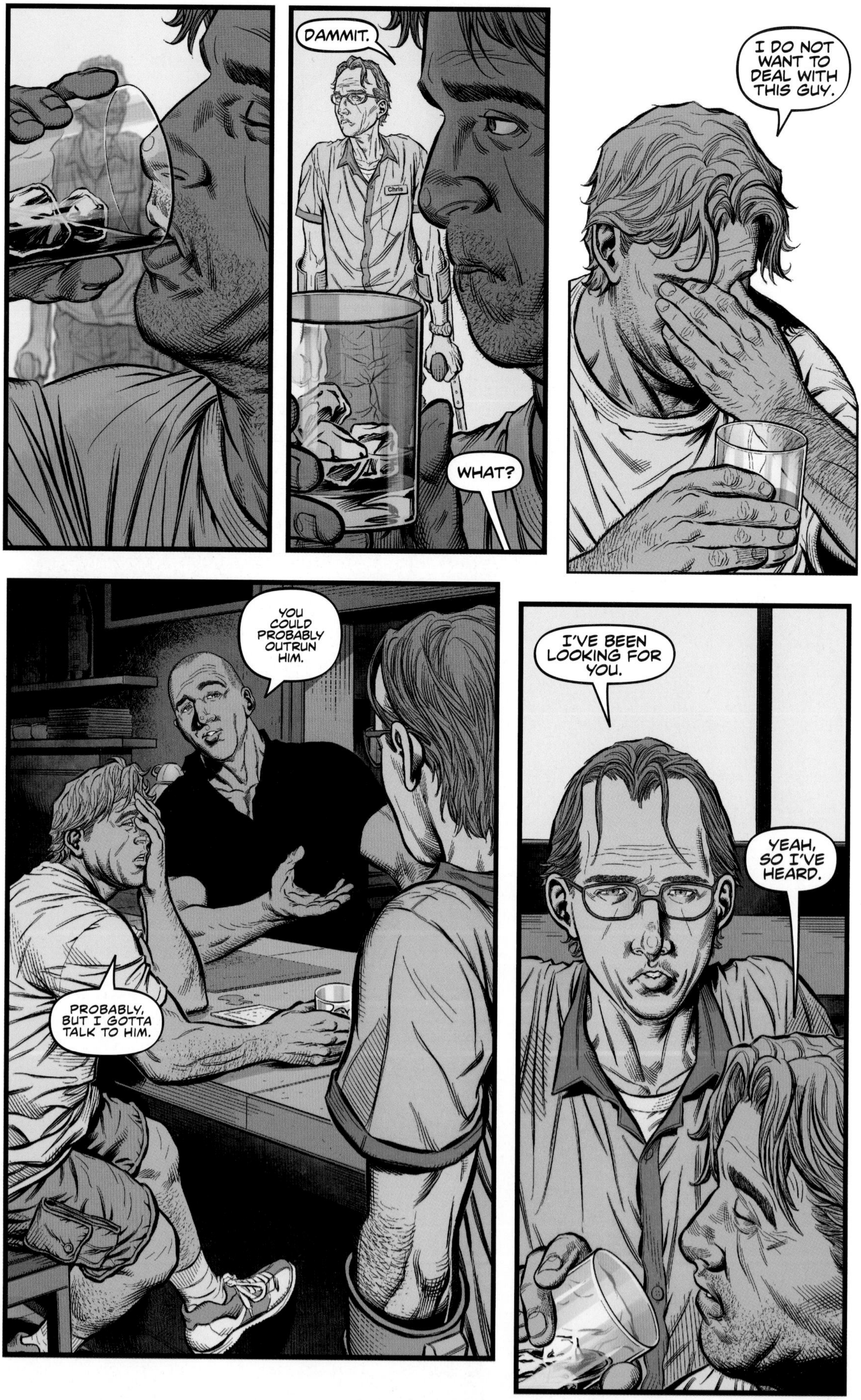
DAMMIT.
Chris
WHAT?
I DO NOT WANT TO DEAL WITH THIS GUY.
YOU COULD PROBABLY OUTRUN HIM.
PROBABLY, BUT I GOTTA TALK TO HIM.
I'VE BEEN LOOKING FOR YOU.
YEAH, SO I'VE HEARD.

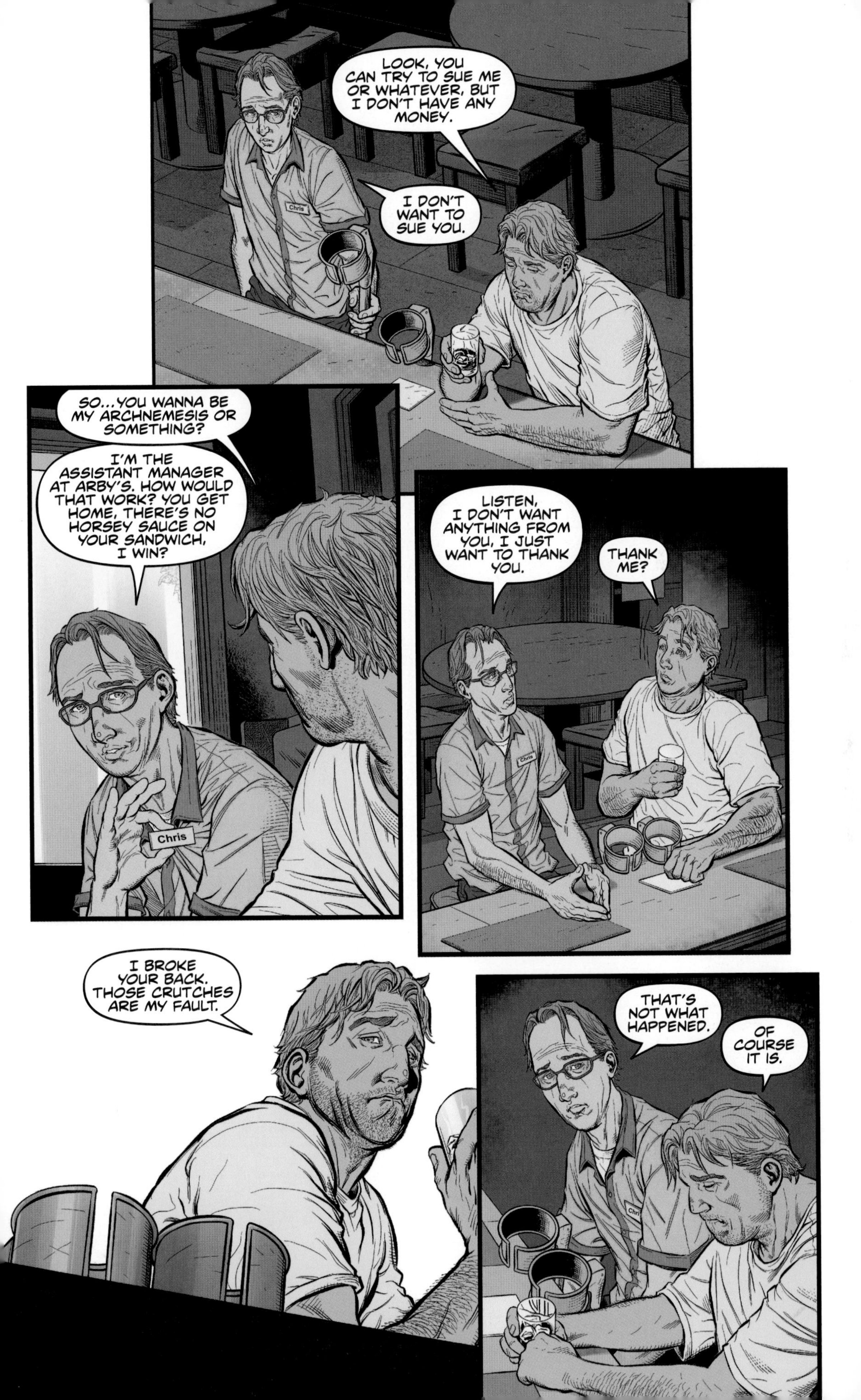
LOOK, YOU CAN TRY TO SUE ME OR WHATEVER, BUT I DON'T HAVE ANY MONEY.
I DON'T WANT TO SUE YOU.
SO...YOU WANNA BE MY ARCHNEMESIS OR SOMETHING?
I'M THE ASSISTANT MANAGER AT ARBY'S. HOW WOULD THAT WORK? YOU GET HOME, THERE'S NO HORSEY SAUCE ON YOUR SANDWICH, I WIN?
Chris
LISTEN, I DON'T WANT ANYTHING FROM YOU, I JUST WANT TO THANK YOU.
THANK ME?
Chris
I BROKE YOUR BACK. THOSE CRUTCHES ARE MY FAULT.
THAT'S NOT WHAT HAPPENED.
OF COURSE IT IS.

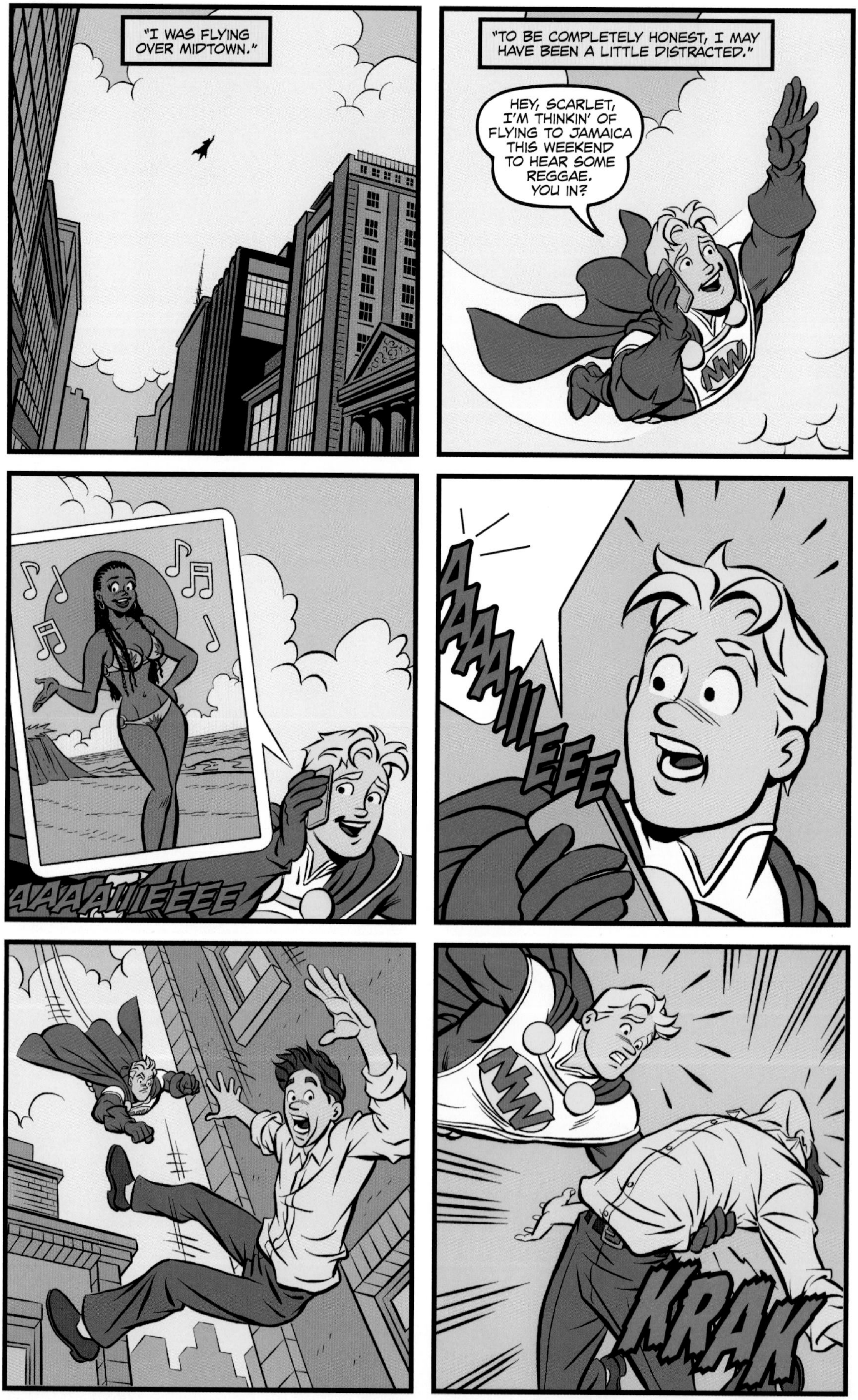
"I WAS FLYING OVER MIDTOWN."
"TO BE COMPLETELY HONEST, I MAY HAVE BEEN A LITTLE DISTRACTED."
HEY, SCARLET, I'M THINKIN' OF FLYING TO JAMAICA THIS WEEKEND TO HEAR SOME REGGAE. YOU IN?
AAAAIIIEEEE
AAAAAIIIEEE
KRAK

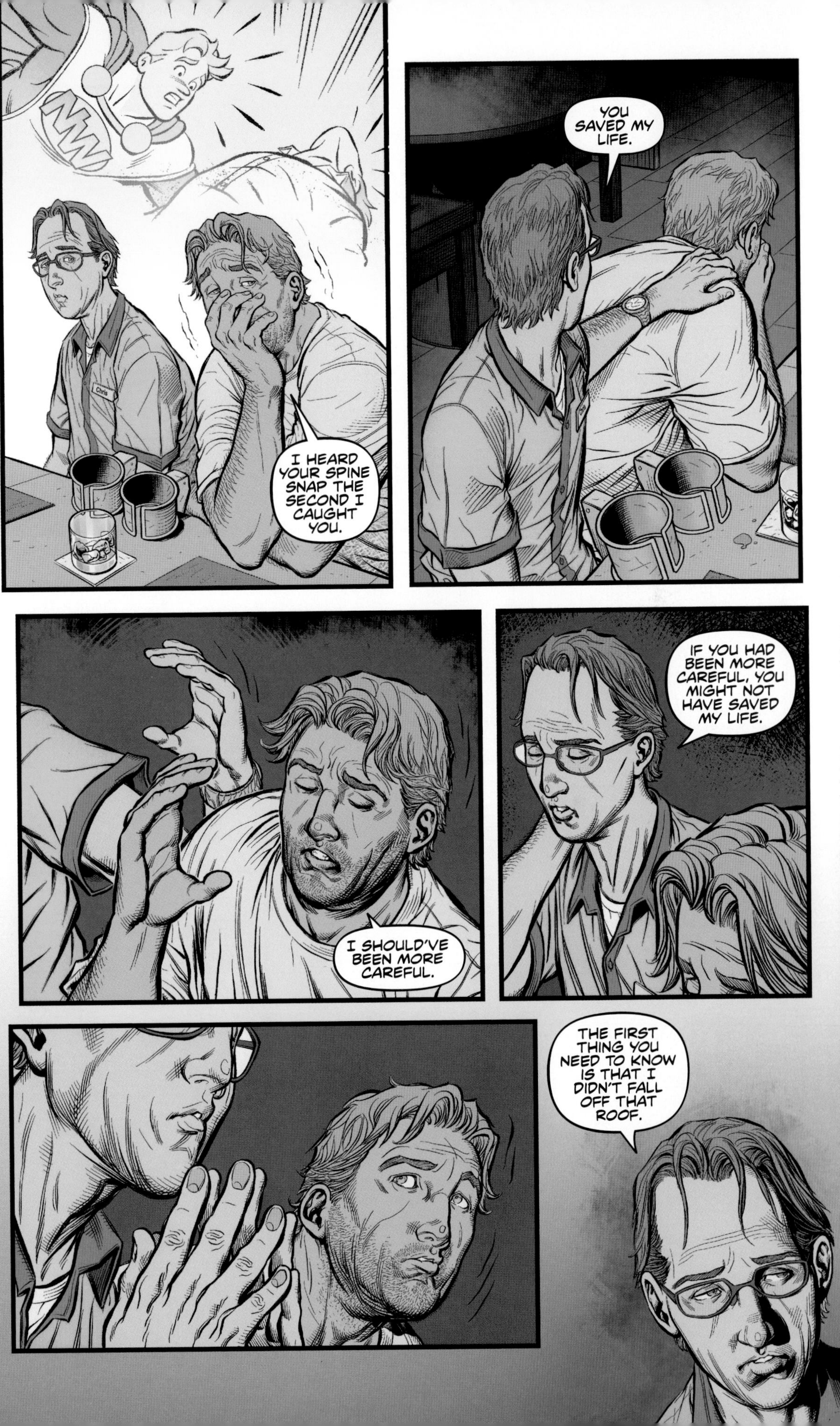

I HEARD YOUR SPINE SNAP THE SECOND I CAUGHT YOU.
YOU SAVED MY LIFE.
I SHOULD'VE BEEN MORE CAREFUL.
IF YOU HAD BEEN MORE CAREFUL, YOU MIGHT NOT HAVE SAVED MY LIFE.
THE FIRST THING YOU NEED TO KNOW IS THAT I DIDN'T FALL OFF THAT ROOF.

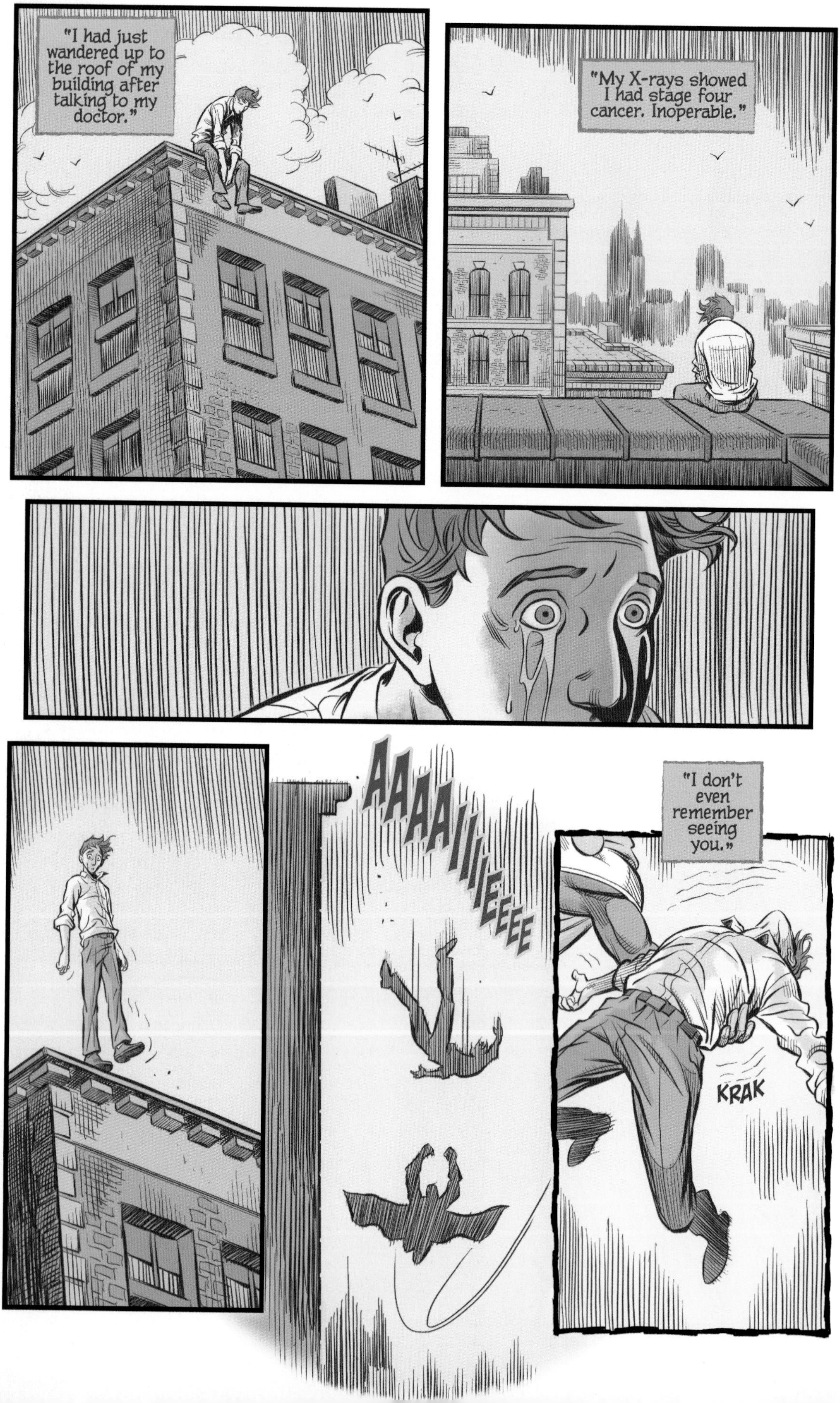
"I had just wandered up to the roof of my building after talking to my doctor."
"My X-rays showed I had stage four cancer. Inoperable."
AAAAIIIIEEEE
"I don't even remember seeing you."
KRAK

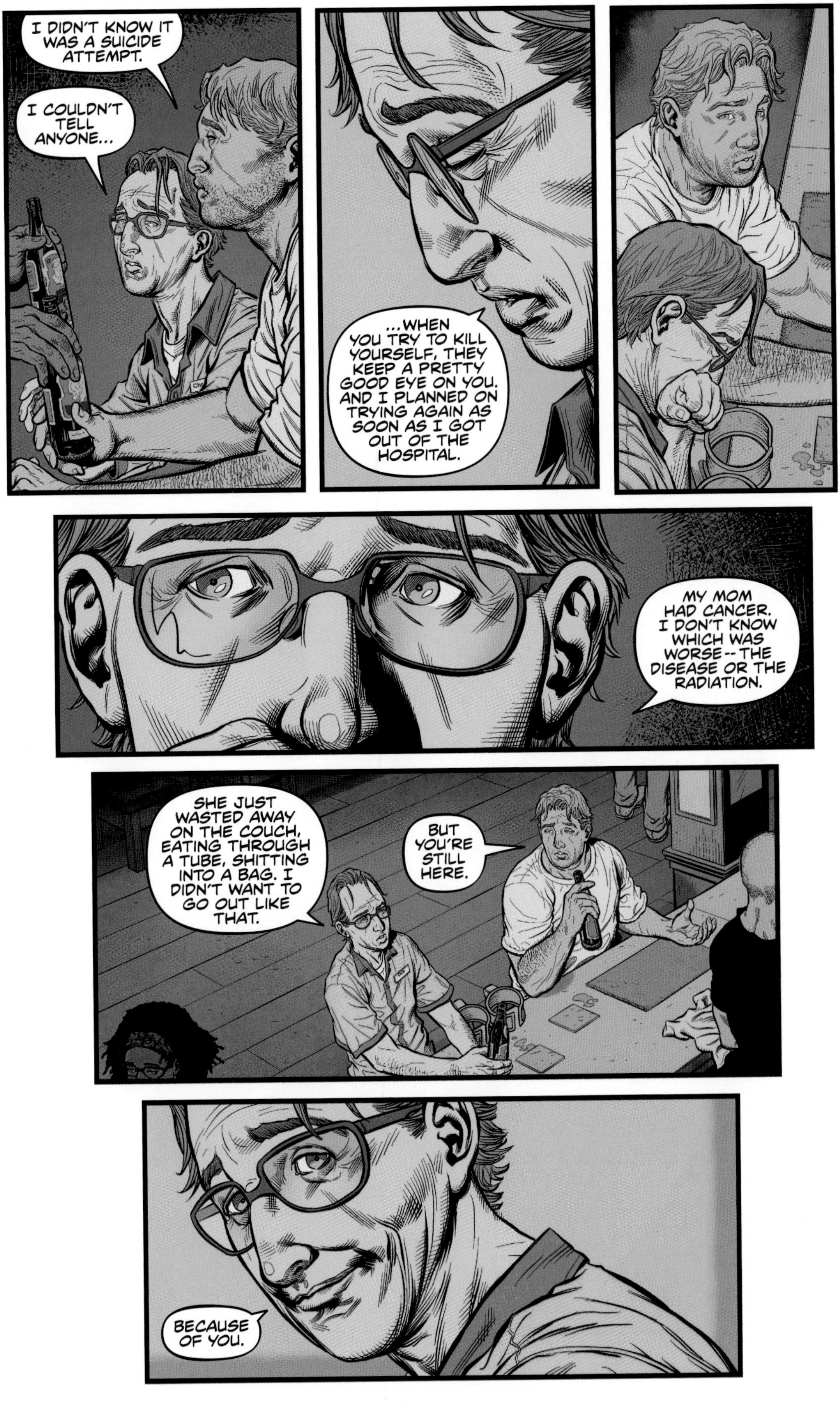
I DIDN'T KNOW IT WAS A SUICIDE ATTEMPT.
I COULDN'T TELL ANYONE...
...WHEN YOU TRY TO KILL YOURSELF, THEY KEEP A PRETTY GOOD EYE ON YOU. AND I PLANNED ON TRYING AGAIN AS SOON AS I GOT OUT OF THE HOSPITAL.
MY MOM HAD CANCER. I DON'T KNOW WHICH WAS WORSE-- THE DISEASE OR THE RADIATION.
SHE JUST WASTED AWAY ON THE COUCH, EATING THROUGH A TUBE, SHITTING INTO A BAG. I DIDN'T WANT TO GO OUT LIKE THAT.
BUT YOU'RE STILL HERE.
BECAUSE OF YOU.

"I was in my hospital bed making a slow recovery and thinking about how much I hated you."

"While I was there, my doctor ran some tests. Turns out I was misdiagnosed."

HOLD ON, YOU DIDN'T HAVE CANCER?

OH, I HAD CANCER. JUST NOT STAGE FOUR.

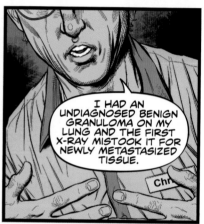

I HAD AN UNDIAGNOSED BENIGN GRANULOMA ON MY LUNG AND THE FIRST X-RAY MISTOOK IT FOR NEWLY METASTASIZED TISSUE.

WHAT WAS IT, THEN?

STAGE ONE AND TOTALLY TREATABLE.

BUT I NEVER WOULD'VE KNOWN THAT IF I HAD GONE SPLAT OR IF I WASN'T STUCK IN THE HOSPITAL WITH BUSTED LEGS.

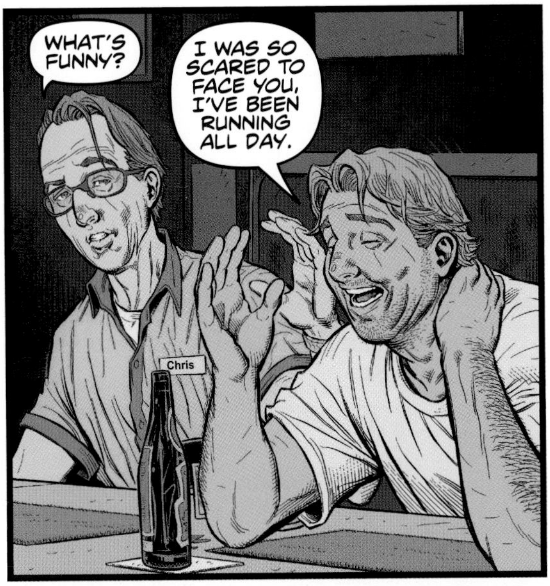
WHAT'S FUNNY?
I WAS SO SCARED TO FACE YOU, I'VE BEEN RUNNING ALL DAY.
Chris

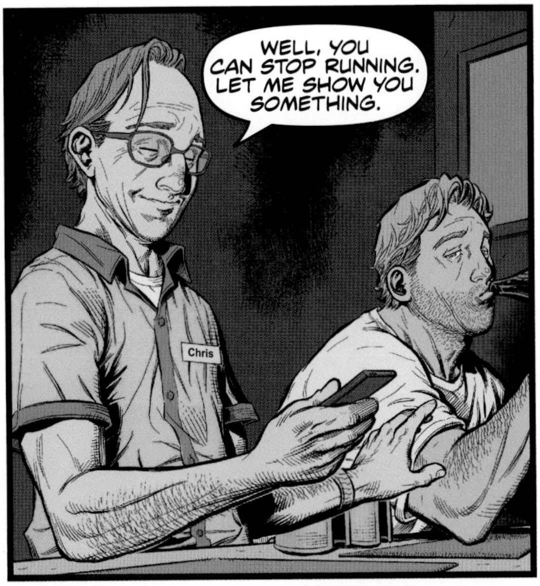
WELL, YOU CAN STOP RUNNING. LET ME SHOW YOU SOMETHING.
Chris

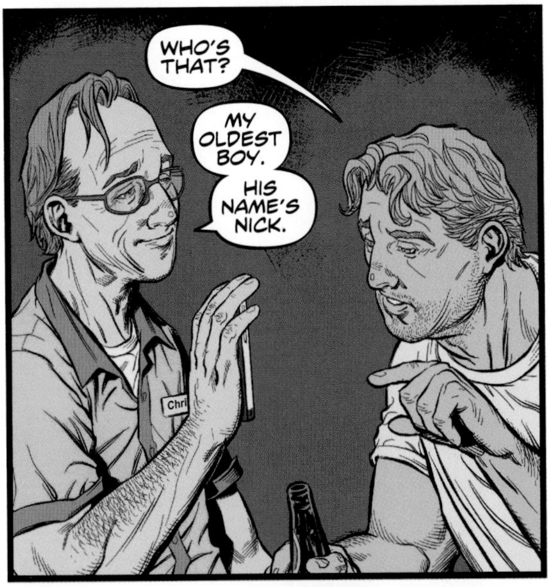
WHO'S THAT?
MY OLDEST BOY.
HIS NAME'S NICK.

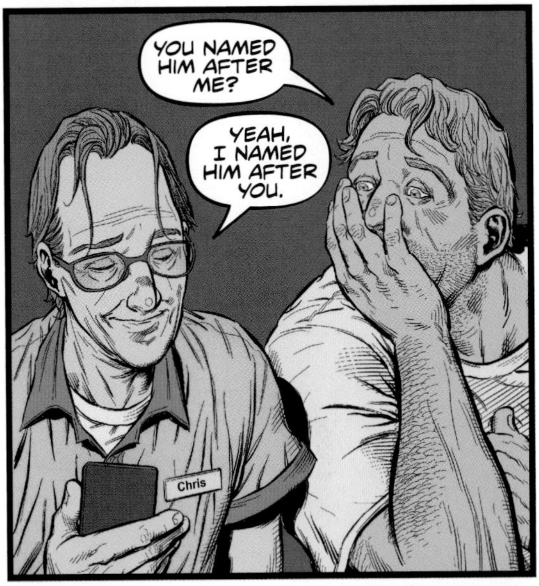
YOU NAMED HIM AFTER ME?
YEAH, I NAMED HIM AFTER YOU.
Chris

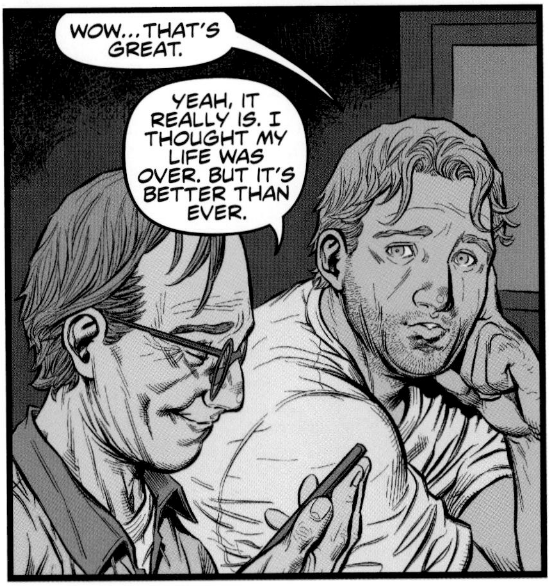
WOW...THAT'S GREAT.
YEAH, IT REALLY IS. I THOUGHT MY LIFE WAS OVER. BUT IT'S BETTER THAN EVER.

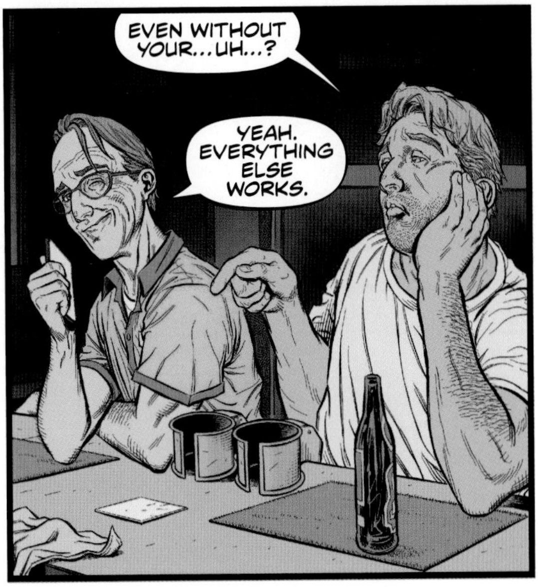
EVEN WITHOUT YOUR...UH...?
YEAH. EVERYTHING ELSE WORKS.

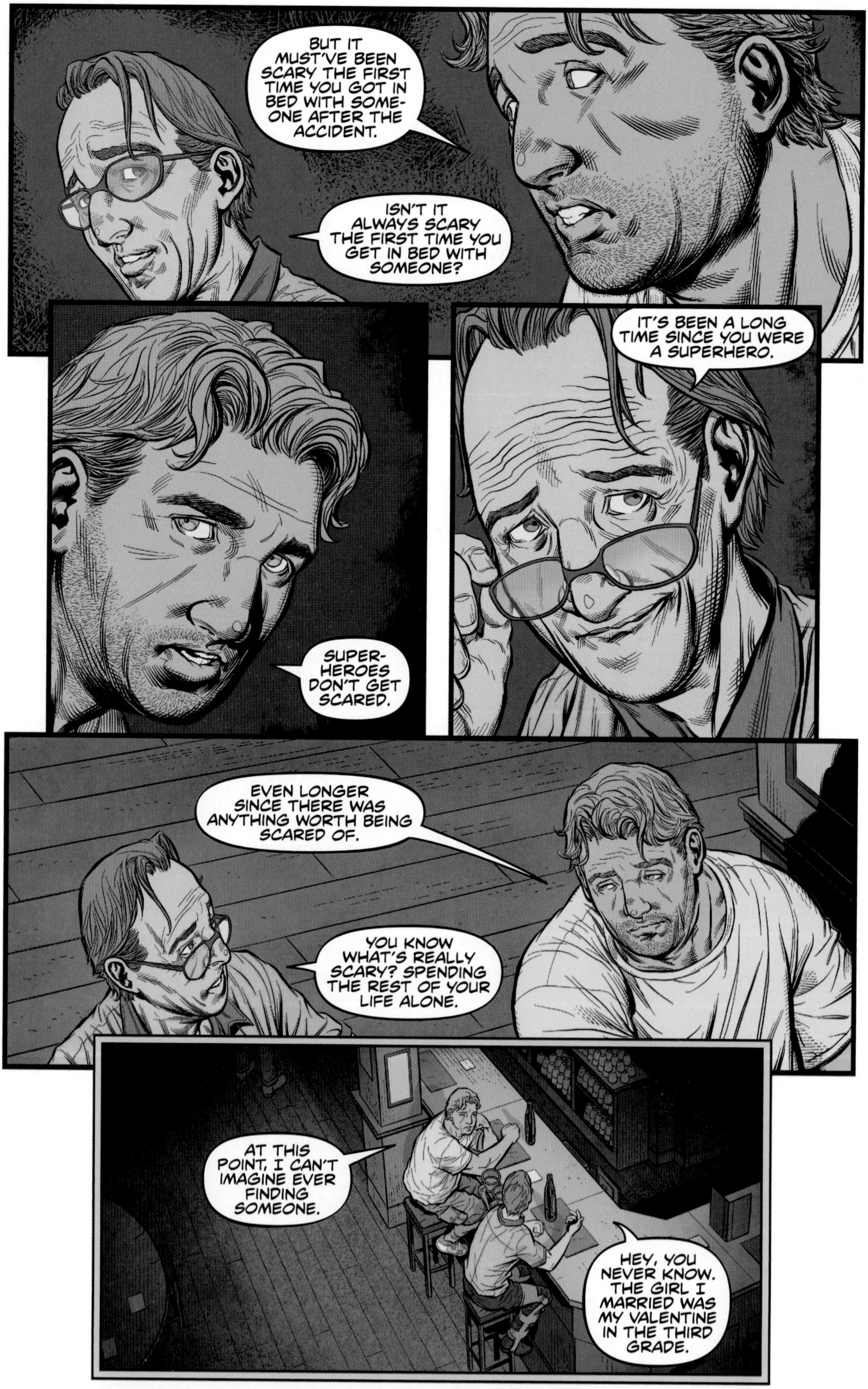
BUT IT MUST'VE BEEN SCARY THE FIRST TIME YOU GOT IN BED WITH SOME-ONE AFTER THE ACCIDENT.
ISN'T IT ALWAYS SCARY THE FIRST TIME YOU GET IN BED WITH SOMEONE?
SUPER-HEROES DON'T GET SCARED.
IT'S BEEN A LONG TIME SINCE YOU WERE A SUPERHERO.
EVEN LONGER SINCE THERE WAS ANYTHING WORTH BEING SCARED OF.
YOU KNOW WHAT'S REALLY SCARY? SPENDING THE REST OF YOUR LIFE ALONE.
AT THIS POINT, I CAN'T IMAGINE EVER FINDING SOMEONE.
HEY, YOU NEVER KNOW. THE GIRL I MARRIED WAS MY VALENTINE IN THE THIRD GRADE.

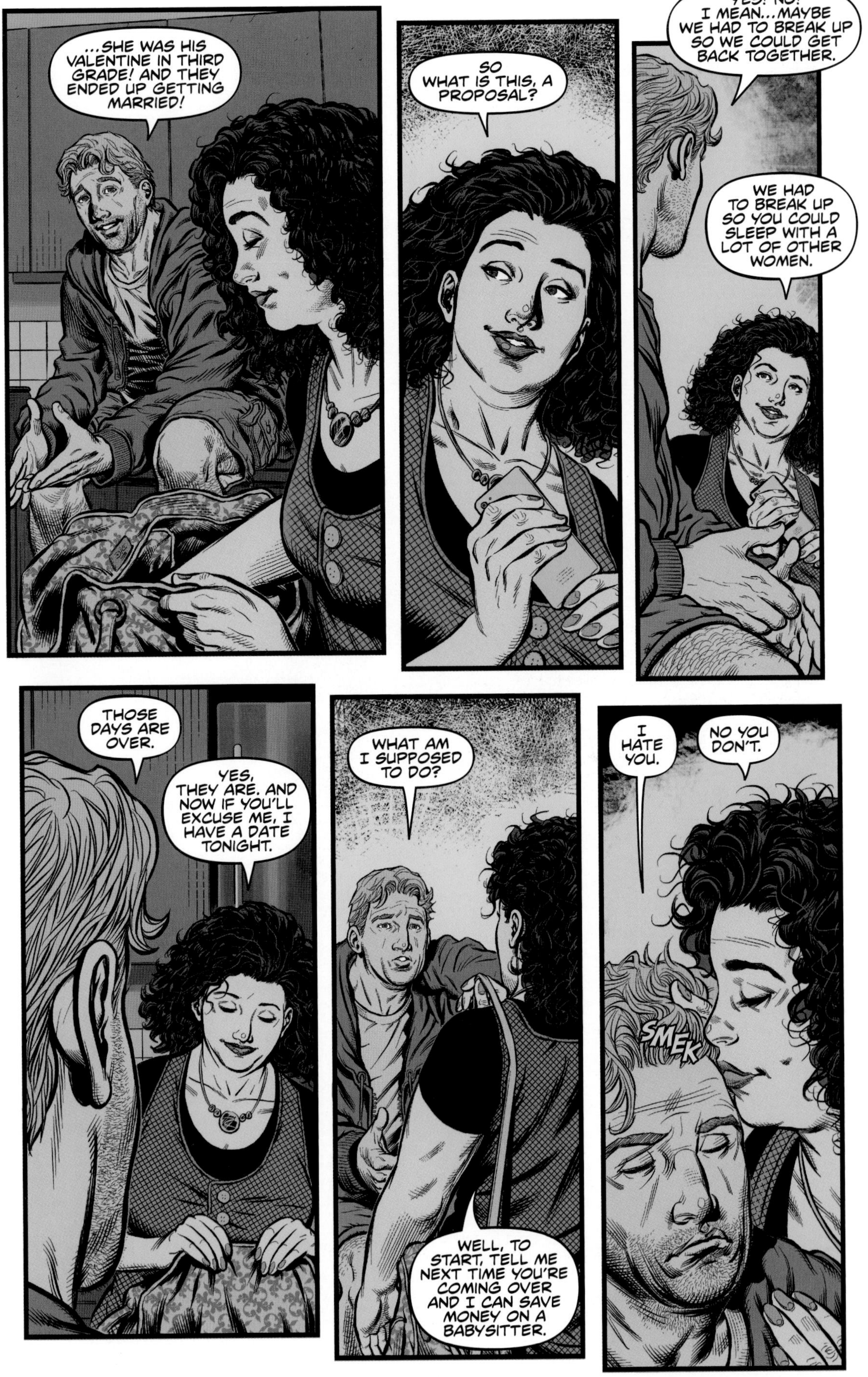
...SHE WAS HIS VALENTINE IN THIRD GRADE! AND THEY ENDED UP GETTING MARRIED!
SO WHAT IS THIS, A PROPOSAL?
YES! NO! I MEAN...MAYBE WE HAD TO BREAK UP SO WE COULD GET BACK TOGETHER.
WE HAD TO BREAK UP SO YOU COULD SLEEP WITH A LOT OF OTHER WOMEN.
THOSE DAYS ARE OVER.
YES, THEY ARE. AND NOW IF YOU'LL EXCUSE ME, I HAVE A DATE TONIGHT.
WHAT AM I SUPPOSED TO DO?
WELL, TO START, TELL ME NEXT TIME YOU'RE COMING OVER AND I CAN SAVE MONEY ON A BABYSITTER.
I HATE YOU.
NO YOU DON'T.
SMEK

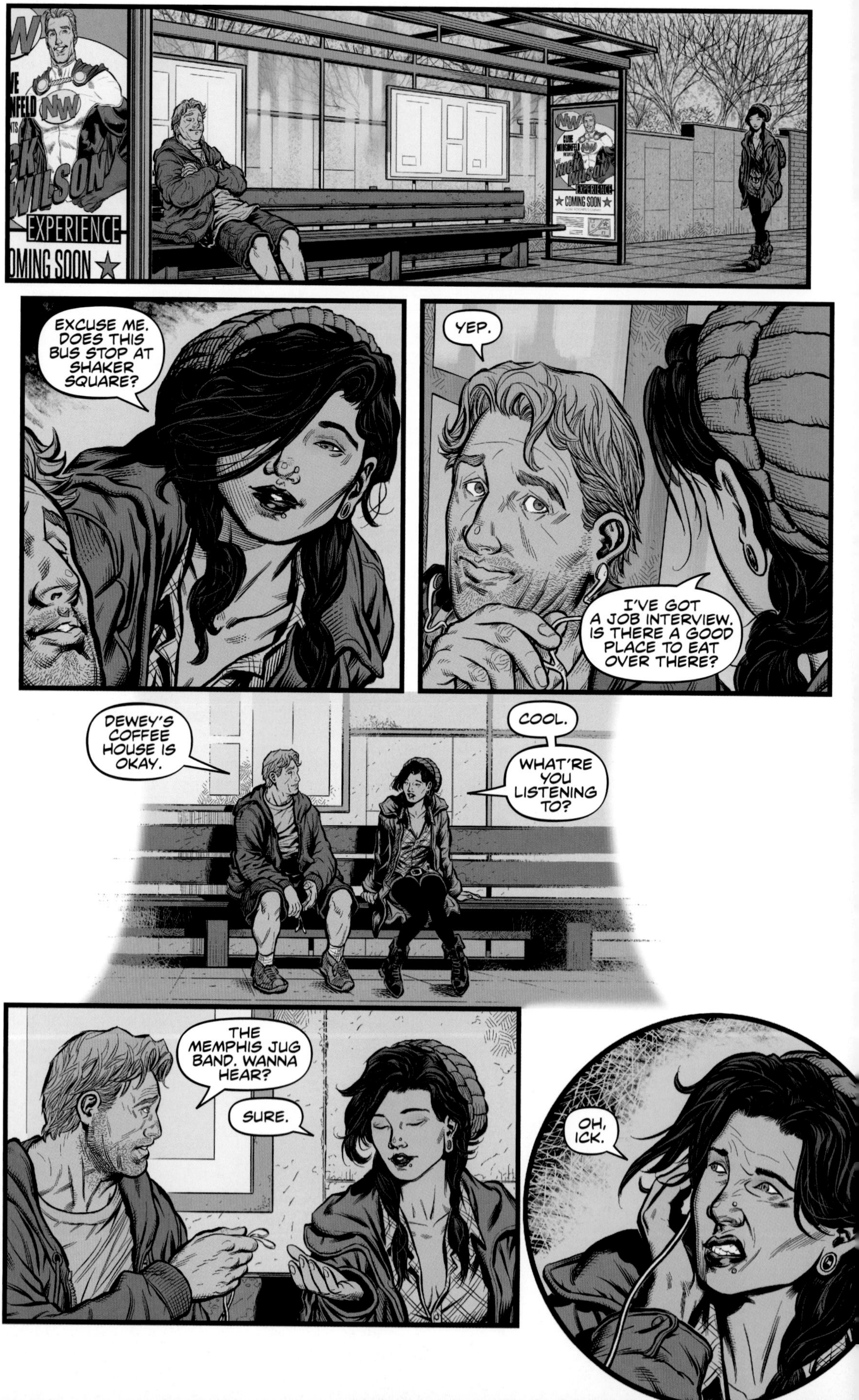
EXPERIENCE
EXCUSE ME. DOES THIS BUS STOP AT SHAKER SQUARE?
YEP.
I'VE GOT A JOB INTERVIEW. IS THERE A GOOD PLACE TO EAT OVER THERE?
DEWEY'S COFFEE HOUSE IS OKAY.
COOL.
WHAT'RE YOU LISTENING TO?
THE MEMPHIS JUG BAND. WANNA HEAR?
SURE.
OH, ICK.

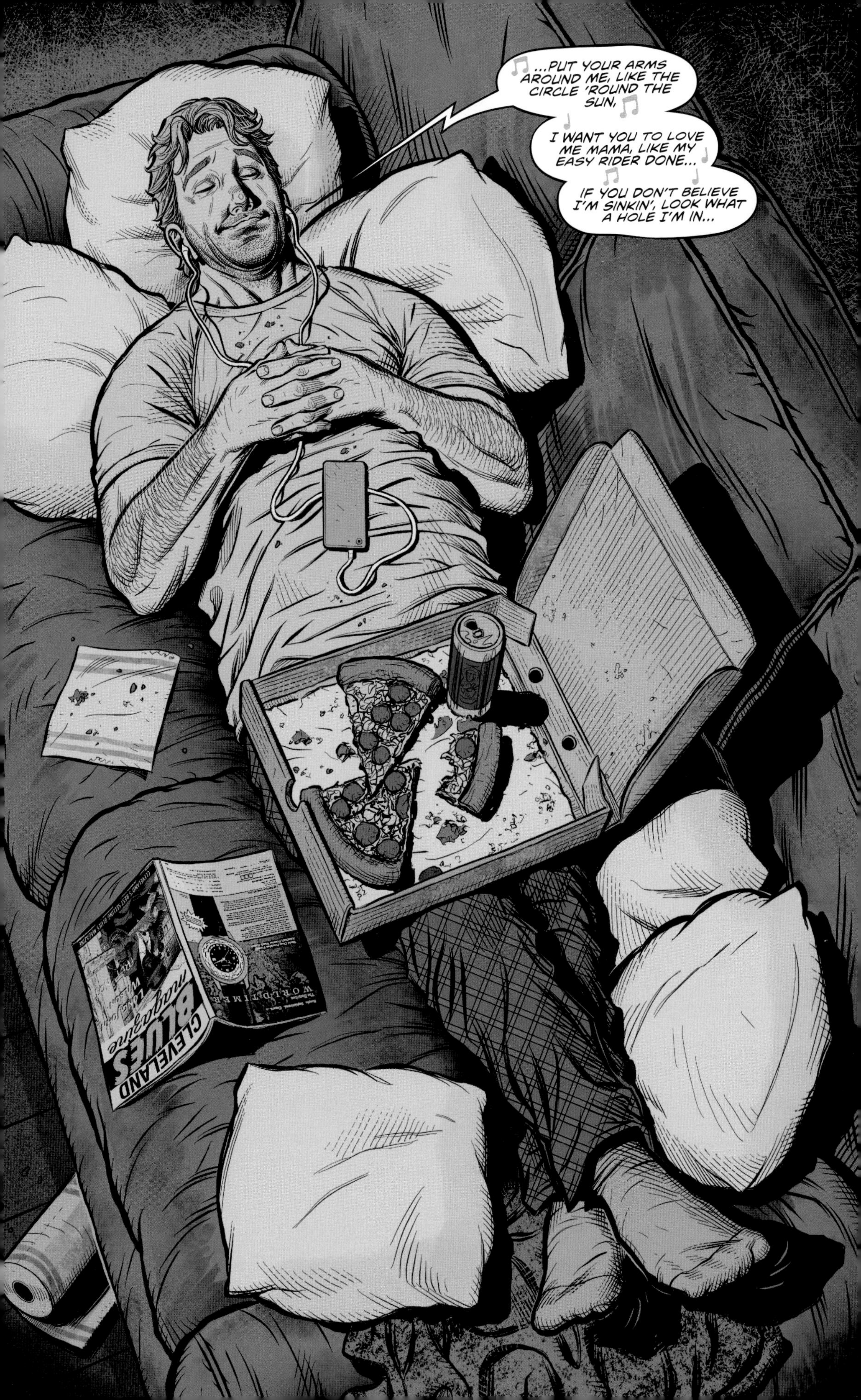
...PUT YOUR ARMS AROUND ME, LIKE THE CIRCLE 'ROUND THE SUN,
I WANT YOU TO LOVE ME MAMA, LIKE MY EASY RIDER DONE...
IF YOU DON'T BELIEVE I'M SINKIN', LOOK WHAT A HOLE I'M IN...
CLEVELAND BLUES magazine

DRIVING ARTISTS *CRAZY!*

3:15 pm
Xavier
CHIME
3:15 pm
Xavier
IT'S XAVIER. I'M BEING SUMMONED.

Why on earth would you put a word balloon there?

Ian Churchill did a terrific job stepping in on this issue when we had scheduling problems. Fortunately Stephen Sadowski was able to return for issue five and wrap up the great job he had started. If we had to use a fill-in artist, it was extremely fortuitous that it was for issue four that Ian took up the quill or mouse or combination thereof.

We always knew that various art styles would be used to give a Rashomon effect in this issue and Ian is quite the chameleon—I had seen some of his work in a collaboration with my friend Paul Dini where he did a pitch-perfect portrayal of the earliest incarnation of Mister Mxyzptlk and immediately knew he was the person for the job.

However, I have enough self-awareness to know that I, like most writers, am capable of driving artists, in my case both Stephen and Ian, a bit bonkers so I thought I would share why and how with you. There are a couple of good examples in this issue but trust me, they serve merely as examples of many other instances that appear across the whole series. But first a bit of background...

I usually make TV shows and I work with various departments to get across the message in a script – from wardrobe to make-up to directing to acting. The editing, the post production and so much more all have to be invisible to a degree, not calling too much attention (you don't want anyone humming the furniture) but it all has to be in service of the story you are telling; all working in congress to convey maximum story information within the limited real estate you have to work. In a program that real estate is measured in time, in a book, it is measured in pages and panels.

I'm lucky to work with wonderful actresses. During the course of the week, Anna Faris and Allison Janney work with the director and, through them, an arched eyebrow or a stressed syllable allows me to cut words or complete sentences from the script and what was once clumsy text becomes elegant subtext.

Likewise, a deft choice of a prop or a piece of wardrobe conveys aspects of backstory or personality without having to waste valuable screen time.

The learning curve here, in a new medium, was hard for me. Marc and I weren't in the room with the artists and most of the books the others worked on weren't big on subtext. I know I drove them nuts.

For example, in this issue on page seven Nick gets a text and tells Jane he's been "summoned." Jane replies, "'Summoned' or just wondering why you're not at work?" Ian did a lovely drawing of an iPhone here and why wouldn't he? One problem, though—Ian drew it in such a way where it would be lettered so you could see the actual text.

But in my mind, it ruins the moment if you can see that text—is it angry, full of expletives or just a request? Doesn't matter—what matters is these two know each other so well that Nick is most likely underplaying how much trouble he is in and Jane is not letting him get away with it. It is a small thing but a mark of how well they know each other. Seeing the actual text kinda makes it less interesting.

Once I explained it to Ian, he very generously offered to redraw it but I had already fallen in love with what he had already drawn. I came up with the solution you see where Nick's word balloon covers the actual text, an idea I never would have thought of if Marc hadn't taught me a thing or two about the cool mechanics of balloon placement. I loved learning the physics of comics from him.

The page before that presented a bigger problem—it was the first dip into an artistic stylistic difference and Ian had drawn a beautifully composed page. Again, I loved it but I thought it ruined the device and broke the storytelling.

The different artistic styles throughout the book show people's relation to the story of Chris falling off the building—without giving too much away, Nick tells it a couple of times himself and his awareness changes. This first time he tells it, he's remembering himself in primary colors as a blithe superhero. That soon changes. In Ian's first attempt at the sequence, the moody elongated head (shades of Boston Brand) that triggers us into the memory is too self-reflective. He's ahead of the story and it leaves us nowhere to go emotionally.

The new page eight is simpler but it tells the story clearer. You may prefer the first attempt as a piece of art but I don't think it conveys the story as well.

I could tell you just as many tales of how I tortured Stephen in the other issues but I will spare myself the embarrassment.

I share these not to aggrandize the writing but for two other reasons—to shine a light on the artists and the letterers and colorists and everyone else who helped put this book together and show how every decision they make helps tell the story a bit more precisely. Their hard work shines on every page and getting an email from them with new work was like receiving a birthday gift several times a month.

But also I wish to point out that every panel of every graphic story you read has this much thought and work by artists like these and, in this kind of book, much of the best of it is invisible. But that doesn't mean it isn't beautiful. In many ways it is harder to put two people on a couch and make them believable and interesting than it is to wage a pan-galactic battle between Skrulls and Qwardians—and yes, I know I am mixing cultures there.

So this is an apology for driving those talented folks crazy and a love letter for the quiet beauty and elegance of their work. I know Marc joins me in thanking all of them for making these characters come alive.

As always, thanks for reading and see you next month where hopefully, we'll get around to talking about some more records.

eddie gorodetsky
los feliz

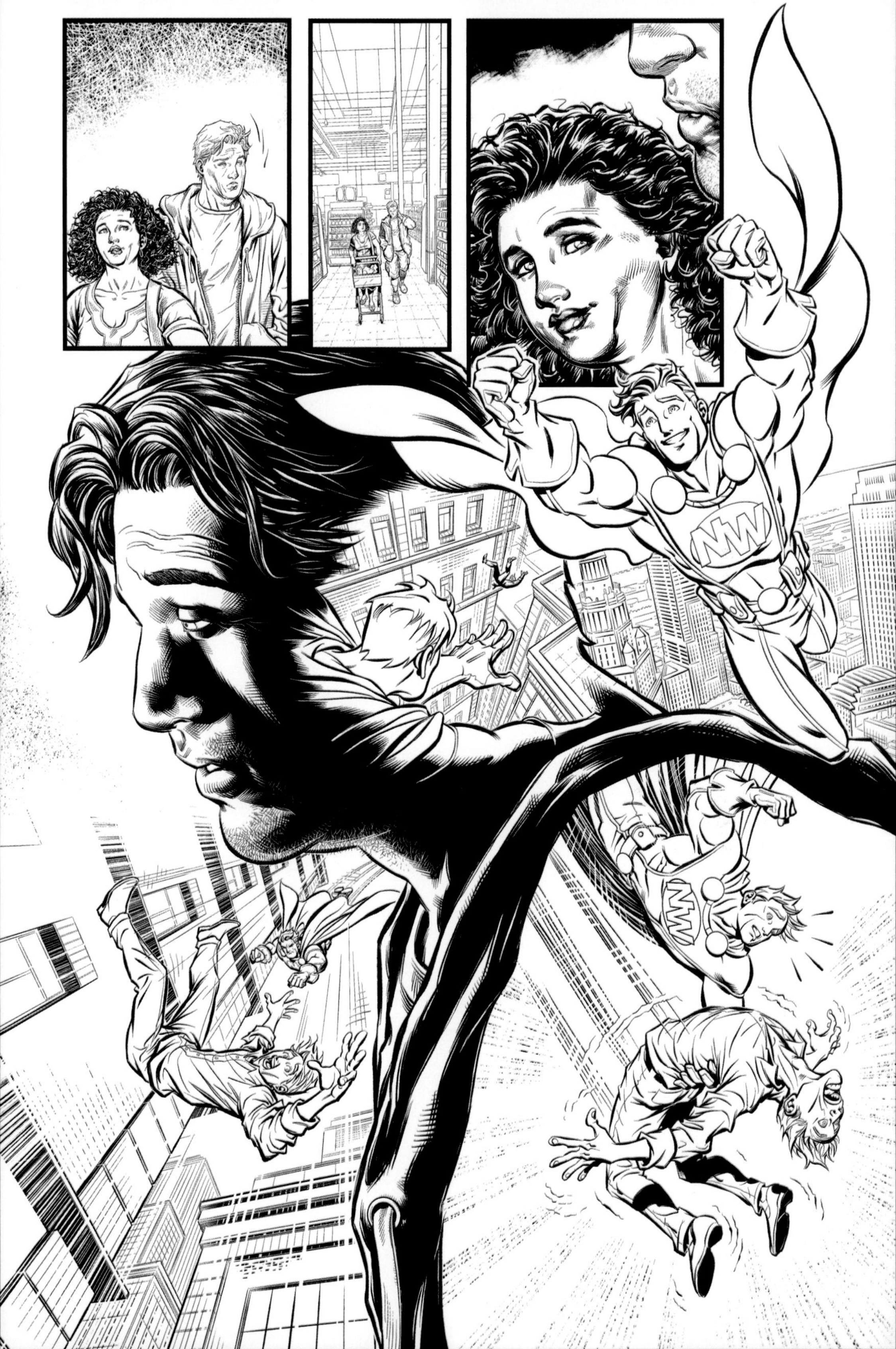

Why on earth wouldn't you use this beautiful piece of art?

THE BOYS & GIRLS OF AMERICA
know that this famous symbol...
NW
...IS THEIR GUARANTEE
of the BEST
IN COMICS READING!
NO. 9
NICK WILSON SERIES
Nick Wilson's PALS 'N' GALS
25¢
OH BOY!
EVEN WITH NO SUPER-POWERS JANE HAS FOUND AN ARCH ENEMY!
YOU LIKE, TOTALLY SAVED MY LIFE! HOW CAN I EVER THANK YOU?
TOMB OF TERROR
IMAGE COMICS GROUP
25¢ 65 APR
TOMB OF TERROR FEATURING
NICK WILSON
JANE IS UNDER THE SPELL OF THE ZOMBIE JUG BAND'S MELODY...
I WANT TO LISTEN TO THAT BLUES MOO-DOO TOO, BUT IF I DO THEN BOTH OF US ARE DOOMED!
NICK WILSON
IMAGE COMICS GROUP
25¢ 190 JAN
NICK WILSON
YOU MAY HAVE BEATEN MY FEMDROIDS, WILSON...
...BUT, VICTORY SHALL BE MINE!
THE ADVENTURES OF
12¢
NICK WILSON
OCT. NO. 77
Featuring "THE COLOSSUS OF CLEVELAND!"
EEEKK! NICK! HELP ME!
HOLY CATS! JANE IS A GIANT!
I HAVE TO FIND A WAY TO SHRINK HER, BUT HOW?!
IF IT'S
NICK WILSON
-IT'S GOT TO BE
GOOD!
THE ADVENTURES OF NICK WILSON #26
APRIL $3.50
GORODETSKY ANDREYKO SADOWSKI CHURCHILL
THE ADVENTURES OF
12¢
NICK WILSON
Featuring "THE DEVILISH DOUBLE!"
I'M FREE!
NICK WILSON, HERO? HAH! SOON YOU'LL BE RUINED-- FOREVER!
THAT RAY HAS CREATED AN EVIL DOUBLE OF... ME!
NICK WILSON
NICK WILSON
SEPTEMBER 1966
THE ADVENTURES OF NICK WILSON #32
APRIL $3.50
GORODETSKY ANDREYKO SADOWSKI CHURCHILL
FROM THE LEADERS IN image INATION!

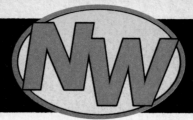

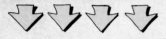

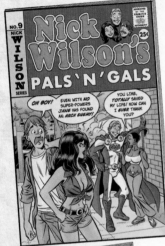

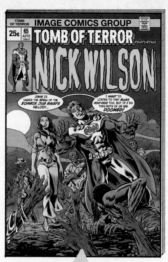

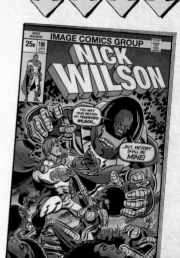

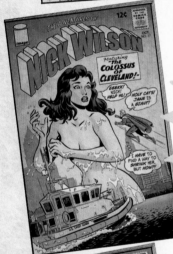

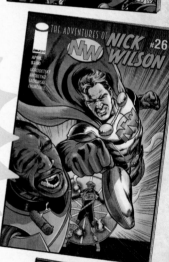

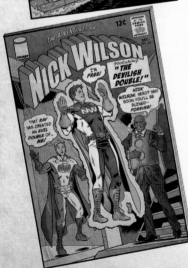

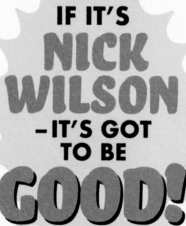

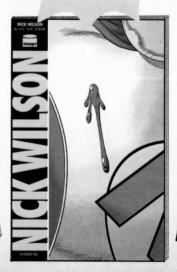

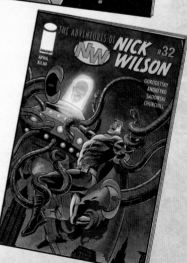

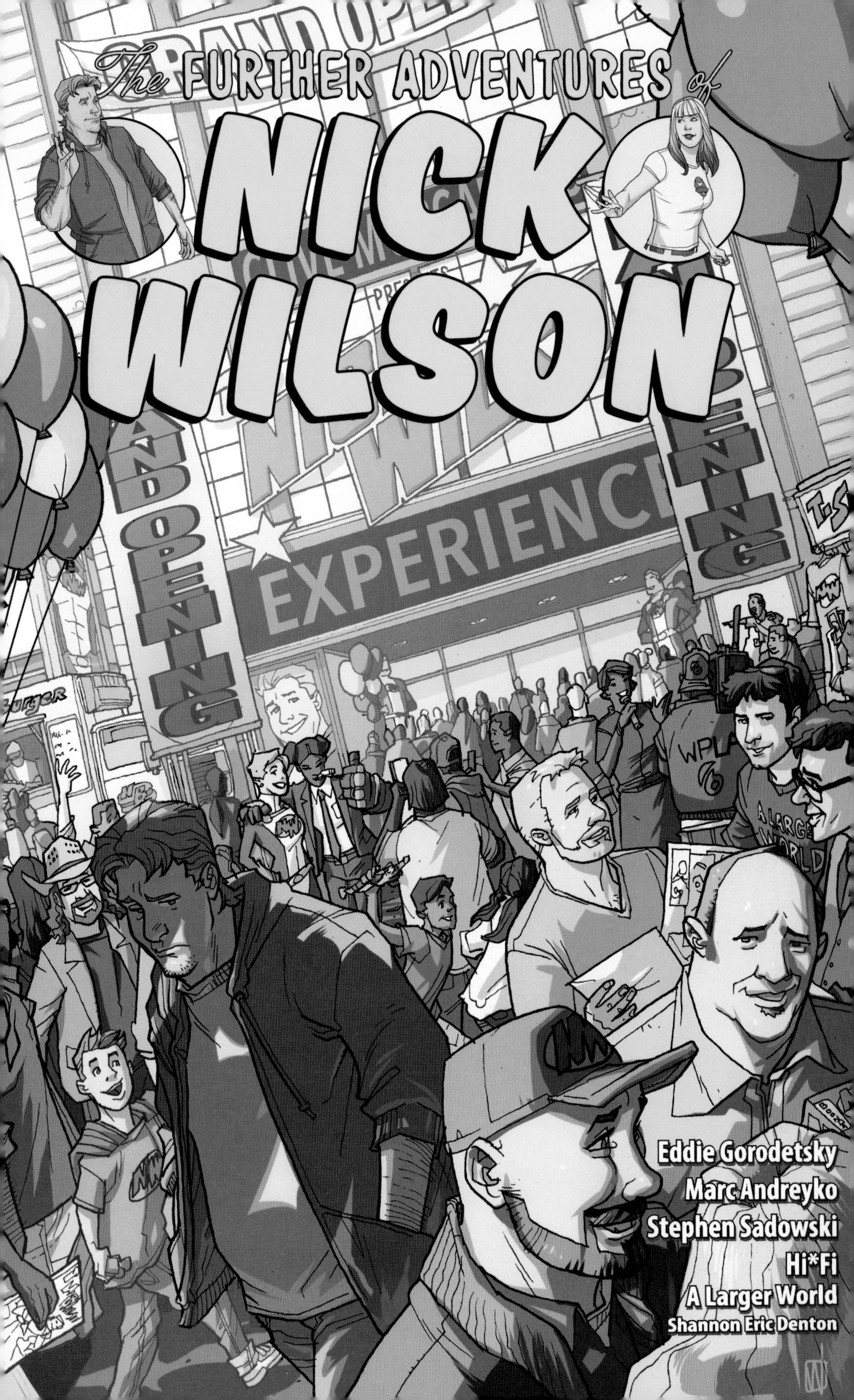

The FURTHER ADVENTURES of
NICK WILSON
EXPERIENCE
Eddie Gorodetsky
Marc Andreyko
Stephen Sadowski
Hi*Fi
A Larger World
Shannon Eric Denton

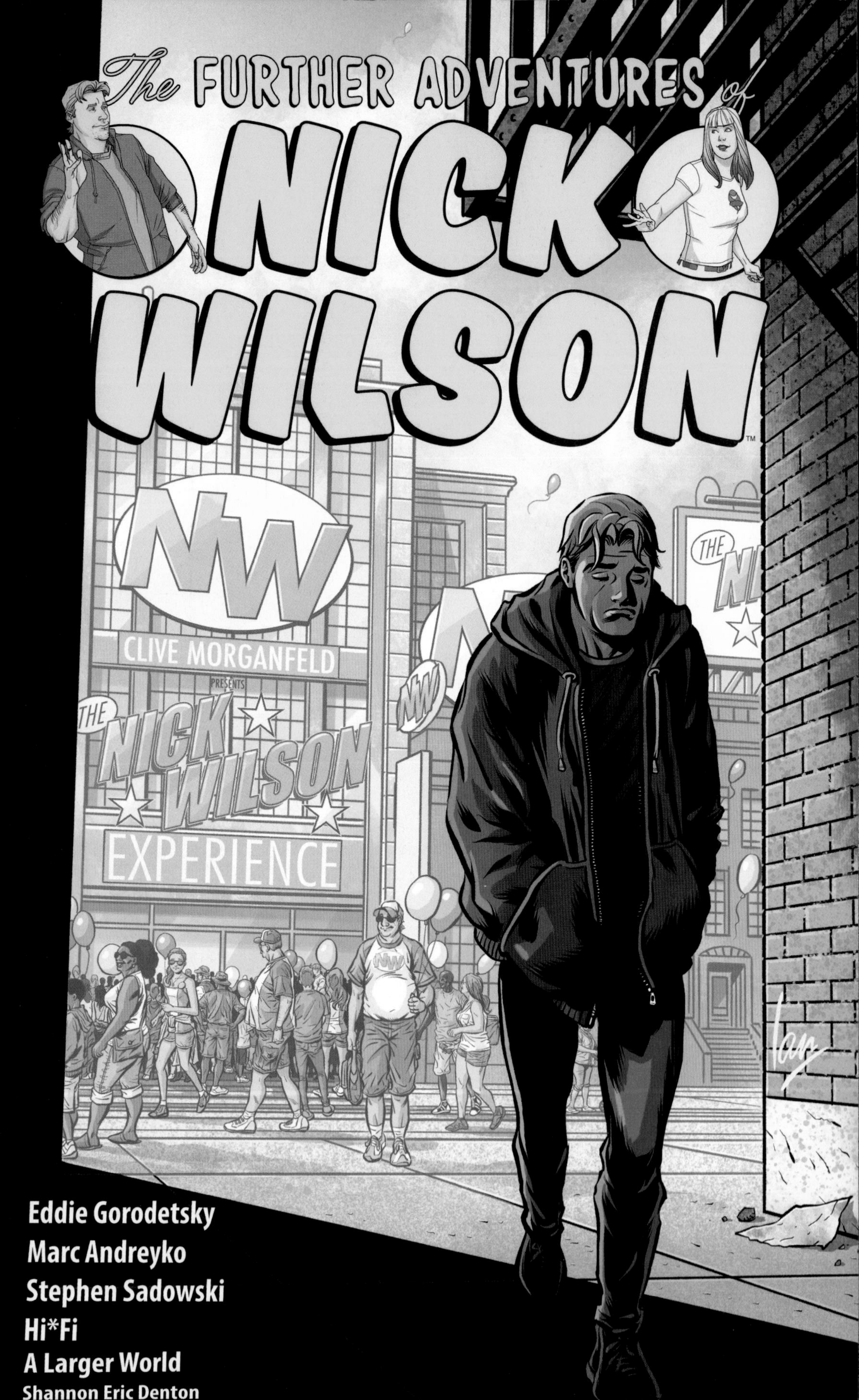
The FURTHER ADVENTURES of
NICK WILSON™
NW
CLIVE MORGANFELD
PRESENTS
THE NICK WILSON EXPERIENCE
THE
NW

Eddie Gorodetsky
Marc Andreyko
Stephen Sadowski
Hi*Fi
A Larger World
Shannon Eric Denton

THE WHOLE WORLD IS WATCHING, T-MINUS FOUR HOURS UNTIL THE OPENING OF CLEVELAND'S LATEST TOURIST ATTRACTION-- THE NICK WILSON EXPERIENCE CHRONICLING THE BRIEF CAREER OF EARTH'S FIRST, AND THUS FAR ONLY, SUPERHERO!

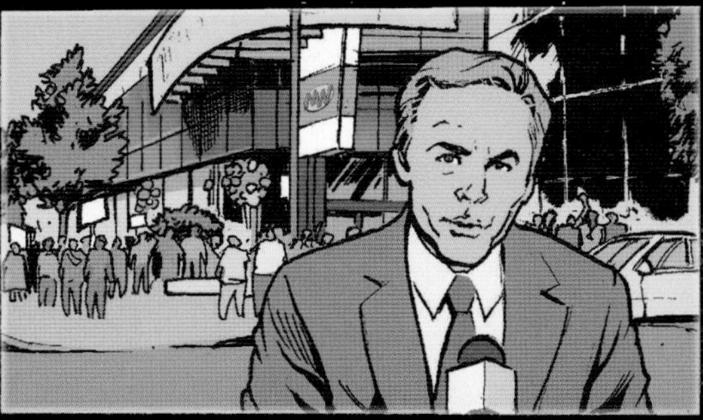

IT SEEMS LIKE ONLY YESTERDAY THAT NICK BURST ONTO THE SCENE, EXHIBITING WHAT CAN ONLY BE CALLED "SUPER-POWERS": FLIGHT, STRENGTH, LASER VISION, INVULNERABILITY...

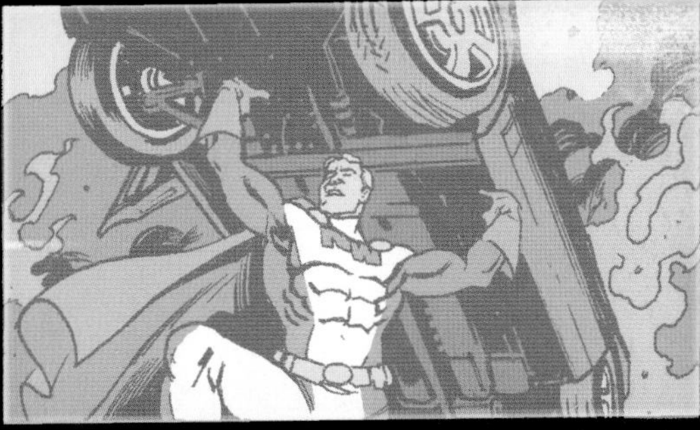

...NICK'S STAR ROSE ALMOST AS FAST AND AS HIGH AS HIS NEWFOUND FLYING ABILITIES. HE HOBNOBBED WITH POLITICAL LEADERS....

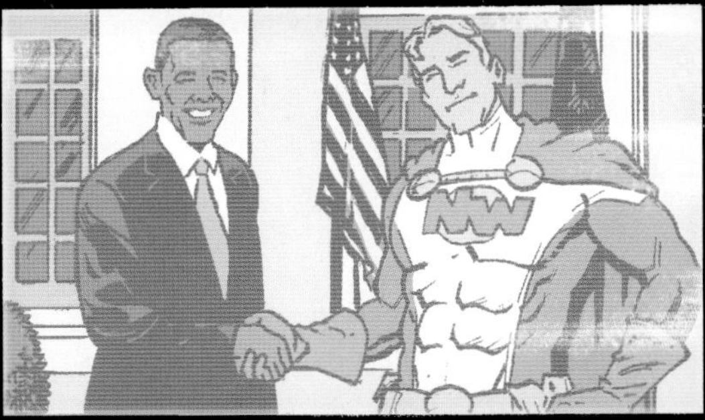
NW

...TOOK HOLLYWOOD BY STORM....

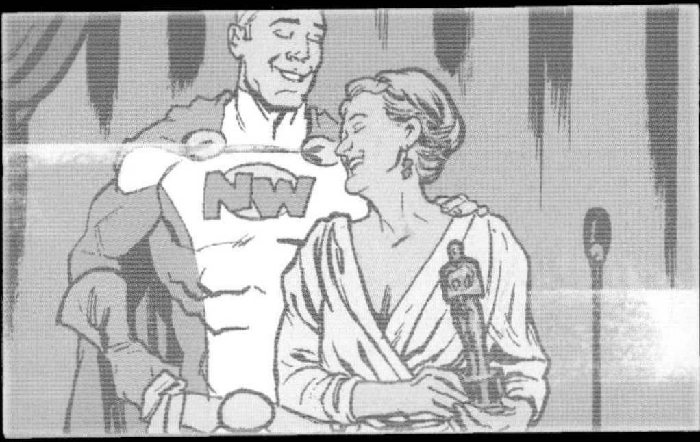
NW

BUT, AS QUICKLY AND MYSTERIOUSLY AS HE GAINED SUPERHUMAN ABILITIES, HE LOST THEM.

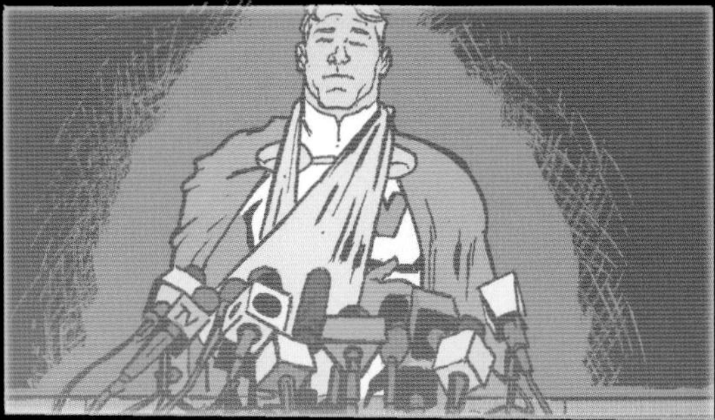
TV

AND NICK WILSON WENT FROM HEADLINE NEWS TO "WHATEVER HAPPENED TO...?" IN AN INSTANT. WHICH BRINGS US HERE TO THIS MUSEUM...

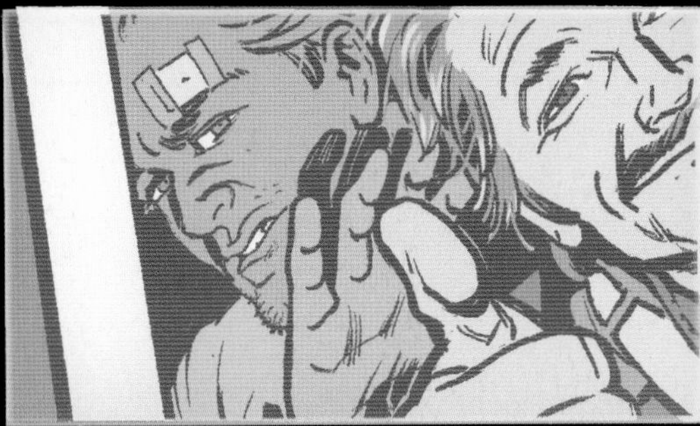

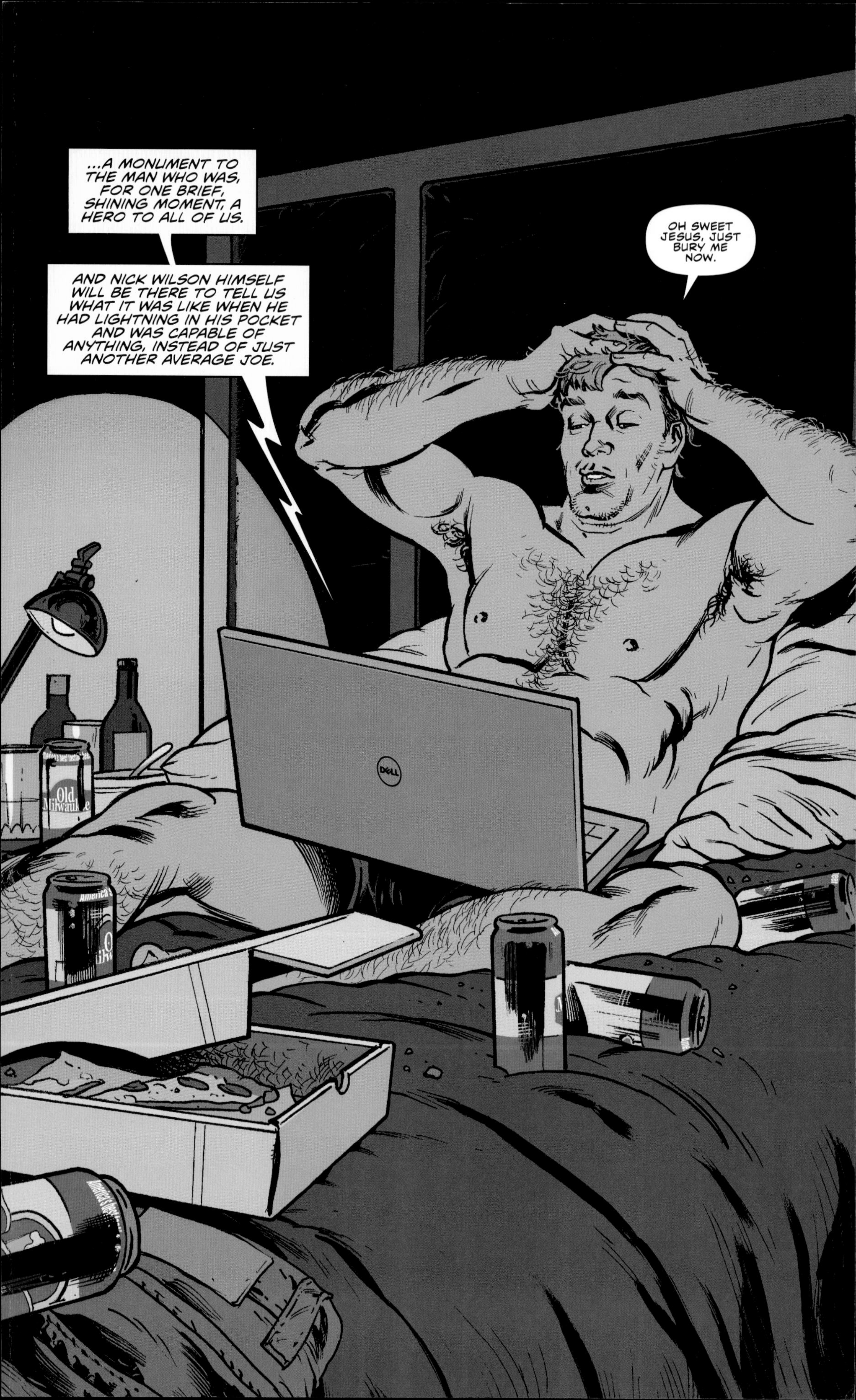
...A MONUMENT TO THE MAN WHO WAS, FOR ONE BRIEF, SHINING MOMENT, A HERO TO ALL OF US.
AND NICK WILSON HIMSELF WILL BE THERE TO TELL US WHAT IT WAS LIKE WHEN HE HAD LIGHTNING IN HIS POCKET AND WAS CAPABLE OF ANYTHING, INSTEAD OF JUST ANOTHER AVERAGE JOE.
OH SWEET JESUS, JUST BURY ME NOW.

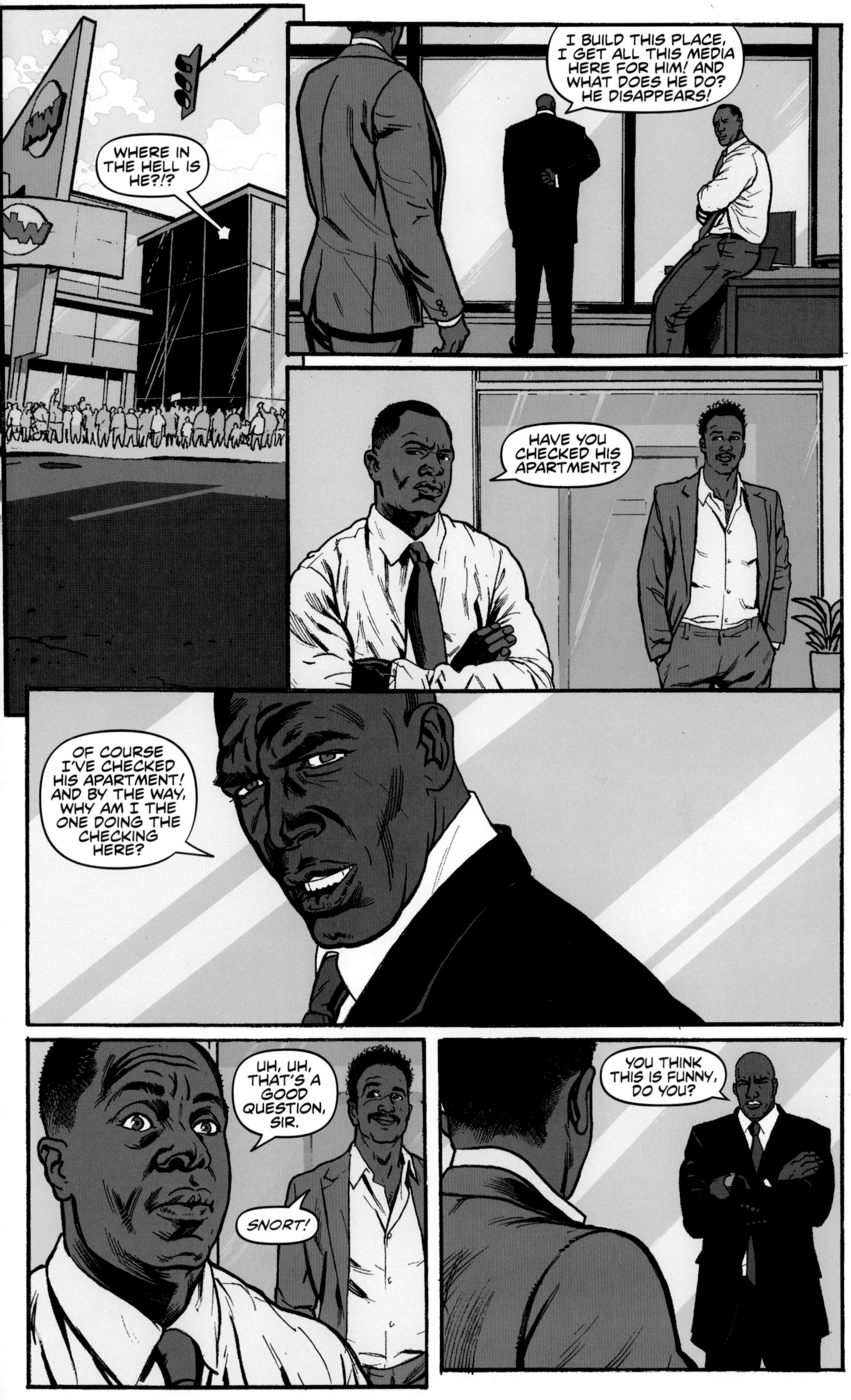
WHERE IN THE HELL IS HE?!?
I BUILD THIS PLACE, I GET ALL THIS MEDIA HERE FOR HIM! AND WHAT DOES HE DO? HE DISAPPEARS!
HAVE YOU CHECKED HIS APARTMENT?
OF COURSE I'VE CHECKED HIS APARTMENT! AND BY THE WAY, WHY AM I THE ONE DOING THE CHECKING HERE?
UH, UH, THAT'S A GOOD QUESTION, SIR.
SNORT!
YOU THINK THIS IS FUNNY, DO YOU?

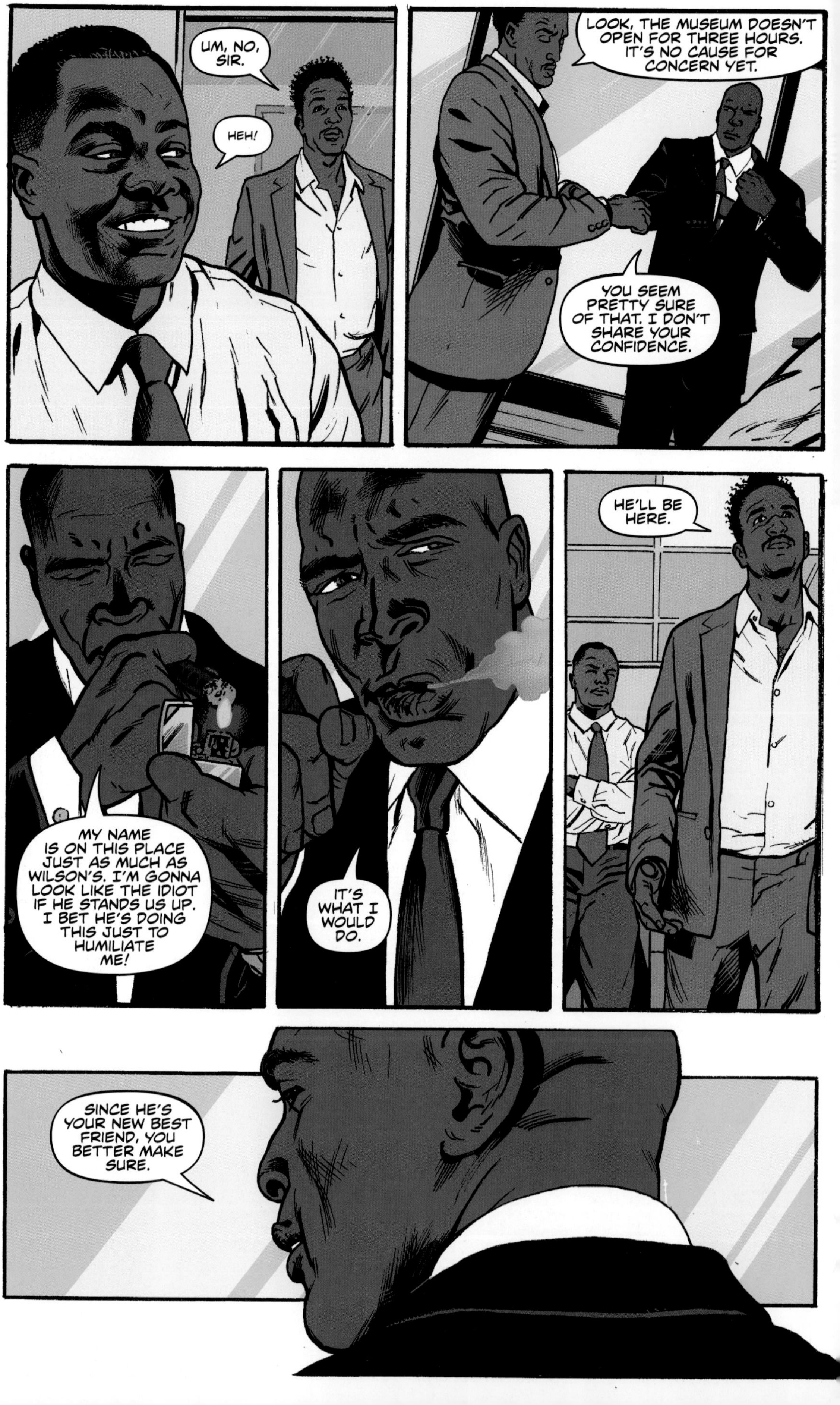
UM, NO, SIR.
HEH!
LOOK, THE MUSEUM DOESN'T OPEN FOR THREE HOURS. IT'S NO CAUSE FOR CONCERN YET.
YOU SEEM PRETTY SURE OF THAT. I DON'T SHARE YOUR CONFIDENCE.
MY NAME IS ON THIS PLACE JUST AS MUCH AS WILSON'S. I'M GONNA LOOK LIKE THE IDIOT IF HE STANDS US UP. I BET HE'S DOING THIS JUST TO HUMILIATE ME!
IT'S WHAT I WOULD DO.
HE'LL BE HERE.
SINCE HE'S YOUR NEW BEST FRIEND, YOU BETTER MAKE SURE.

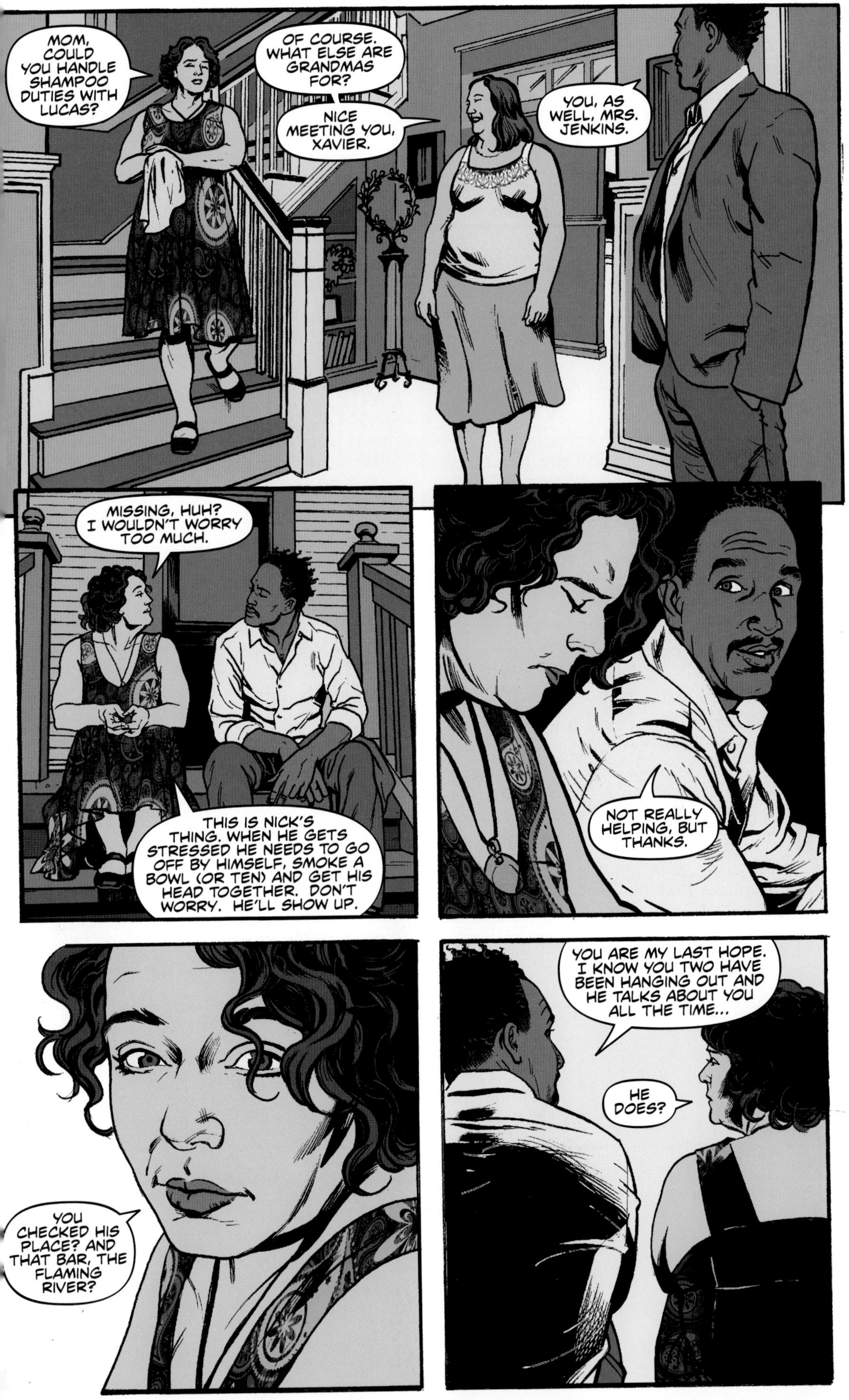
MOM, COULD YOU HANDLE SHAMPOO DUTIES WITH LUCAS?
OF COURSE. WHAT ELSE ARE GRANDMAS FOR?
NICE MEETING YOU, XAVIER.
YOU, AS WELL, MRS. JENKINS.
MISSING, HUH? I WOULDN'T WORRY TOO MUCH.
THIS IS NICK'S THING. WHEN HE GETS STRESSED HE NEEDS TO GO OFF BY HIMSELF, SMOKE A BOWL (OR TEN) AND GET HIS HEAD TOGETHER. DON'T WORRY. HE'LL SHOW UP.
NOT REALLY HELPING, BUT THANKS.
YOU CHECKED HIS PLACE? AND THAT BAR, THE FLAMING RIVER?
YOU ARE MY LAST HOPE. I KNOW YOU TWO HAVE BEEN HANGING OUT AND HE TALKS ABOUT YOU ALL THE TIME...
HE DOES?

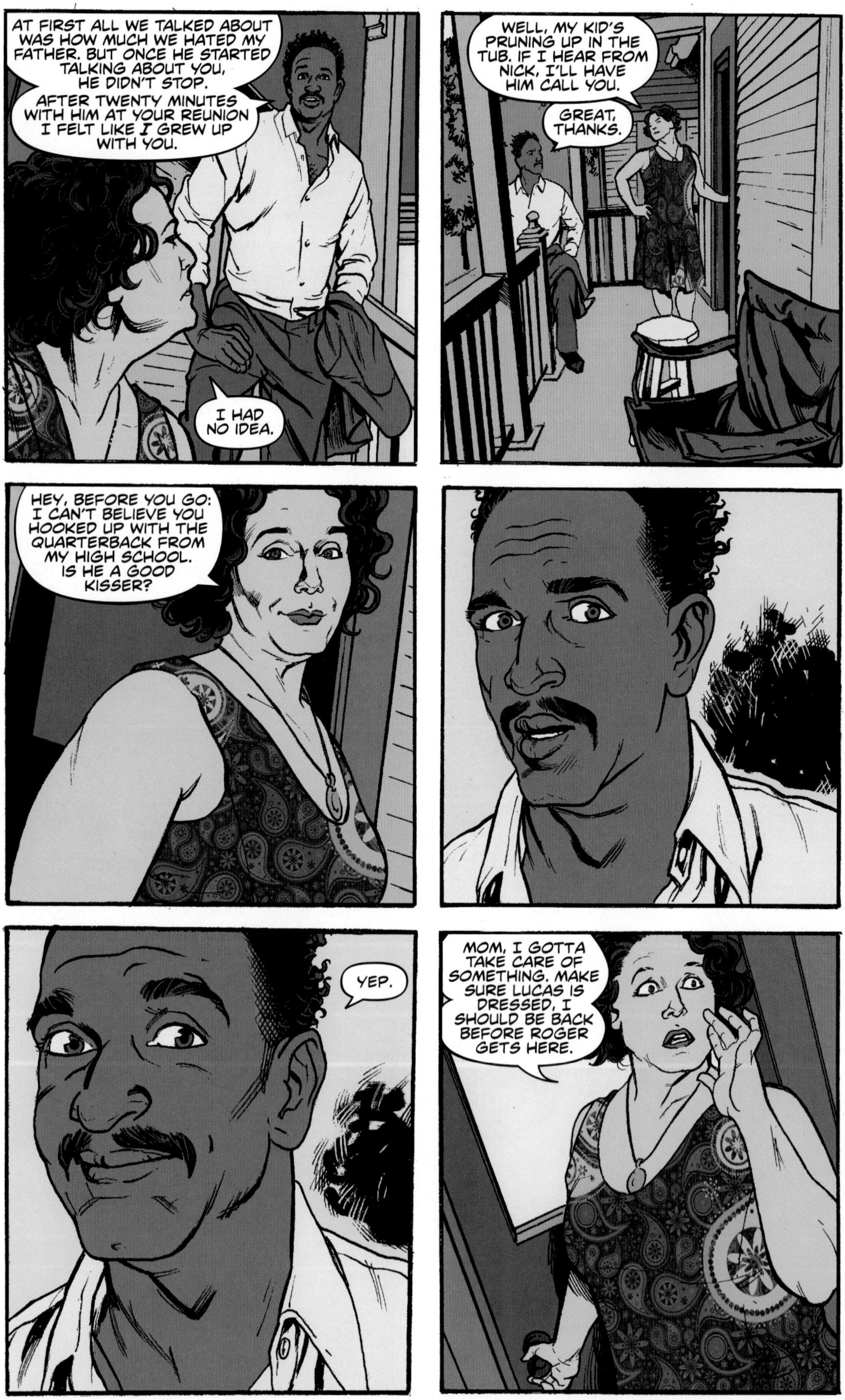
AT FIRST ALL WE TALKED ABOUT WAS HOW MUCH WE HATED MY FATHER. BUT ONCE HE STARTED TALKING ABOUT YOU, HE DIDN'T STOP.
AFTER TWENTY MINUTES WITH HIM AT YOUR REUNION I FELT LIKE *I* GREW UP WITH YOU.
I HAD NO IDEA.
WELL, MY KID'S PRUNING UP IN THE TUB. IF I HEAR FROM NICK, I'LL HAVE HIM CALL YOU.
GREAT, THANKS.
HEY, BEFORE YOU GO: I CAN'T BELIEVE YOU HOOKED UP WITH THE QUARTERBACK FROM MY HIGH SCHOOL. IS HE A GOOD KISSER?
YEP.
MOM, I GOTTA TAKE CARE OF SOMETHING. MAKE SURE LUCAS IS DRESSED, I SHOULD BE BACK BEFORE ROGER GETS HERE.

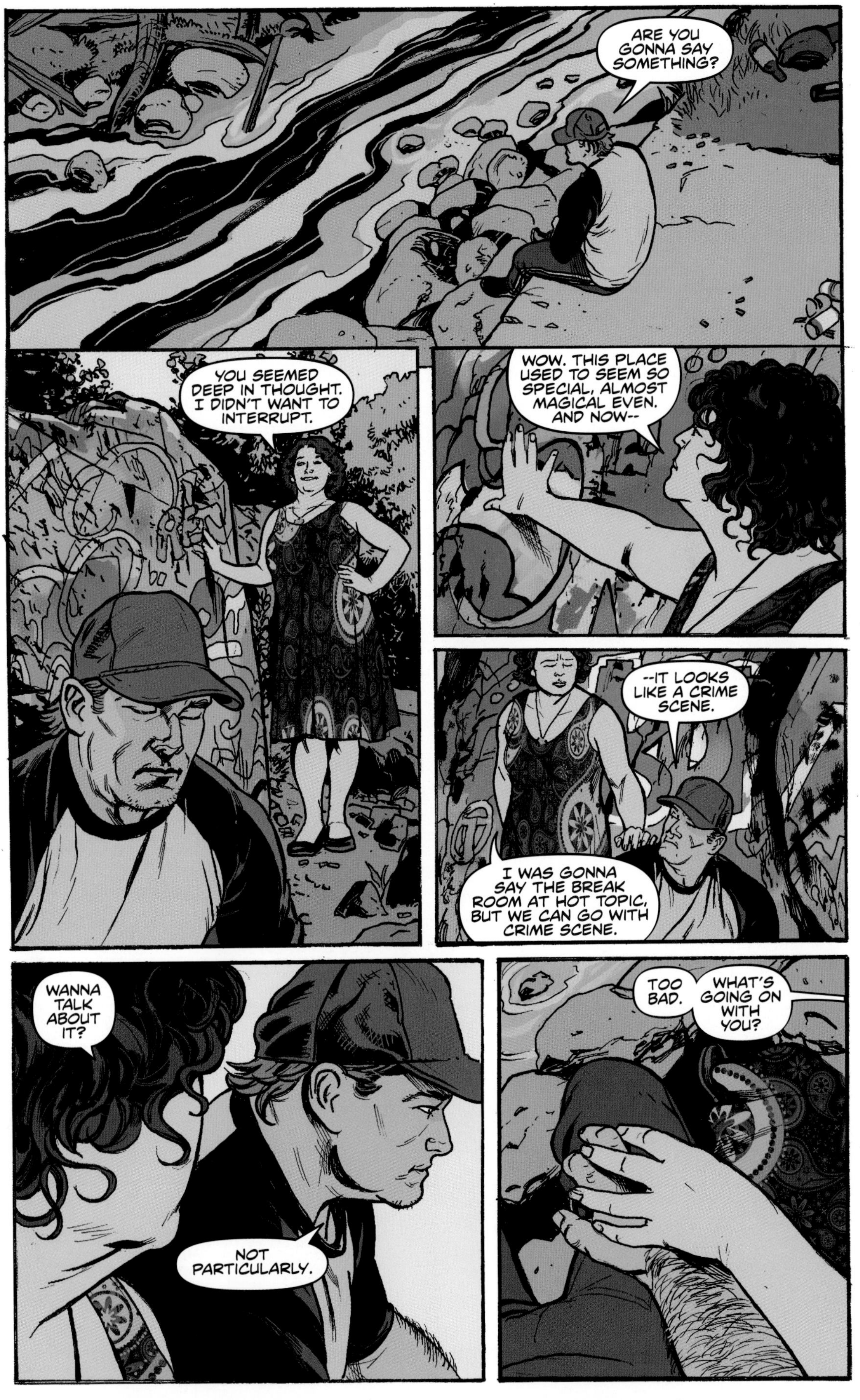
ARE YOU GONNA SAY SOMETHING?
YOU SEEMED DEEP IN THOUGHT. I DIDN'T WANT TO INTERRUPT.
WOW. THIS PLACE USED TO SEEM SO SPECIAL, ALMOST MAGICAL EVEN. AND NOW--
--IT LOOKS LIKE A CRIME SCENE.
I WAS GONNA SAY THE BREAK ROOM AT HOT TOPIC, BUT WE CAN GO WITH CRIME SCENE.
WANNA TALK ABOUT IT?
NOT PARTICULARLY.
TOO BAD.
WHAT'S GOING ON WITH YOU?

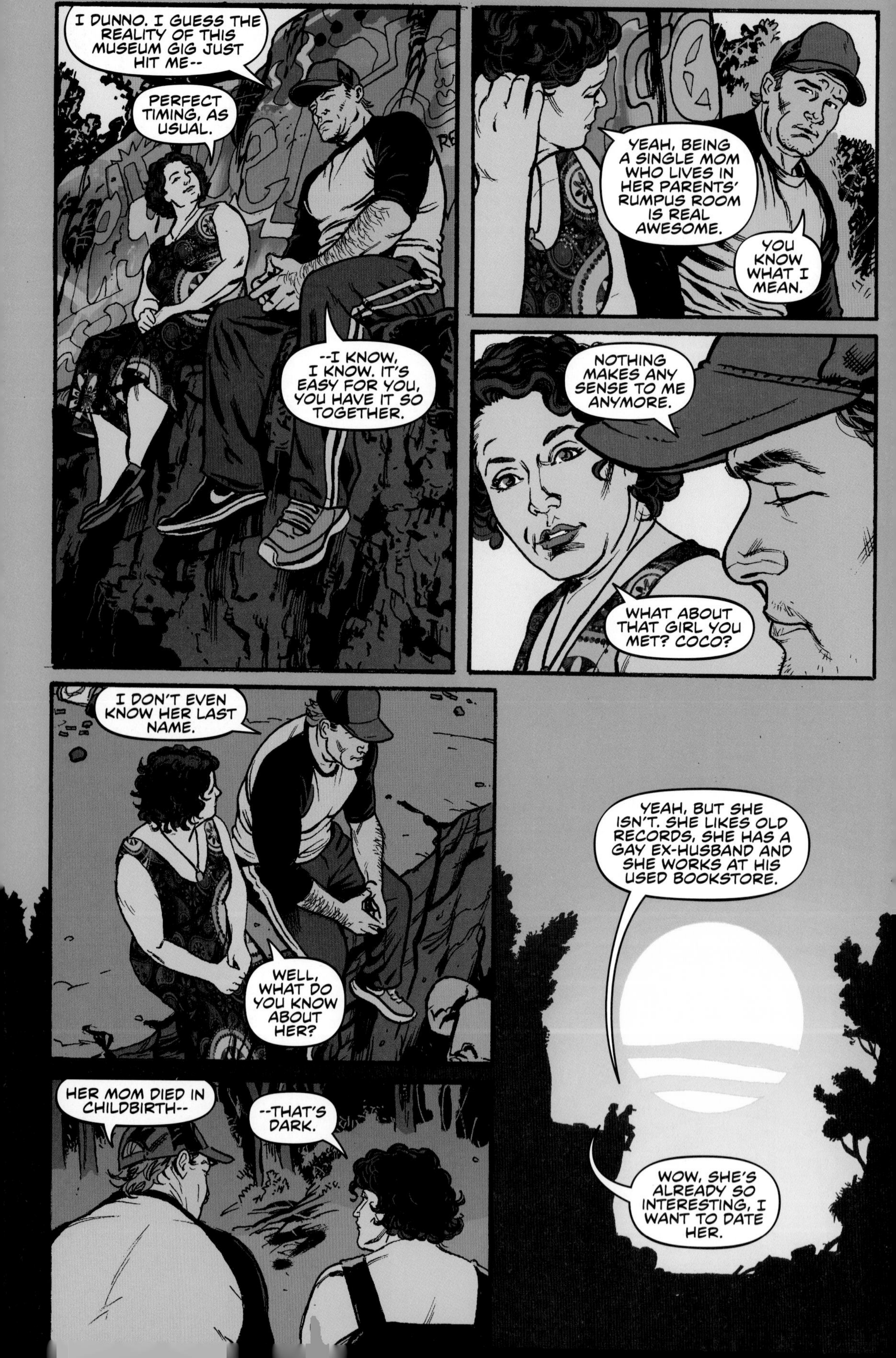
I DUNNO. I GUESS THE REALITY OF THIS MUSEUM GIG JUST HIT ME--
PERFECT TIMING, AS USUAL.
--I KNOW, I KNOW. IT'S EASY FOR YOU, YOU HAVE IT SO TOGETHER.
YEAH, BEING A SINGLE MOM WHO LIVES IN HER PARENTS' RUMPUS ROOM IS REAL AWESOME.
YOU KNOW WHAT I MEAN.
NOTHING MAKES ANY SENSE TO ME ANYMORE.
WHAT ABOUT THAT GIRL YOU MET? COCO?
I DON'T EVEN KNOW HER LAST NAME.
WELL, WHAT DO YOU KNOW ABOUT HER?
HER MOM DIED IN CHILDBIRTH--
--THAT'S DARK.
YEAH, BUT SHE ISN'T. SHE LIKES OLD RECORDS, SHE HAS A GAY EX-HUSBAND AND SHE WORKS AT HIS USED BOOKSTORE.
WOW, SHE'S ALREADY SO INTERESTING, I WANT TO DATE HER.

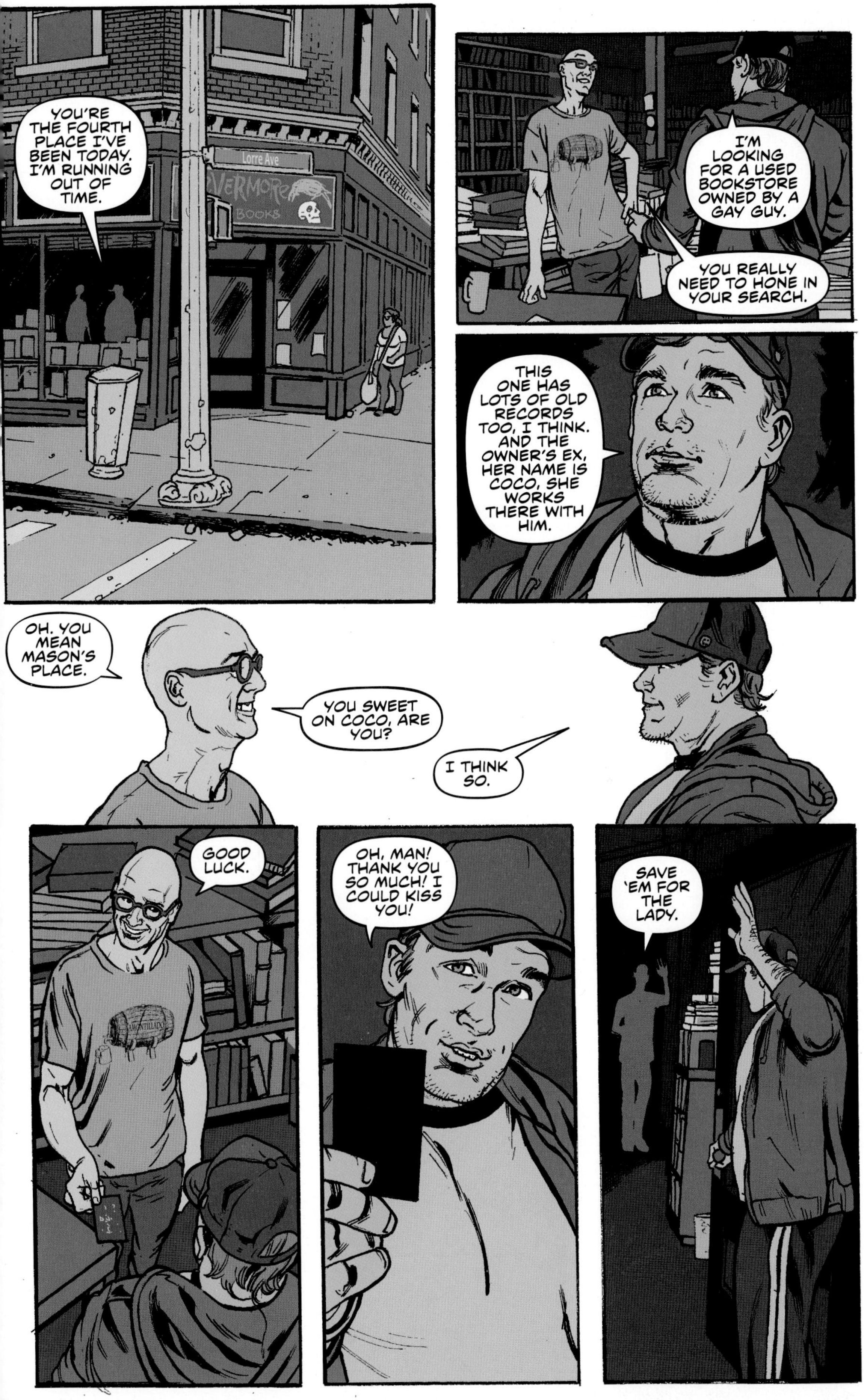

Lorre Ave
VERMORE BOOKS
YOU'RE THE FOURTH PLACE I'VE BEEN TODAY. I'M RUNNING OUT OF TIME.
I'M LOOKING FOR A USED BOOKSTORE OWNED BY A GAY GUY.
YOU REALLY NEED TO HONE IN YOUR SEARCH.
THIS ONE HAS LOTS OF OLD RECORDS TOO, I THINK. AND THE OWNER'S EX, HER NAME IS COCO, SHE WORKS THERE WITH HIM.
OH. YOU MEAN MASON'S PLACE.
YOU SWEET ON COCO, ARE YOU?
I THINK SO.
GOOD LUCK.
OH, MAN! THANK YOU SO MUCH! I COULD KISS YOU!
SAVE 'EM FOR THE LADY.

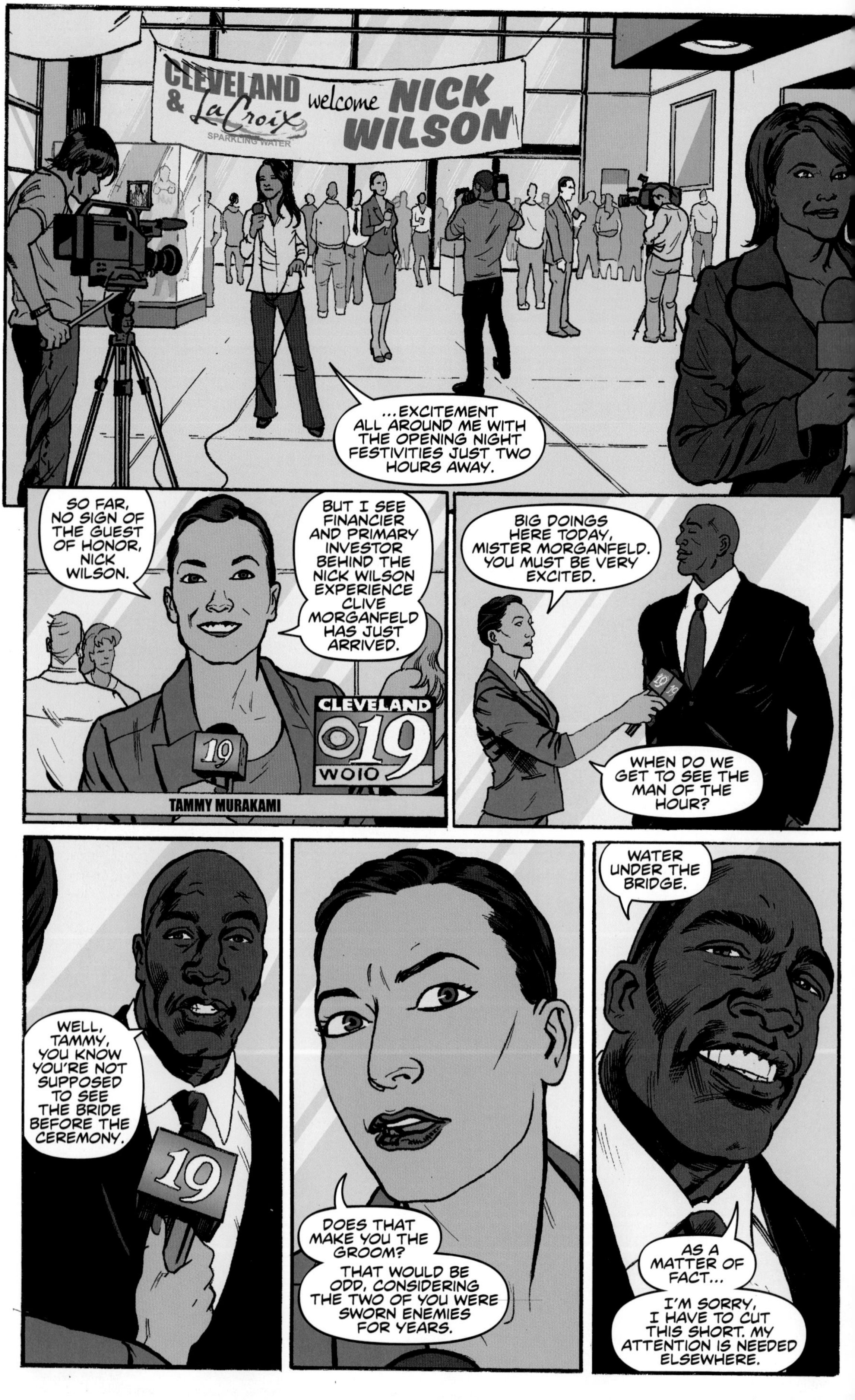
CLEVELAND & LaCroix SPARKLING WATER welcome NICK WILSON
...EXCITEMENT ALL AROUND ME WITH THE OPENING NIGHT FESTIVITIES JUST TWO HOURS AWAY.
SO FAR, NO SIGN OF THE GUEST OF HONOR, NICK WILSON.
BUT I SEE FINANCIER AND PRIMARY INVESTOR BEHIND THE NICK WILSON EXPERIENCE CLIVE MORGANFELD HAS JUST ARRIVED.
19
CLEVELAND 19 WOIO
TAMMY MURAKAMI
BIG DOINGS HERE TODAY, MISTER MORGANFELD. YOU MUST BE VERY EXCITED.
WHEN DO WE GET TO SEE THE MAN OF THE HOUR?
WELL, TAMMY, YOU KNOW YOU'RE NOT SUPPOSED TO SEE THE BRIDE BEFORE THE CEREMONY.
19
DOES THAT MAKE YOU THE GROOM?
THAT WOULD BE ODD, CONSIDERING THE TWO OF YOU WERE SWORN ENEMIES FOR YEARS.
WATER UNDER THE BRIDGE.
AS A MATTER OF FACT...
I'M SORRY, I HAVE TO CUT THIS SHORT. MY ATTENTION IS NEEDED ELSEWHERE.

DID YOU FIND HIM?

NO.

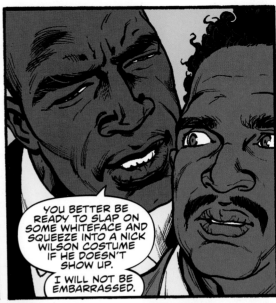

YOU BETTER BE READY TO SLAP ON SOME WHITEFACE AND SQUEEZE INTO A NICK WILSON COSTUME IF HE DOESN'T SHOW UP.

I WILL NOT BE EMBARRASSED.

AND YOU DON'T FIND WHITEFACE EMBARRASSING?

YOU'RE PICKING THE WRONG TIME TO GROW A PAIR.

MISTER MORGANFELD!

MISTER MORGANFELD!

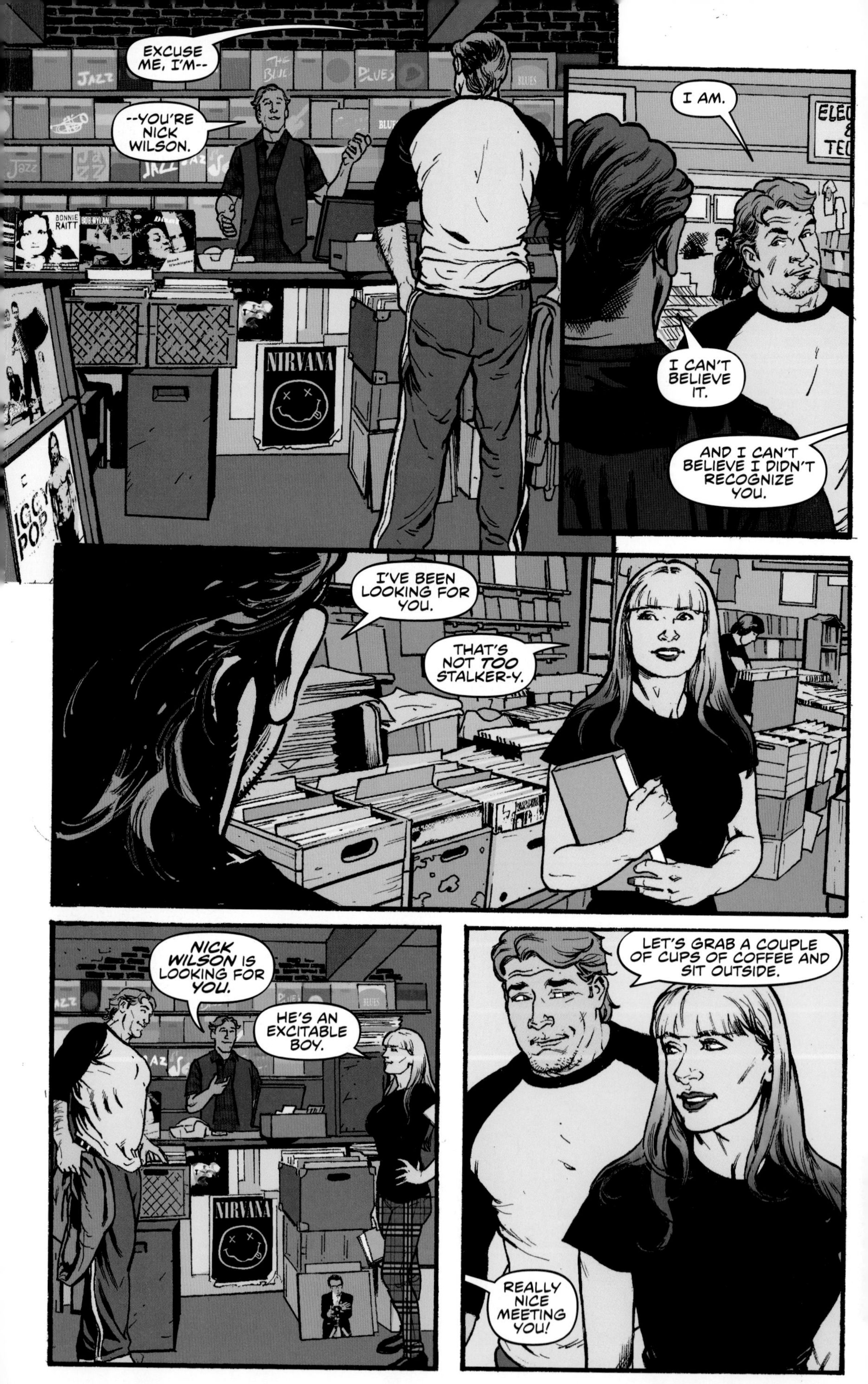
EXCUSE ME, I'M--
--YOU'RE NICK WILSON.
JAZZ
BLUES
BONNIE RAITT
BOB DYLAN
NIRVANA
IGGY POP
I AM.
I CAN'T BELIEVE IT.
AND I CAN'T BELIEVE I DIDN'T RECOGNIZE YOU.
I'VE BEEN LOOKING FOR YOU.
THAT'S NOT *TOO* STALKER-Y.
NICK WILSON IS LOOKING FOR *YOU.*
HE'S AN EXCITABLE BOY.
NIRVANA
LET'S GRAB A COUPLE OF CUPS OF COFFEE AND SIT OUTSIDE.
REALLY NICE MEETING YOU!

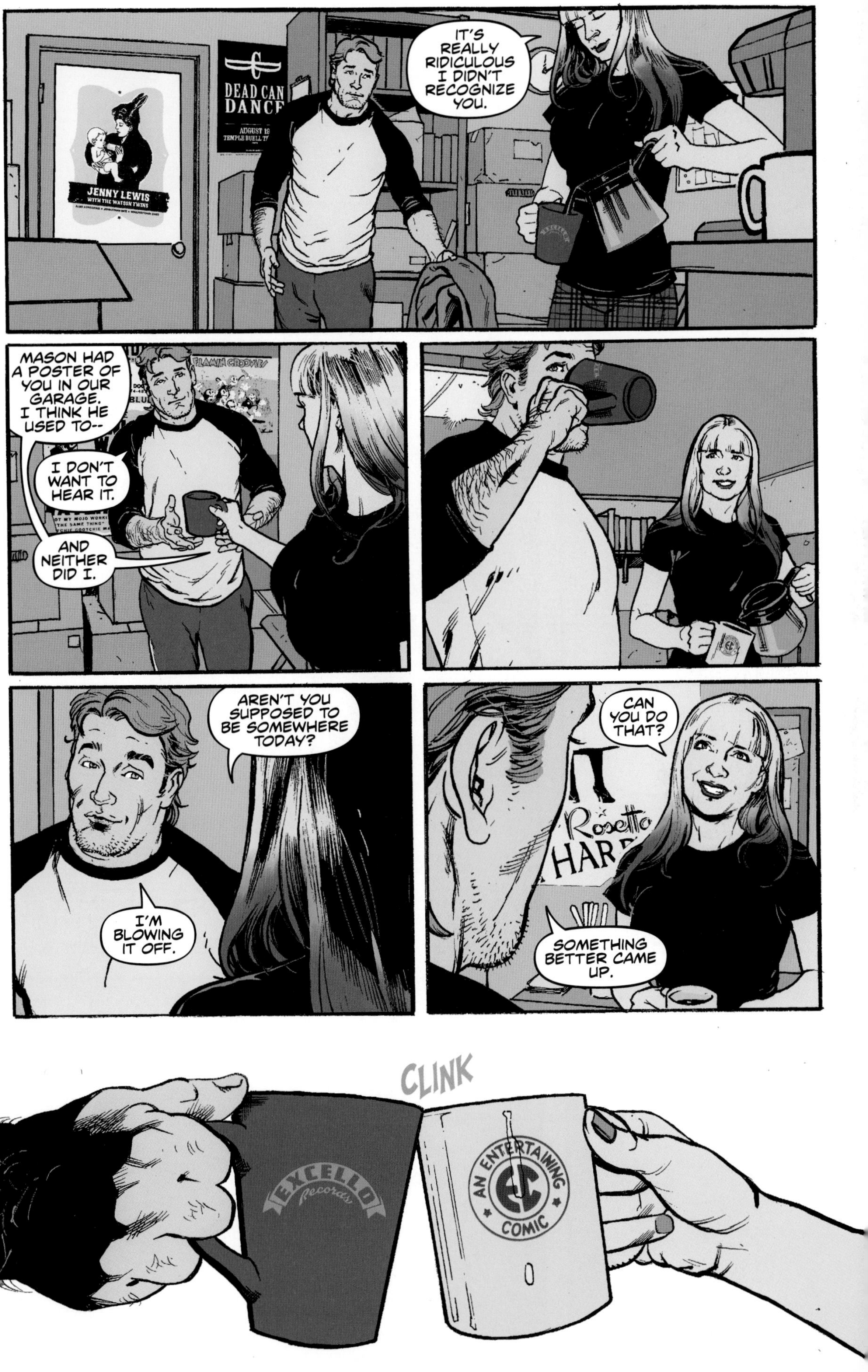
JENNY LEWIS
WITH THE WATSON TWINS
DEAD CAN DANCE
AUGUST 19
TEMPLE BUELL T
IT'S REALLY RIDICULOUS I DIDN'T RECOGNIZE YOU.
FLAMIN GROOVIES
MASON HAD A POSTER OF YOU IN OUR GARAGE. I THINK HE USED TO--
I DON'T WANT TO HEAR IT.
AND NEITHER DID I.
AREN'T YOU SUPPOSED TO BE SOMEWHERE TODAY?
I'M BLOWING IT OFF.
CAN YOU DO THAT?
Rosetta
SOMETHING BETTER CAME UP.
CLINK
EXCELLO Records
AN ENTERTAINING EC COMIC

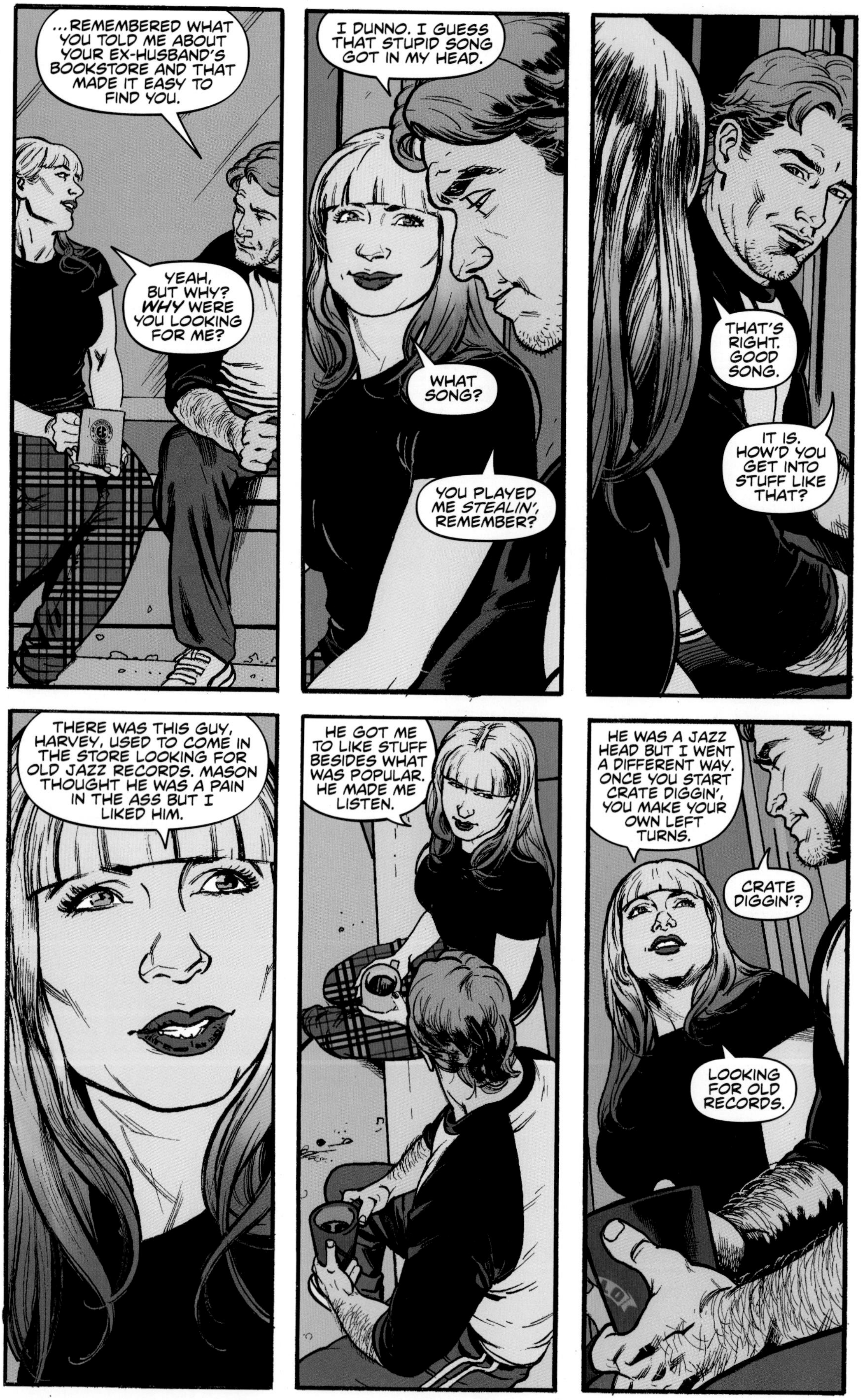
...REMEMBERED WHAT YOU TOLD ME ABOUT YOUR EX-HUSBAND'S BOOKSTORE AND THAT MADE IT EASY TO FIND YOU.
YEAH, BUT WHY? *WHY* WERE YOU LOOKING FOR ME?
I DUNNO. I GUESS THAT STUPID SONG GOT IN MY HEAD.
WHAT SONG?
YOU PLAYED ME *STEALIN'*, REMEMBER?
THAT'S RIGHT. GOOD SONG.
IT IS. HOW'D YOU GET INTO STUFF LIKE THAT?
THERE WAS THIS GUY, HARVEY, USED TO COME IN THE STORE LOOKING FOR OLD JAZZ RECORDS. MASON THOUGHT HE WAS A PAIN IN THE ASS BUT I LIKED HIM.
HE GOT ME TO LIKE STUFF BESIDES WHAT WAS POPULAR. HE MADE ME LISTEN.
HE WAS A JAZZ HEAD BUT I WENT A DIFFERENT WAY. ONCE YOU START CRATE DIGGIN', YOU MAKE YOUR OWN LEFT TURNS.
CRATE DIGGIN'?
LOOKING FOR OLD RECORDS.

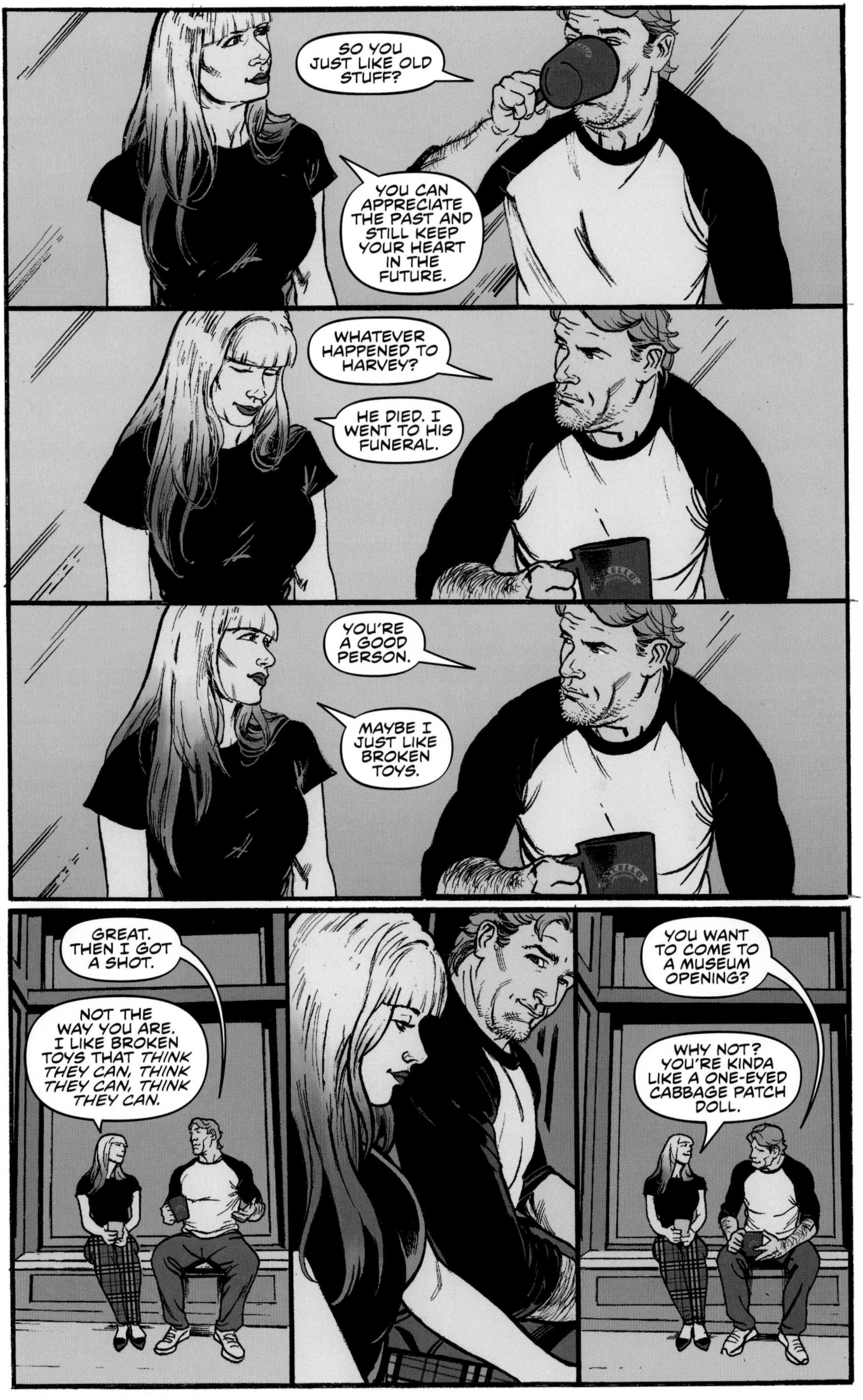
SO YOU JUST LIKE OLD STUFF?
YOU CAN APPRECIATE THE PAST AND STILL KEEP YOUR HEART IN THE FUTURE.
WHATEVER HAPPENED TO HARVEY?
HE DIED. I WENT TO HIS FUNERAL.
YOU'RE A GOOD PERSON.
MAYBE I JUST LIKE BROKEN TOYS.
GREAT. THEN I GOT A SHOT.
NOT THE WAY YOU ARE. I LIKE BROKEN TOYS THAT *THINK* THEY CAN, THINK THEY CAN, THINK THEY CAN.
YOU WANT TO COME TO A MUSEUM OPENING?
WHY NOT? YOU'RE KINDA LIKE A ONE-EYED CABBAGE PATCH DOLL.

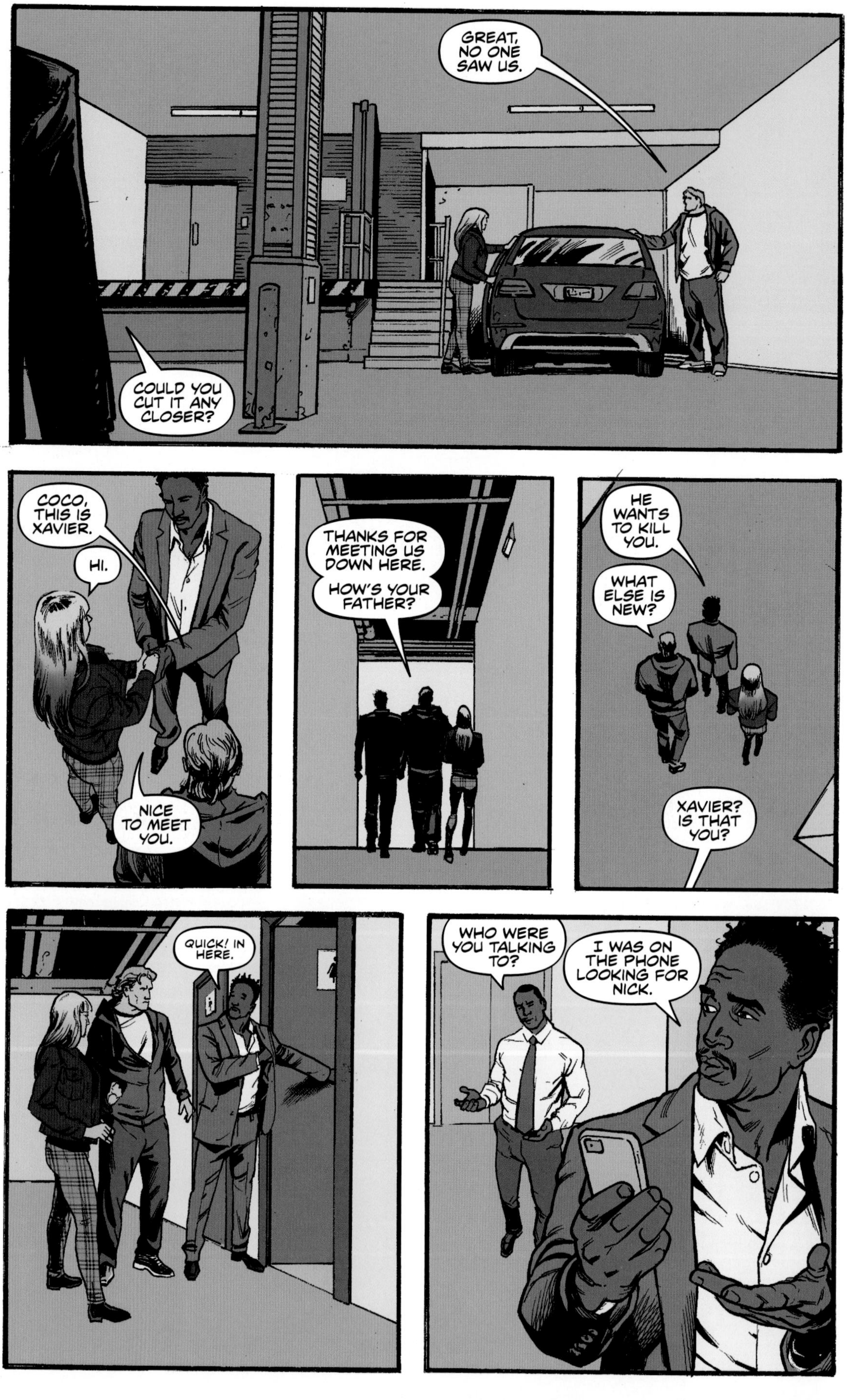
GREAT, NO ONE SAW US.
COULD YOU CUT IT ANY CLOSER?
COCO, THIS IS XAVIER.
HI.
NICE TO MEET YOU.
THANKS FOR MEETING US DOWN HERE.
HOW'S YOUR FATHER?
HE WANTS TO KILL YOU.
WHAT ELSE IS NEW?
XAVIER? IS THAT YOU?
QUICK! IN HERE.
WHO WERE YOU TALKING TO?
I WAS ON THE PHONE LOOKING FOR NICK.

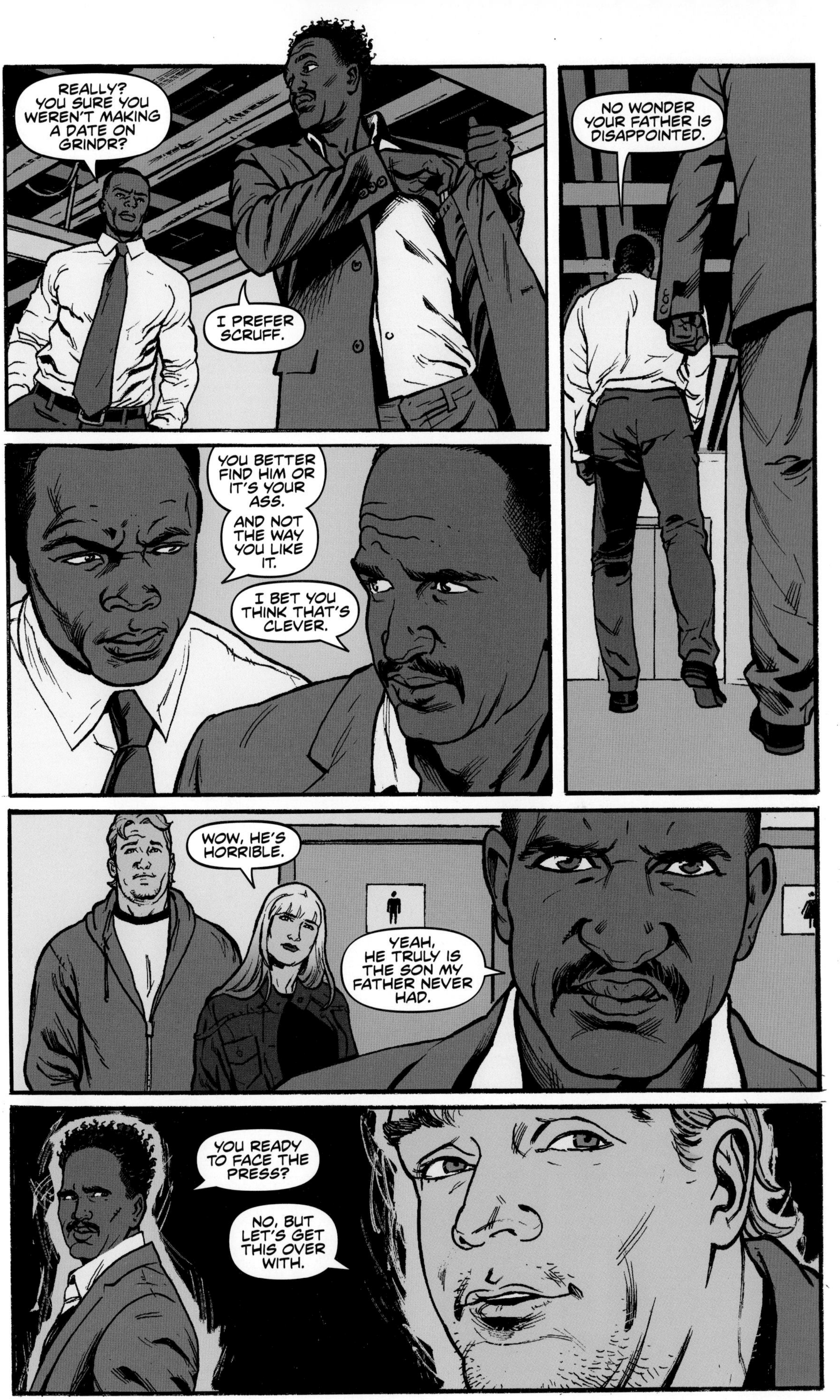
REALLY? YOU SURE YOU WEREN'T MAKING A DATE ON GRINDR?
I PREFER SCRUFF.
NO WONDER YOUR FATHER IS DISAPPOINTED.
YOU BETTER FIND HIM OR IT'S YOUR ASS.
AND NOT THE WAY YOU LIKE IT.
I BET YOU THINK THAT'S CLEVER.
WOW, HE'S HORRIBLE.
YEAH, HE TRULY IS THE SON MY FATHER NEVER HAD.
YOU READY TO FACE THE PRESS?
NO, BUT LET'S GET THIS OVER WITH.

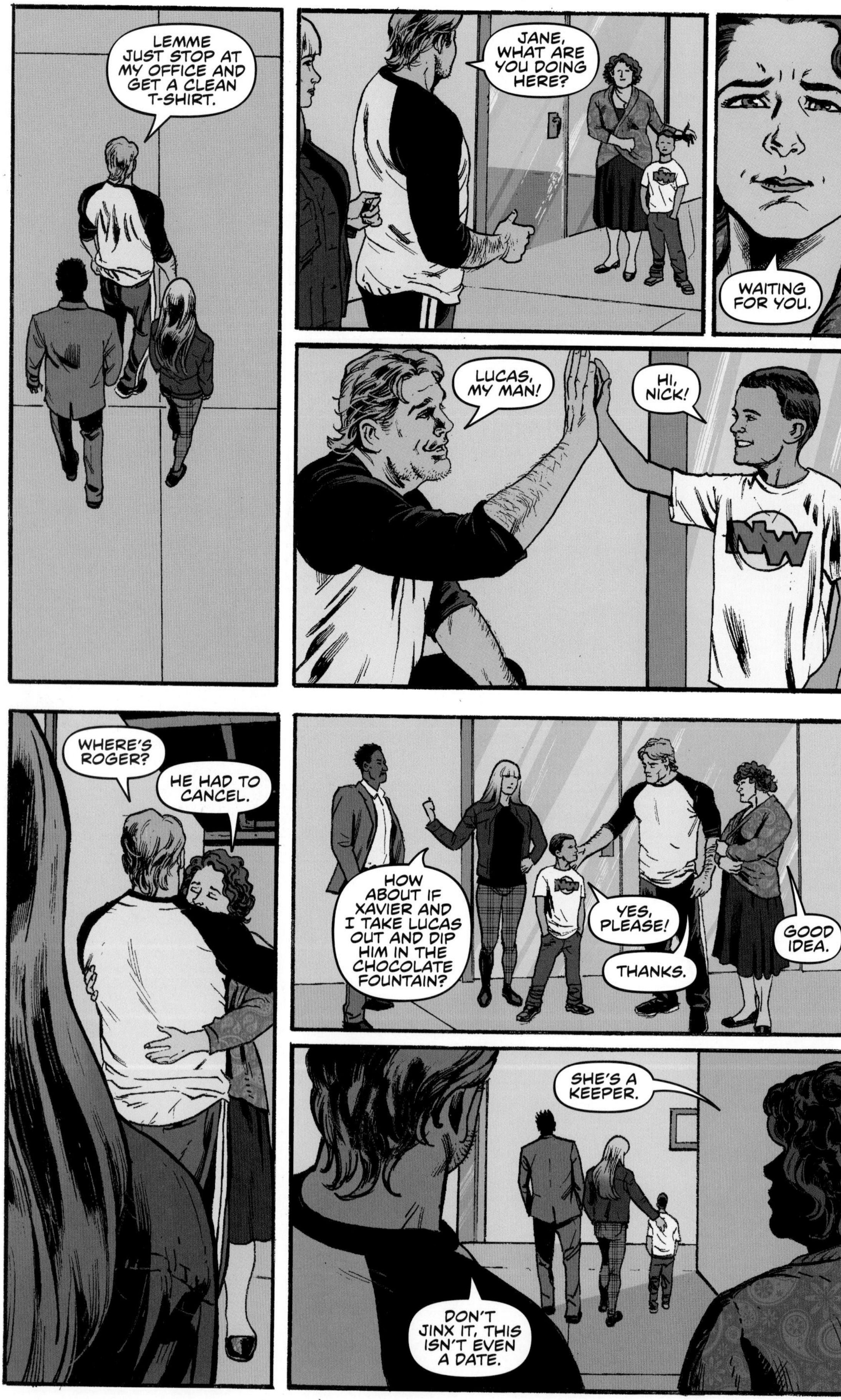
LEMME JUST STOP AT MY OFFICE AND GET A CLEAN T-SHIRT.
JANE, WHAT ARE YOU DOING HERE?
WAITING FOR YOU.
LUCAS, MY MAN!
HI, NICK!
WHERE'S ROGER?
HE HAD TO CANCEL.
HOW ABOUT IF XAVIER AND I TAKE LUCAS OUT AND DIP HIM IN THE CHOCOLATE FOUNTAIN?
YES, PLEASE!
THANKS.
GOOD IDEA.
SHE'S A KEEPER.
DON'T JINX IT, THIS ISN'T EVEN A DATE.

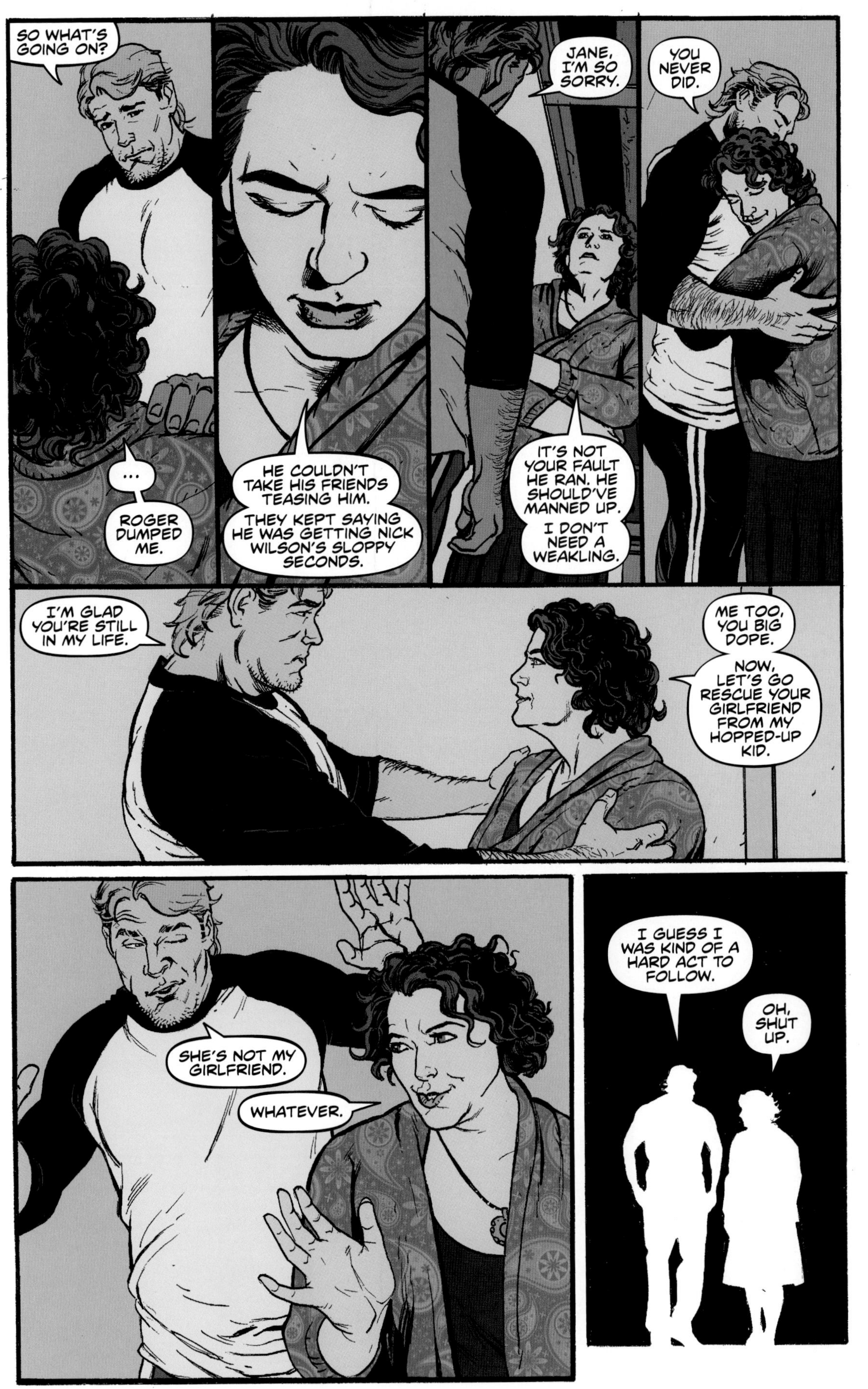
SO WHAT'S GOING ON?
...
ROGER DUMPED ME.
HE COULDN'T TAKE HIS FRIENDS TEASING HIM.
THEY KEPT SAYING HE WAS GETTING NICK WILSON'S SLOPPY SECONDS.
JANE, I'M SO SORRY.
IT'S NOT YOUR FAULT HE RAN. HE SHOULD'VE MANNED UP.
I DON'T NEED A WEAKLING.
YOU NEVER DID.
I'M GLAD YOU'RE STILL IN MY LIFE.
ME TOO, YOU BIG DOPE.
NOW, LET'S GO RESCUE YOUR GIRLFRIEND FROM MY HOPPED-UP KID.
SHE'S NOT MY GIRLFRIEND.
WHATEVER.
I GUESS I WAS KIND OF A HARD ACT TO FOLLOW.
OH, SHUT UP.

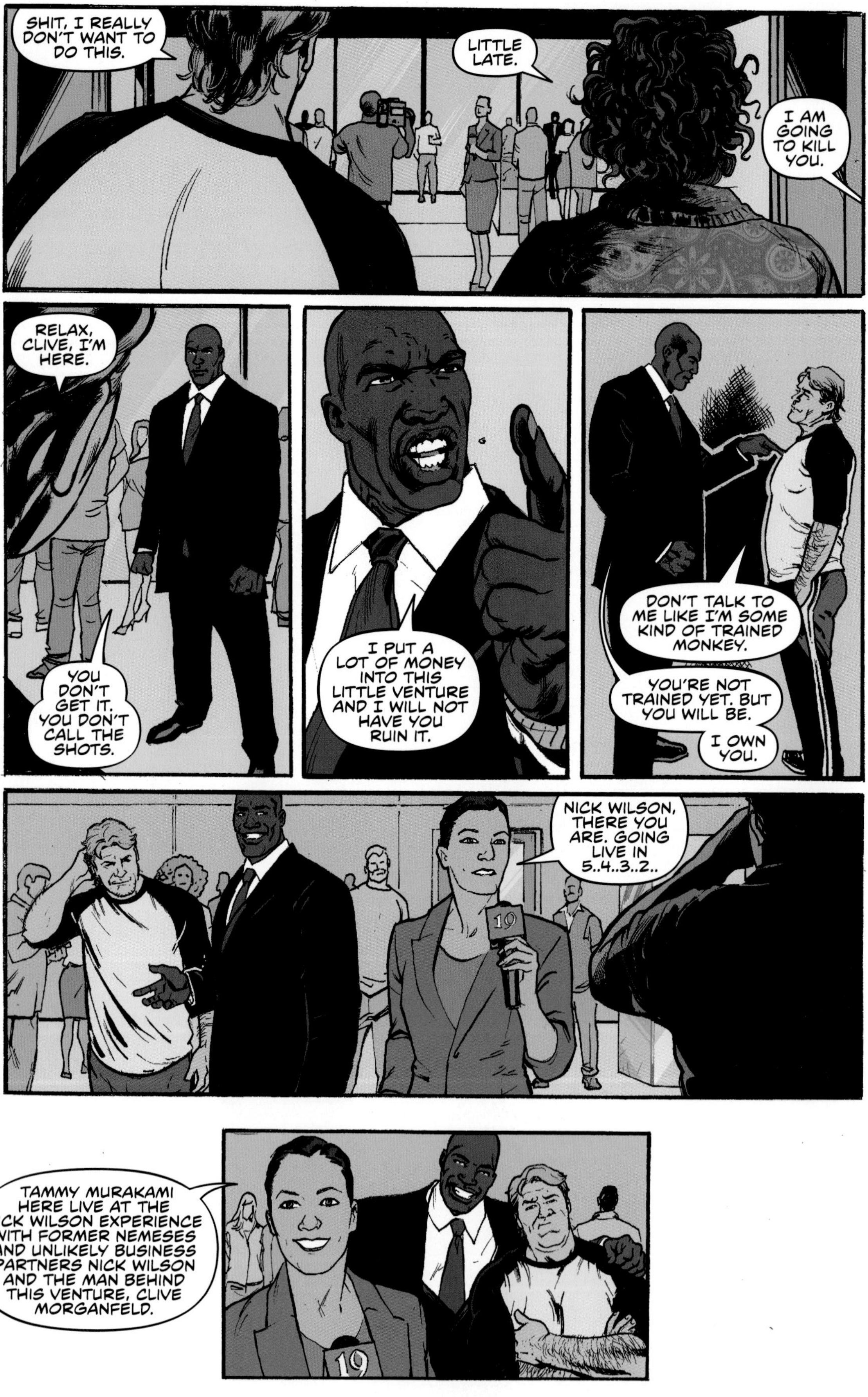
SHIT, I REALLY DON'T WANT TO DO THIS.
LITTLE LATE.
I AM GOING TO KILL YOU.
RELAX, CLIVE, I'M HERE.
YOU DON'T GET IT. YOU DON'T CALL THE SHOTS.
I PUT A LOT OF MONEY INTO THIS LITTLE VENTURE AND I WILL NOT HAVE YOU RUIN IT.
DON'T TALK TO ME LIKE I'M SOME KIND OF TRAINED MONKEY.
YOU'RE NOT TRAINED YET. BUT YOU WILL BE.
I OWN YOU.
NICK WILSON, THERE YOU ARE. GOING LIVE IN 5..4..3..2..
19
TAMMY MURAKAMI HERE LIVE AT THE NICK WILSON EXPERIENCE WITH FORMER NEMESES AND UNLIKELY BUSINESS PARTNERS NICK WILSON AND THE MAN BEHIND THIS VENTURE, CLIVE MORGANFELD.
19

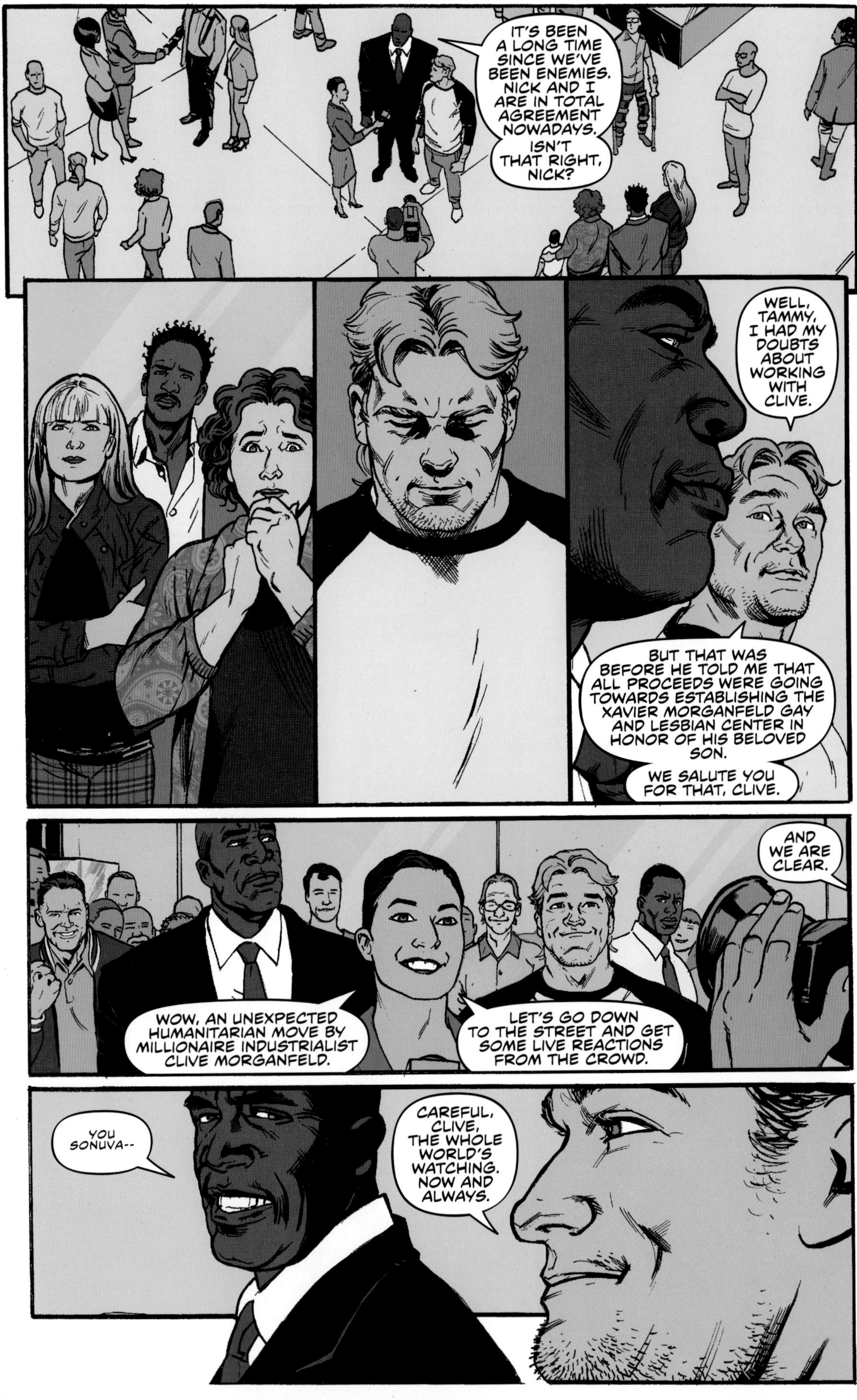
IT'S BEEN A LONG TIME SINCE WE'VE BEEN ENEMIES. NICK AND I ARE IN TOTAL AGREEMENT NOWADAYS.
ISN'T THAT RIGHT, NICK?
WELL, TAMMY, I HAD MY DOUBTS ABOUT WORKING WITH CLIVE.
BUT THAT WAS BEFORE HE TOLD ME THAT ALL PROCEEDS WERE GOING TOWARDS ESTABLISHING THE XAVIER MORGANFELD GAY AND LESBIAN CENTER IN HONOR OF HIS BELOVED SON.
WE SALUTE YOU FOR THAT, CLIVE.
WOW, AN UNEXPECTED HUMANITARIAN MOVE BY MILLIONAIRE INDUSTRIALIST CLIVE MORGANFELD.
LET'S GO DOWN TO THE STREET AND GET SOME LIVE REACTIONS FROM THE CROWD.
AND WE ARE CLEAR.
YOU SONUVA--
CAREFUL, CLIVE, THE WHOLE WORLD'S WATCHING. NOW AND ALWAYS.

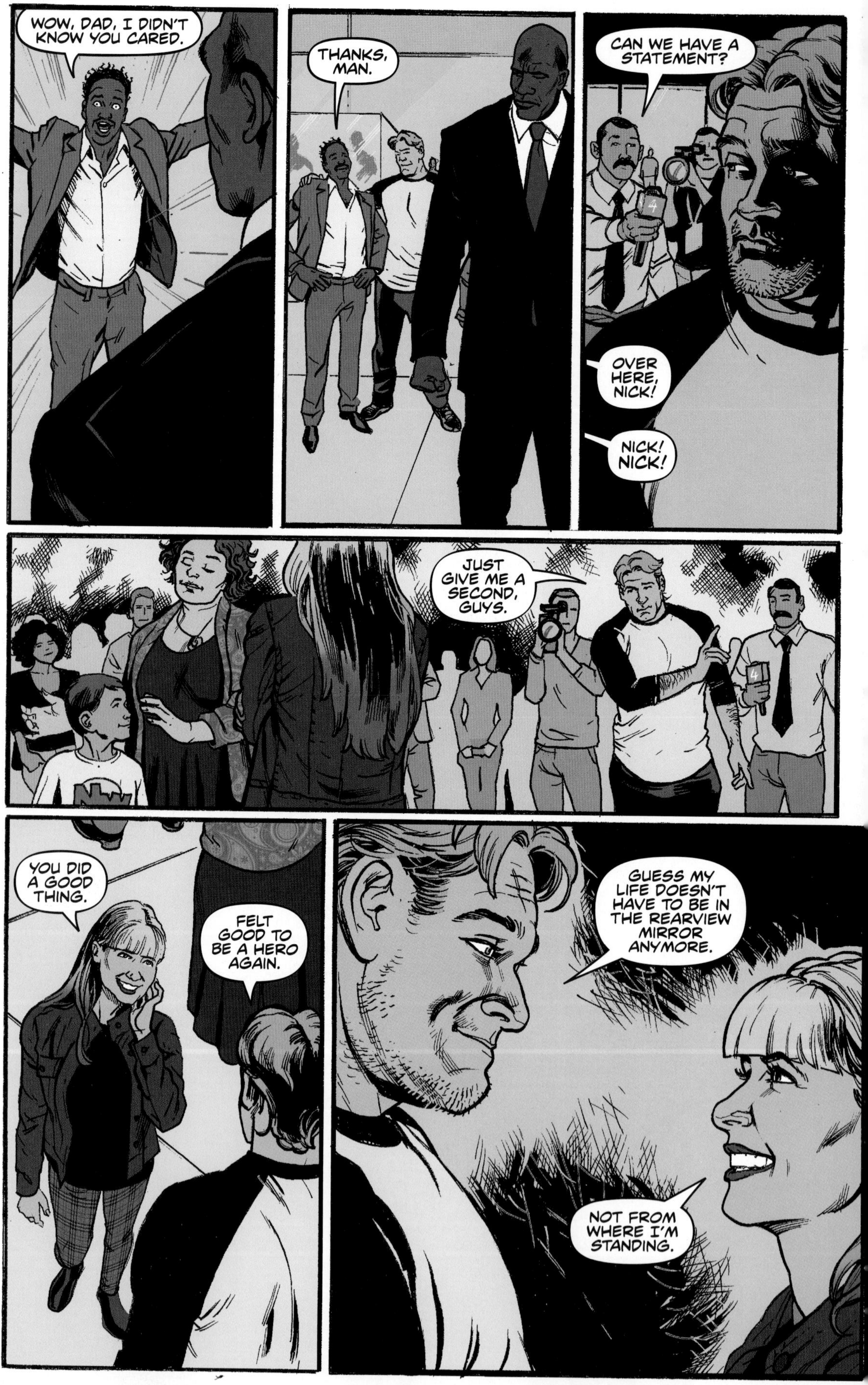
WOW, DAD, I DIDN'T KNOW YOU CARED.
THANKS, MAN.
CAN WE HAVE A STATEMENT?
OVER HERE, NICK!
NICK! NICK!
JUST GIVE ME A SECOND, GUYS.
YOU DID A GOOD THING.
FELT GOOD TO BE A HERO AGAIN.
GUESS MY LIFE DOESN'T HAVE TO BE IN THE REARVIEW MIRROR ANYMORE.
NOT FROM WHERE I'M STANDING.

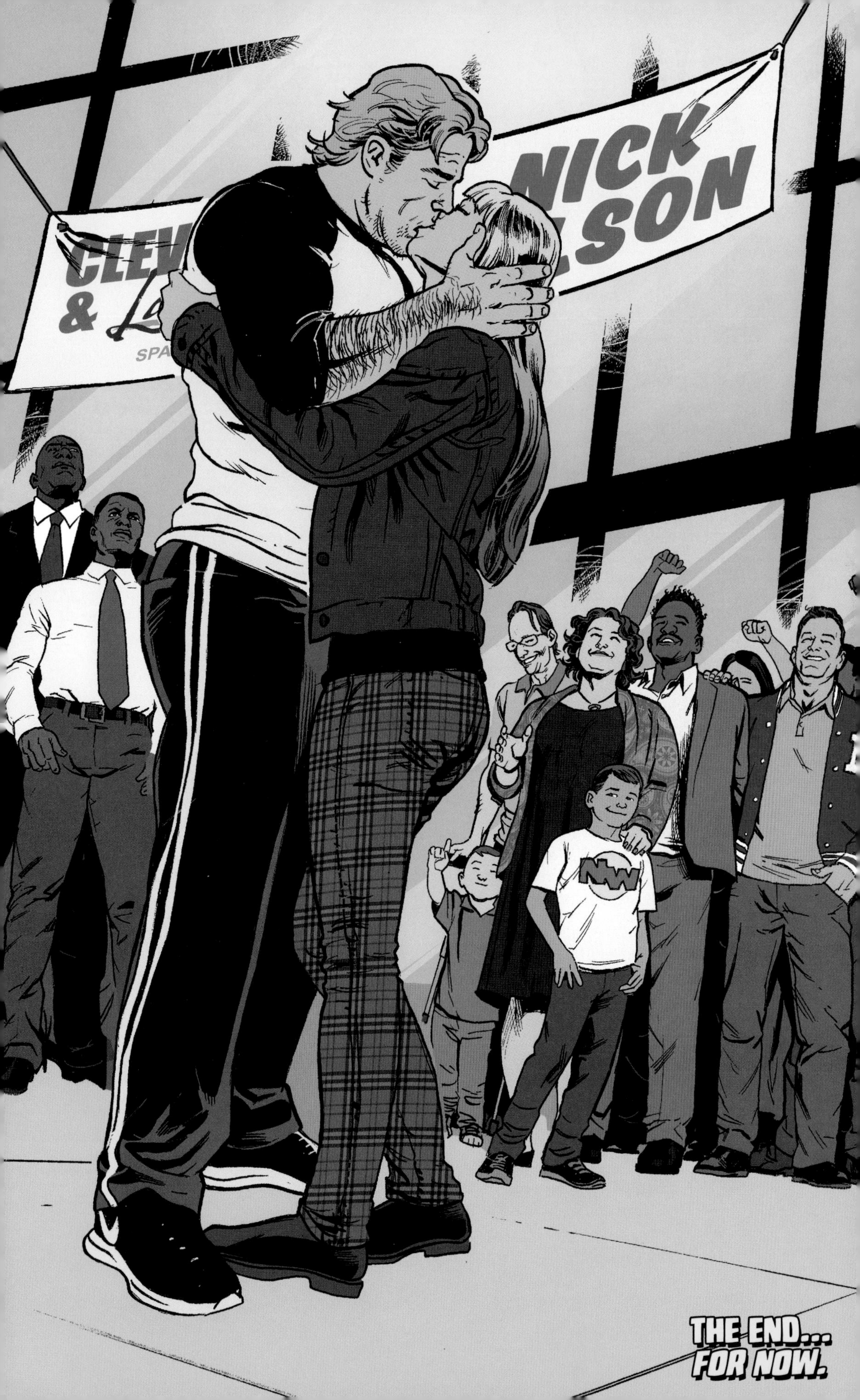

NICK
SON
CLEV
&
SPA
NW
THE END...
FOR NOW.

Cleveland
ARCANA

SO, HERE WE ARE at the end of the first "Nick Wilson" mini-series. I have to say, I was thrilled beyond measure to collaborate with Eddie on his first dive into comics (and I learned more about sitcom structure and organic joke writing than I would have as a grad student at USC!).

Now, writing this final text page, I'm actually a bit misty at not knowing when I will visit Nick and Jane and Xavier… hell, even Clive. But there is one character I definitely don't want to forget to thank:

THE CITY OF CLEVELAND.

As a kid growing up in Mentor, Ohio (about 40 minutes outside of Cleveland), I heard all the jokes about the city: the Cuyahoga River catching on fire, our then-beleaguered sports teams (well, except for the Browns. They seem eternally beleaguered.), the Rust Belt…and on and on.

But, Cleveland is where superheroes were born. In 1938, two gents from Cleveland brought us Superman and changed the world of pop culture in ways they never would have dreamed.

Having Nick, his Earth's only real superhero, be a Clevelander seemed like a no-brainer and a nice tip of the hat to Mssrs. Siegel and Shuster.

And once I started down that path, Eddie suggested we pepper in actual Cleveland locales and references to make the city one of our leads. So, for those unwashed in Northeast Ohio trivia, here's a handy-dandy guide of things you can do on your own NICK WILSON tour of Cleveland:

THE BIG EGG. A legendary diner open all hours and the perfect capper to a night out dancing as a college student. Most of the clubs of my era (U4ia, The Aquilon, Visions….) are but memories, but the Big Egg (and its egg-shaped menus) prevails. And has great omelettes.

THE FLAMING RIVER PUB. No, it ain't real, but I always wanted to reclaim the whole "river on fire" thing from all the lazy jokes (it was almost 50 years ago, folks). Hmm, maybe I should open a bar….

WKYC. My local NBC affiliate. Bit of deep-cut trivia: in the '80s, Al Roker was our weatherman!

JOHNNY MANZIEL. Poor kid. All that attention, all the expectations. Zero delivery. Maybe a cheap shot, but in keeping with the feelings of most of the city. I'm sure his model wife and all that money ease his pain.

THE PLAIN DEALER. Cleveland's last surviving major newspaper. Still not sure what its title means, but an old warhorse of journalism nonetheless.

AND EDDIE EVEN JOINED IN! He made Coco's mentor (revealed in the issue in your hands) that well-known record collector, autobiographical comics genius, and Cleveburg native, Harvey Pekar.

Looking at this list, I realize there are dozens of other Cleveland-centric locales, people (a Toby Radloff cameo, anyone? Or MSB reference?), and weather (oh, those September-to-May winters. I miss them not.) that could be part of…ahem…Even Further Adventures of Nick Wilson.

Although I haven't been back to the former "mistake on the lake" in years, I still cherish growing up there and will always think fondly about good ol' Cleveland.*

Thanks for reading. Hope to see you all soon.

Marc

Los Angeles, CA. April, 2018.

*Except for that awful attempt at mid-1980s branding: "If NYC is the Big Apple, Cleveland's a Plum". What does that mean? Did someone get paid to come up with that?

ANDREA DEL SARTO & THE RESTLESS NATURE OF CREATIVITY

I was excited when Marc and I were laying out this final issue because I knew the sequences in the used book & record stores would give us chances to show record covers and give me an opportunity to write about odd singles. But as I started laying out my notes I realized I would not get very far. I compiled a hundred-song list of songs about comic strip and book characters I gotta find something to do with now. Because I have other things on my mind.

For, like Nick, I find myself at a crossroads…But I'm getting ahead of myself, Let's at least start by talking about music. I told our eminent artist Mister Sadowski to include some of his favorite artists in Coco and Mason's store. The Nirvana poster is his. The poorly printed blotch above it is supposed to be Tom Waits' "Bone Machine" with its lovely cover photo by Jesse Dylan.

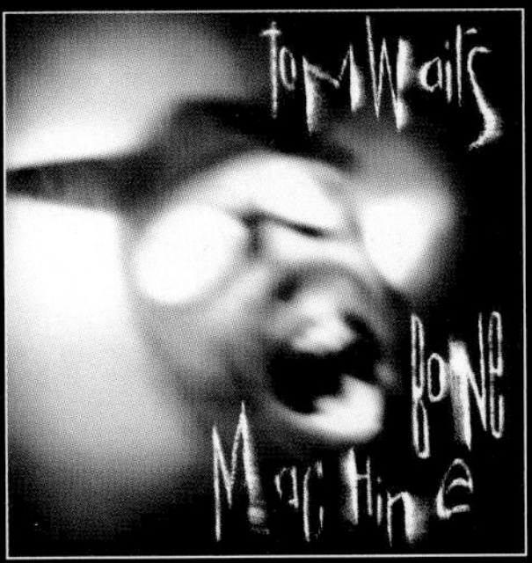
Tom Waits
Bone
Machine
Better in non-blob form.

Now many people separate Tom's career into two halves — the early singer-songwriter — the junkyard poet lord of the Tropicana Motel versus the post "One From Heart" clanging bohemian — equal parts Harry Partch and Captain Beefheart, all broken glass and barbed wire.

I, myself, was totally totally guilty of rejecting what I considered his faux boho early works in favor of what I thought his more authentic later material. It's taken me years to realize I was wrong — across the board, his work is brilliant and beautiful, the living embodiment of the restless spirit of creativity. I was the one that was full of shit.

Growing up somewhat feral in Providence, Rhode Island, I gravitated towards a scene of hipsters and art students, from Rhode Island School of Design. Like all hipsters and art students they had little use for what's happening contemporaneously. Through them I accrued my life-long love of earlier musical forms from jump blues to hillbilly, jug band, country blues and beyond. It was a valuable lesson that showed me that, freed from the trappings of faddishness, the complexities of passions and desire are expressed just as eloquently by contemporaries of Shakespeare as they are by ASAP Rocky if fans of either are willing to look on the other side of the street.

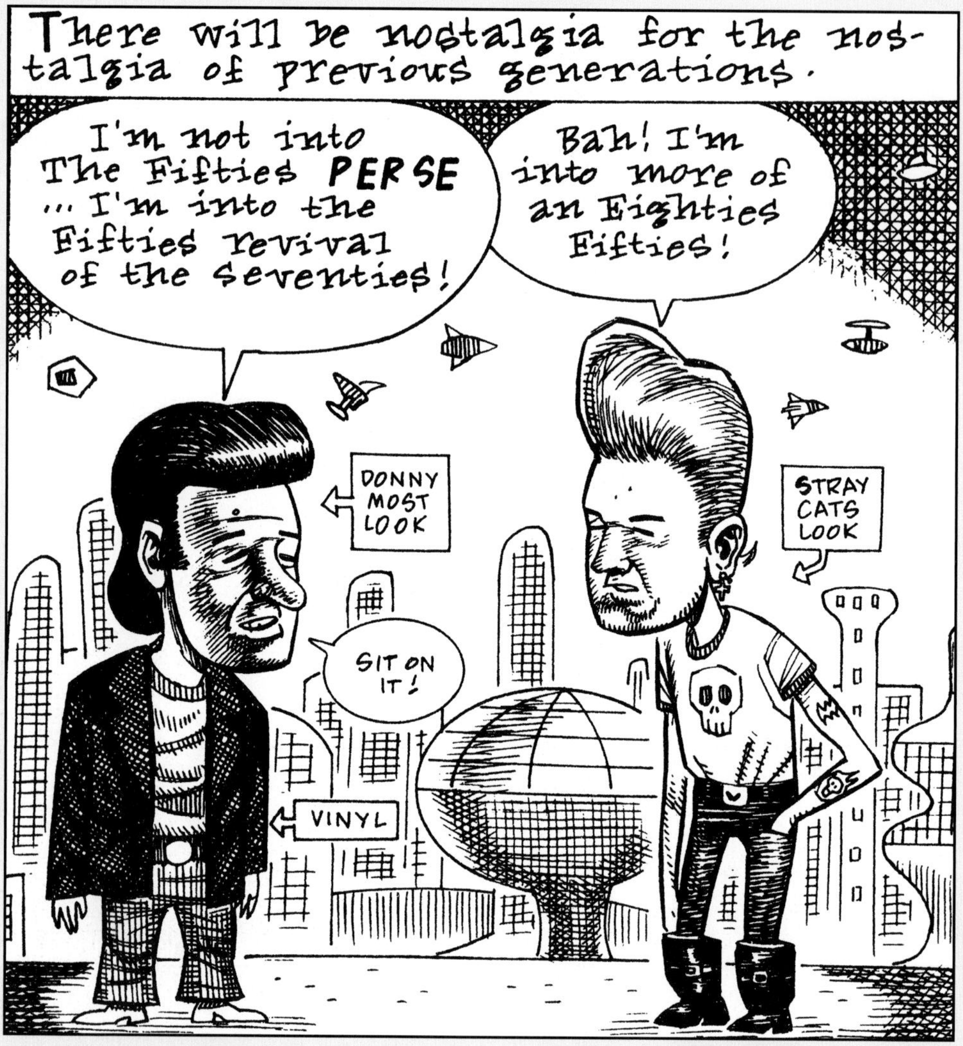
There will be nostalgia for the nostalgia of previous generations.
I'm not into The Fifties PERSE ... I'm into the Fifties revival of the seventies!
Bah! I'm into more of an Eighties Fifties!
DONNY MOST LOOK
STRAY CATS LOOK
SIT ON IT!
VINYL

Daniel Clowes demonstrates the succinctness of form. (Panel from "The Future" in Eightball #4)

For many years I was sure my quest down the rabbit hole was more authentic than Tom's; he recorded after I was born, how could he be any good? This bizarre authenticity one-upmanship conundrum was distilled down to a single panel by Dan Clowes when he had a Stray Cats fan argue with a fan over whose version of the fifties was better — again proving the succinct greatness of comics in the right hands. The only reason I even saw Tom Waits the first time was because I heard that Herb Hardesty, a New Orleans sax player who had been on some of my favorite r&b records was touring with him. I didn't want to admit that I liked Mister Waits back then, I snobbishly footnoted all of his influences to my friends as if my ability to identify his sources somehow limited him instead of me.

But the truth is to eschew those early records is to rob myself of songs like "Tom Traubert's Blues," "On the Nickel," "Ol' 55" and "Looking For the Heart of Saturday Night." But I tried for years to pretend those records meant nothing to me.

I realize now the reason I love Tom Vaits so much is that he doesn't seem dependent on the applause of an audience. In fact, he seems somewhat skeptical of it. He's not unlike Lenny Bruce's Lone Ranger, the Masked Man who won't stop for a "thank you" for fear the adulation is too heady a juice and to accept it is to expect it and down that road is suffocation and death.

Or perhaps I'm reading in.

But, unfortunately, my quest for authenticity had led me into quite the cul-de-sac. My purist love of the arcane allowed me to appreciate some great music but I knew nobody was going to make a country record as good as Hank Williams or sing jump blues like Wynonie Harris. I wasn't satisfied and I didn't know why. I hadn't yet figured out that in some ways I was listening to a fished-out pond — the music itself was timeless but I needed something that was happening in real time. Listening to only old music was in danger of becoming as much of an affectation as slavishly following the charts.

But in 1977 a couple of records came out that changed my life. The first Clash singles had the spiky excitement that those first Beatles and Stones records must have had for a generation more than a dozen years earlier before rock'n'roll got smothered by big business, bad drugs, classic-rock tropes and self-indulgence.

But more importantly, Elvis Costello released his first single. Everyone talks about the A-side — "Less Than Zero" but it was the B-side "Radio Sweetheart" I played incessantly. A country rock sing-along that obviously recognized the past without being a slavish imitation and deftly painted a last call tableau of despair and self-loathing loneliness. The words slip by

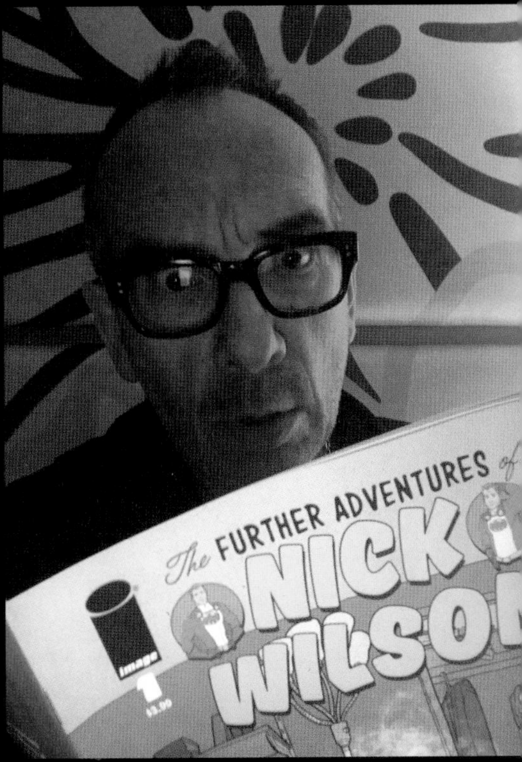
The FURTHER ADVENTURES
NICK
image

What a pal.

easily because the music is so catchy bu look at this:

My head is spinning and my
legs are weak
Goose step dancing, can't hear
myself speak
Hope in the eyes of the ugly girls
That settle for the lies of the
last chancers
When slow motion drunks pick
wallflower dancers

By the time "This Years Model" came ou four months later, I had worn out the grooves on the single and it wasn't even on the album. And that made sense because Elvis embodies, like Waits and Bob Dylan and a few others, that restless creative spirit. Some perceive it as willful, I suppose, but I respec the journey more than the goal, the eterna curiosity to find the next thing around the

Post *Mom*, Chuck and I still eyeing the horizon.

bend. It's why I can go see some artists perform multiple times or read everything they write or see every film they make and give up on others after one taste.

All these years later, Elvis remains an inspiration to me, not just as an artist but also as a person, as I have been fortunate enough to become a close friend with him over the years. Thus "This Years Model" on display in this issue.

Meanwhile, in another part of town in another panel on another page in this issue a street sign reads Lorre Ave. I had to give a shout-out to Chuck Lorre because he is another person with the same restless creative spirit who has been an inspiration and a boon to me for two decades. He is as much of a chameleon as Waits, Elvis or Dylan though he is unfairly pigeonholed for making one type of program.

As a matter of fact, the enthusiasm he has recently shown in embracing a new form and his discipline in learning it instead of resting on his considerable laurels has been instrumental in my decision to move on myself from a comfortable job and leap into the abyss of exploration.

But Chuck has always encouraged me, both by example and actual tutelage. I often say that when I met him, my meager skill set was not unlike a fire hydrant hit by a car in an urban neighborhood on a hot summer day; everyone loved jumping around in the chaotic streams of water. But god forbid there was an actual fire; the water pressure would most likely be depleted. Chuck taught me how to put a nozzle on the hose and for that I will be always be grateful.

He and I often talk about being comfortable in our own discomfort, knowing that quite often writing, perhaps especially writing comedy, comes from being willing to go off without a map and not give in to the panic. There is no way I can repay him for all he helped me do.

And there are others, some I know personally, some strangers, some contemporaries, others long dead — fellow travelers on the open

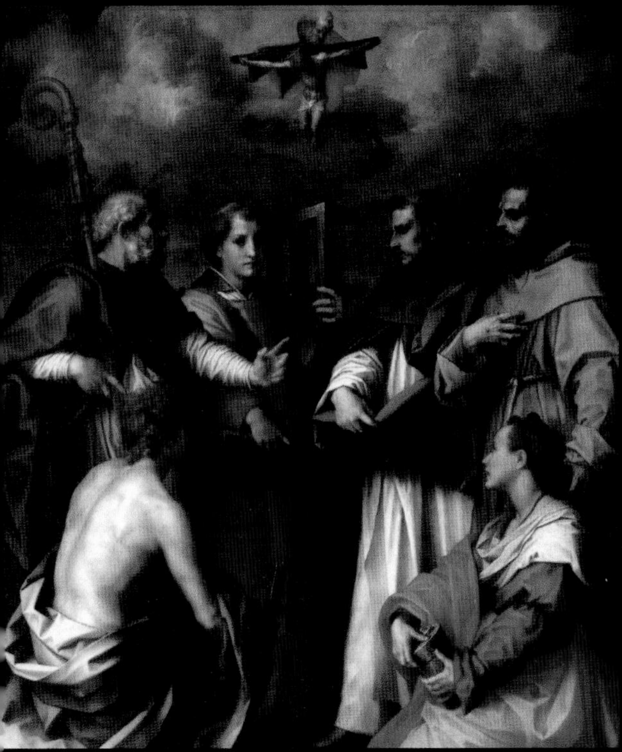

Andrea del Sarto—imagine how good he would have been if he had tried.

sea who realize a groove can quickly become a rut and the fear of failure, though palpable, is preferable to the torpor of repetition. Aside from Tom, Elvis and Chuck, there is Dylan (always Dylan) as well as people like Phillip Guston, Jordan Peele, Hannah Höch, Sonny Rollins, Sarah Silverman, Ida Lupino, Donald Glover and many others who steer off onto roads that others may not recognize immediately.

Not that I am anywhere as self-aggrandizing that I think for a moment that I breathe the same rarefied air as any of them but their journeys are always an inspiration, their refusals to be limited always an example, their resilience in moments of temporary setback models of bravery.

I yearn for their grace because I know good enough is never good enough. And even a hardened atheist like myself understands what Robert Browning meant when he threw shade at the painter Andrea del Sarto when he wrote in his eponymous poem from 1855 "Ah, a man's reach must exceed his grasp/or what's a heaven for?"

So, what will happen to Nick Wilson next, I'm not sure. I'm not even sure what I'm gonna do next. But I do have lots of ideas for this motley band of characters. But to tell them in comic book form or somewhere else, that is a question.

I thought a comic book would be a quick respite from making a TV show but it actually took longer — I was able to generate close to two seasons of *Mom* in the time between the writing and actual production and publishing of this short series. I love these characters and writing is communication so I hope they found a place in your heart as well.

I think there's a bit of Nick in all of us, trying to regain equilibrium in reduced circumstances, to dig out of a public embarrassment. Sure, his was more extreme but we all know the feeling.

This was not a book about a superhero. It was book about a person, who just happened to be super once. He started off as fearful but when he opened his heart he found courage.

This isn't the end of the story. It's the beginning.

What will happen to Nick Wilson?

Watch the signs...

Yer ol pal

eddie gorodetsky

los feliz, summer 2018

(Most of all, thank you, Coco

A QUICK TIP O' THE HAT

This collected edition gives Marc and myself a chance to thank people who otherwise may have fallen through the cracks or who have extended themselves above and beyond.

Every issue has credits and most of those people were really helpful to us. You can see Stephen Sadowski and Pete Wood's work in every panel and every cover but they were so helpful in making Nick and his world come to life, I cannot thank them enough.

I do have to take a second, though, to thank Ian Churchill. He kept surprising me and went the extra mile with wit and dexterity. The fake Nick Wilson covers on the front of this book give you a small idea of his skills.

Britté Anchor has worked with me on more than one television program and she brought those same skills to this book. She was an asset and a help on every level, and writing issue four with her was probably more fun for me than it was for her.

Paul Dini, one of my favorite comic book writers and longtime friend must be given special thanks for being the midwife that brought Marc and me together. Paul manages to infuse humanity and a touch of humor into every book he touches.

I also want to thank everyone who was generous enough to give a blurb to our little project. The ones plucked from reviews, of course, are exciting because it means somebody said something nice about our work.

But many of the others came from friends who offered kind and quotable phrases. They also make wonderful creative things across a spectrum of mediums—music, stand-up, film, TV and more. Marc and I had a rule that we wouldn't publish a blurb unless we liked the person's work so it is with a clear conscience that we encourage you to seek out work by all of them.

I must also thank my accountant, Alan. He was a giant help, making sure everyone got paid immediately as opposed to what some of the bigger companies do. Freelancers work hard and Alan was terrific in making sure work was rewarded as quickly as possible.

Jeff Rosen is more comfortable in the shadows but without him, this thing would have died on the vine at least once an issue. Thank you, Jeff.

Coco Shinomiya dodged deadlines for her regular labors to help make much of this book work. And I have insight into her personal time allotment because I am lucky enough to be married to her.

She also reminds me to give thanks for the hard-working production team including A Larger World and Hi-Fi Colour. Also, Shannon.

And finally, as always, thanks to you guys and gals reading this. I have always considered communication important in what I write. Without you to complete the circuit, it becomes pure wankery.

To me, its not about whether or not a tree falling makes any noise if no one is there to hear it. Who really cares? Without someone there to hear it, it's just an intellectual exercise. You, the reader, makes it sing. Thanks.

And finally, I need to thank Marc—without him this idea I had been carrying around would've just been another unfulfilled thought. He taught me much and allowed me my craziness. Who could ask for more?

Keep your eyes, ears and heart open...
eddie gorodetsky
los feliz 2018

The **FURTHER ADVENTURES** *of*

NICK WILSON

Created by
EDDIE GORODETSKY & MARC ANDREYKO

Trade Paperback Cover Art
IAN CHURCHILL

Trade Paperback Design:
COCO SHINOMIYA, IAN CHURCHILL,
A LARGER WORLD STUDIO & SEAN TEJARATCHI

· ·

ISSUES 1,2,5
Written by Eddie Gorodetsky & Marc Andreyko

ISSUE 3
Story by Eddie Gorodetsky & Marc Andreyko
Written by Marc Andreyko

ISSUE 4
Story by Eddie Gorodetsky & Marc Andreyko
Written by Eddie Gorodetsky & Brittè Anchor

ISSUES 1, 2, 3, 5
Illustrated by Stephen Sadowski

ISSUE 4
Illustrated by Ian Churchill

COLORED BY
Hi-Fi Colour Design

LETTERING/DESIGN
A Larger World Studio

AMANUENSIS
Brittè Anchor

ADDITIONAL DESIGN
Coco Shinomiya & Zen Hcmp

EDITED BY
Shannon Eric Denton

COVER ARTISTS
ISSUE 1: Pete Woods / Ian Churchill
ISSUE 2: Pete Woods / Ian Churchill
ISSUE 3: Pete Woods/ Ian Churchill
ISSUE 4: Pete Woods / Ian Churchill
ISSUE 5: Pete Woods / Ian Churchill

Look for THEFURTHERADVENTURESOFNICKWILSON.COM

"In the NICK WILSON stories Eddie Gorodetsky has created the superhero that probably lurks within each of us; flawed beneath a thin disguise of skin and wrestling with a legend that was pressed upon us all."
ELVIS COSTELLO

"A sometimes funny, always touching parable about the pitfalls of early success, cloaked in the tale of a one-time hero who believes his best days are behind him."
PAUL DINI

"Eddie Gorodetsky is the funniest man in the world...He knows everything about, well everything, but especially music, comedy, and comics. He writes the most successful comedy on TV. Now, he's written the best ex-superhero comic ever."
PENN JILLETTE of Penn & Teller

"Funny, smart...a clever take on how hard falling from grace can be, especially when you used to be able to fly."
TARAN KILLAM,
actor/director, "SNL", "Killing Gunther"

"THE FURTHER ADVENTURES OF NICK WILSON is a well-produced piece of entertainment that continues to defy what a superhero comic is supposed to be. Nick's exploits are at times funny, sad, hopeful, and endearing. I have to say I'm hooked."
ENRIQUE REA, SPARTANTOWN.NET

"One of the biggest surprises of the year."
LASERTIMEPODCAST.COM

"Funny and fast and human. Truly Excellent. Grade: A."
FORCESOFGEEK.COM

"Skillful script-writing storytelling by Eddie Gorodetsky and Marc Andreyko. Stephen Sadowski proves the perfect artistic partner. 10 out of 10."
EXPLORETHEMULTIVERSE.COM

"I knew it from Manhunter, Torso, and Love Is Love. Now, NICK WILSON will show you that Marc Andreyko is one of the best writers and most unique voices in comics. This book is earthy and honest."
BRIAN MICHAEL BENDIS

"A funny human comic about what it means to go from 'super' to 'human.'"
PATTON OSWALT

"I love this comic book by Eddie Gorodetsky. If you love comic books you will for reals love this."
SARAH SILVERMAN

"I really fell in love with this book. Very recommended!"
DAVID MANDEL,
Emmy-winning Executive Producer/Writer "Veep"

"This book really got to me. It pretends to be cynical, but there's a beautiful, beating heart at the center of it. Give NICK WILSON a shot. For sure."
BRAD MELTZER,
bestselling author of "The Escape Artist"

"Nick Wilson used to change the course of mighty rivers and bend steel with his mighty hands. Now he's sitting on his couch, getting high in Cleveland. Andreyko and Gorodetsky may have the final word on superheroes, and they do it with one who's powerless, penniless and so sad, it's hilarious."
POPCULTUREMAVEN.COM

"Impressive writing talent here...Stephen Sadowski's art is masterfully natural, smooth, and funny. Definitely take a look. 10 out of 10."
COMICSGRINDER.COM

"Wildly fun, completely original and with some of the best storytelling around right now [NICK WILSON] is one you need in your life."
READINGWITHAFLIGHTRING.WEEBLY.COM